Grammar Sense

Sense

2

SERIES DIRECTOR
Susan Kesner Bland

Cheryl Pavlik

OXFORD
UNIVERSITY PRESS

OXFORD
UNIVERSITY PRESS

198 Madison Avenue
New York, NY 10016 USA

Great Clarendon Street
Oxford OX2 6DP England

Oxford New York
Auckland Bangkok Buenos Aires Cape Town Chennai
Dar es Salaam Delhi Hong Kong Istanbul Karachi Kolkata
Kuala Lumpur Madrid Melbourne Mexico City Mumbai
Nairobi São Paulo Shanghai Taipei Tokyo Toronto

OXFORD is a trademark of Oxford University Press.

Copyright © 2004 Oxford University Press
ISBN 0-19-436571-9

Library of Congress Cataloging-in-Publication Data

Pavlik, Cheryl, 1949-
   Grammar sense 2 / series director, Susan Kesner Bland ;
Cheryl Pavlik.
      p. cm.
   Includes index.
   ISBN 0-19-436571-9
   1. English language—Textbooks for foreign speakers. 2. English
language—Grammar—Problems, exercises, etc. I. Title: Grammar
sense two. II. Bland, Susan Kesner. III. Title.

PE1128.P375 2004
428.2'4—dc21
                                        2003051757

Editorial Manager: Janet Aitchison
Senior Editor: Stephanie Karras
Editor: Diane Flanel Piniaris
Associate Editor: Kim Steiner
Art Director: Lynn Luchetti
Design Project Manager: Mary Chandler
Designer (cover): Lee Anne Dollison
Senior Art Buyer: Jodi Waxman
Art Buyer: Judi DeSouter
Production Manager: Shanta Persaud
Production Controller: Eve Wong

Book design: Bill Smith Studio
Composition: Compset, Inc.
Indexer: Leonard Neufeld

Printing (last digit): 10 9 8 7 6 5 4 3 2 1

Printed in Hong Kong.

Acknowledgments
Cover image: © Kevin Schafer / Peter Arnold, Inc.

Illustrations by:
Barbara Bastian, Lyndall Culbertson, Mike Hortens
Design, Patrick Faricy, Paul Hampson, Randy Jones,
Jon Keegan, Laura Hartman Maestro, Tom Newsom,
Roger Penwill, Alan Reingold, Don Stewart, Bill
Thomson, Scott Tysick / Masterfile, Bob Wilson

*The publisher would like to thank the following for
their permission to reproduce photographs:*
Macduff Everton / CORBIS; Tom Brakefield / Bruce
Coleman, Inc.; Wally McNamee / CORBIS; Ron
Russell / ImageState; photograph of Voyager: NASA,
JPL, and Caltech; Associated Press; Hulton Archive /
Getty Images; Ted Streshinsky / CORBIS; Rosenberg
Library, Galveston, Texas; Keith Black / Index Stock
Imagery; PhotoDisc; Comstock; Robin Lynne Gibson /
Getty Images; Eric Futran / FoodPix; Bettmann /
CORBIS; Patrick Robert / Corbis Sygma; W. Bibikow /
Jonarnold.com; EyeWire / Getty Images; Rob Gage /
Getty Images; Ken Reid / Getty Images; Renee Lynn /
Photo Researchers, Inc.; Ron Cohn / The Gorilla
Foundation; Dan Suzio / Photo Researchers, Inc.; Will
and Deni Mcintyre / Getty Images / Stone; Hammecher
Schlemmer; Jodi Waxman / OUP; Roy Morsch /
CORBIS; PhotoAlto / Robert Harding World Imagery;
Pictures Colour Library; Duomo / CORBIS

*The publisher would like to thank the following for
their permission to reproduce these extracts and
adaptations of copyrighted material:*
pp. 4–5. "Mysterious Island." This article first
appeared in *The Christian Science Monitor* on
June 16, 1998, and is reproduced with permission.
© 1998 The Christian Science Publishing Society.
All rights reserved; **pp. 48–49.** "The Decade That
Mattered." ©1991 Time Inc. Reprinted by permission;
pp. 90–91. "This man's been nearly everywhere." This
article first appeared in *The Christian Science Monitor*
on March 10, 1998, and is reproduced with permission.
© 1998 The Christian Science Publishing Society. All
rights reserved; **p. 263.** "Mood Foods." Courtesy
of *Seventeen* magazine / Karen Robinovitz,
www.seventeen.com; **p. 283.** From *Carnivorous Plants*
by Cynthia Overbeck. Text copyright © 1982 by
Lerner Publications, a division of Lerner Publishing
Group. Adapted from a book first published in Japan
by Akane Shobo Publishers (Tokyo) entitled
Insectivorous Plants by Kiyoshi Shimizu. Used by
permission. All rights reserved; **p. 303.** From the
Hammacher Schlemmer catalog; **pp. 318–319.** From
The Personality Compass by Diane Turner. Reprinted
with permission by HarperCollins Publishers Ltd;
pp. 382–383. "10 Easy Ways to Start Saving Money"
by Franny Van Nevel; **p. 413.** Adapted from
"Learn2Fry An Egg" with permission by Learn2.com,
Inc. All rights reserved.

Acknowledgements

It takes a village to write a grammar series. I am humbled by the expertise of all those who have contributed in so many ways.

I am grateful to Cheryl Pavlik for her intellectual curiosity, creativity, wit, and for her friendship. A special thanks goes to Stephanie Karras for putting all of the pieces together with such commitment and superb organizational and problem-solving skills, mixed with just the right amount of levity. I owe a special debt of gratitude to Janet Aitchison for her continued support and encouragement from the very beginning, and for her help with the big issues as well as the small details.

It has been a pleasure working closely with Diane Flanel Piniaris, Pietro Alongi, Andrew Gitzy, James Morgan, Nan Clarke, Randee Falk, and Marietta Urban. Their comments, questions, grammar insights, and creative solutions have been invaluable. Many thanks also go to the talented editorial, production, and design staff at Oxford University Press; to Susan Lanzano for her role in getting this project started; and to Susan Mraz for her help in the early stages.

Finally, I owe everything to my family, Bob, Jenny, and Scott, for always being there for me, as well as for their amusing views about everything, especially grammar.

This book is dedicated to my parents, Sam and Bess Kesner.

Susan Kesner Bland,
Series Director

The Series Director and Publisher would like to acknowledge the following individuals for their invaluable input during the development of this series:

Harriet Allison, Atlanta College of Art, GA; **Alex Baez,** Southwest Texas State University, TX; **Nathalie Bailey,** Lehman College, CUNY, NY; **Jamie Beaton,** Boston University, MA; **Michael Berman,** Montgomery College, MD; **Angela Blackwell,** San Francisco State University, CA; **Vera Bradford,** IBEU, Rio de Janerio, Brazil; **Glenda Bro,** Mount San Antonio Community College, CA; **Jennifer Burton,** University of California, San Francisco, CA; **Magali Duignan,** Augusta State University, GA; **Anne Ediger,** Hunter College, CUNY, NY; **Joyce Grabowski,** Flushing High School, NY; **Virginia Heringer,** Pasadena City College, CA; **Rocia Hernandez,** Mexico City, Mexico; **Nancy Hertfield-Pipkin,** University of California, San Diego, CA; **Michelle Johnstone,** Mexico City, Mexico; **Kate de Jong,** University of California, San Diego, CA; **Pamela Kennedy,** Holyoke Community College, MA; **Jean McConochie,** Pace University, NY; **Karen McRobie,** Golden Gate University, CA; **Elizabeth Neblett,** Union County College, NJ; **Dian Perkins,** Wheeling High School, IL; **Fausto Rocha de Marcos Rebelo,** Recife, Brazil; **Mildred Rugger,** Southwest Texas State University, TX; **Dawn Schmidt,** California State University, San Marcos, CA; **Katharine Sherak,** San Francisco State University, CA; **Lois Spitzer,** University of Nebraska-Lincoln, NE; **Laura Stering,** University of California, San Francisco, CA; **Annie Stumpfhauser,** Morelios, Mexico; **Anthea Tillyer,** Hunter College, CUNY, NY; **Julie Un,** Massasoit Community College, MA; **Susan Walker,** SUNY New Paltz, NY; **Cheryl Wecksler,** California State University, San Marcos, CA; **Teresa Wise,** Georgia State University, GA.

Contents

PART 3: The Future

PART 4: Modals

PART 7: Adjectives and Adverbs

PART 8: Comparatives and Superlatives

Introduction

Grammar Sense: A Discourse-Based Approach

Grammar Sense is a comprehensive three-level grammar series based on the authentic use of English grammar in discourse. The grammar is systematically organized, explained, and practiced in a communicative, learner-centered environment, making it easily teachable and learnable.

Many people ask, why learn grammar? The answer is simple: meaningful communication depends on our ability to connect form and meaning appropriately. In order to do so, we must consider such factors as intention, attitude, and social relationships, in addition to the contexts of time and place. All of these factors make up a discourse setting. For example, we use the present continuous not only to describe an activity in progress (*He's working.*), but also to complain (*He's always working.*), to describe a planned event in the future (*He's working tomorrow.*), and to describe temporary or unusual behavior (*He's being lazy at work.*). It is only through examination of the discourse setting that the different meanings and uses of the present continuous can be distinguished from one another. A discourse-based approach provides students with the tools for making sense of the grammar of natural language by systematically explaining *who, what, where, when, why,* and *how* for each grammatical form.

Systematically Organized Syllabus

Learning grammar is a developmental process that occurs gradually. In *Grammar Sense* the careful sequencing, systematic repetition, recycling, review, and expansion promote grammatical awareness and fluency.

Level 1 (basic level) focuses on building an elementary understanding of form, meaning, and use as students develop basic oral language skills in short conversations and discussions. Level 1 also targets the grammar skills involved in writing short paragraphs, using basic cohesive devices such as conjunctions and pronouns.

At **Level 2 (intermediate level)** the focus turns to expanding the basic understanding of form, meaning, and use in longer and more varied discourse settings, and with more complex grammatical structures and academic themes. Level 2 emphasizes grammar skills beyond the sentence level, as students begin to initiate and sustain conversations and discussions, and progress toward longer types of writing.

Finally, at **Level 3 (high intermediate to advanced level)** the focus moves to spoken and written grammar in academic discourse settings, often in contexts that are conceptually more challenging and abstract. Level 3 emphasizes consistent and appropriate language use, especially of those aspects of grammar needed in extended conversations and discussions, and in longer academic and personal writing.

Introduction of Form Before Meaning and Use

Form is introduced and practiced in a separate section before meaning and use. This ensures that students understand what the form looks like and sounds like at the sentence level, before engaging in more challenging and open-ended activities that concentrate on meaning and use.

Focus on Natural Language Use

Grammar Sense uses authentic reading texts and examples that are based on or quoted verbatim from actual English-language sources to provide a true picture of natural language use. To avoid unnatural language, the themes of the introductory reading texts are only subtly touched upon throughout a chapter. The focus thus remains on typical examples of the most common meanings and uses.

Exposure to authentic language helps students bridge the gap between the classroom and the outside world by encouraging awareness of the "grammar" all around them in daily life: in magazines, newspapers, package instructions, television shows, signs, and so on. Becoming language-aware is an important step in the language-learning process: Students generalize from the examples they find and apply their understanding to their independent language use in daily living, at work, or as they further their education.

Special Sections to Extend Grammatical Knowledge

Understanding grammar as a system entails understanding how different parts of the language support and interact with the target structure. *Grammar Sense* features special sections at strategic points throughout the text to highlight relevant lexical and discourse issues.

- **Beyond the Sentence** sections focus on the structure as it is used in extended discourse to help improve students' writing skills. These sections highlight such issues as how grammatical forms are used to avoid redundancy, and how to change or maintain focus.

- **Informally Speaking** sections highlight the differences between written and spoken language. This understanding is crucial for achieving second language fluency. Reduced forms, omissions, and pronunciation changes are explained in order to improve aural comprehension.

- **Pronunciation Notes** show students how to pronounce selected forms of the target language, such as the regular simple past ending *-ed*.

- **Vocabulary Notes** provide succinct presentations of words and phrases that are commonly used with the target structure, such as time expressions associated with the simple present and simple past.

Student-Centered Presentation and Practice

Student-centered presentation and practice allow learners at all levels to discover the grammar in pairs, groups, and individually, in both the Form and in the Meaning and Use sections of each chapter. Numerous inductive activities encourage students to use their problem-solving abilities to gain the skills, experience, and confidence to use English outside of class and to continue learning on their own.

Flexibility to Suit Any Classroom Situation

Grammar Sense offers teachers great flexibility with hundreds of intellectually engaging exercises to choose from. Teachers may choose to skip chapters or sections within chapters, or teach them in a different order, depending on student needs and time constraints. Each Student Book is self-contained so teachers may choose to use only one book, or the full series, if they wish.

Components at Each Level

- The **Student Book** is intended for classroom use and offers concise charts, level-appropriate explanations, and thorough four-skills practice exercises. Each Student Book is also a useful reference resource with extensive Appendices, a helpful Glossary of Grammar Terms, and a detailed Index.

- The **Audio Cassettes and CDs** feature listening exercises that provide practice discriminating form, understanding meaning and use, and interpreting non-standard forms.

- The **Workbook** has a wealth of additional exercises to supplement those in the Student Book. It is ideal for homework, independent practice, or review. The Answer Key, on easily removable perforated pages, is provided at the back of the book.

- The **Teacher's Book** has many practical ideas and techniques for presenting the Form and the Meaning and Use sections. It also includes troubleshooting advice, cultural notes, and suggestions for additional activities. The Answer Key for the Student Book and the complete Tapescript are also provided.

- **TOEFL®-Style Tests** and Answer Keys, along with advice on conducting the tests and interpreting the results, are available for teachers to download from the Internet. (See *Grammar Sense Teacher's Book 2* for the website address.)

Tour of a Chapter

Each chapter in *Grammar Sense* follows this format:

The **Grammar in Discourse** section introduces the target structure in its natural context via a high-interest authentic reading text.

• *Authentic reading texts show how language is really used.*

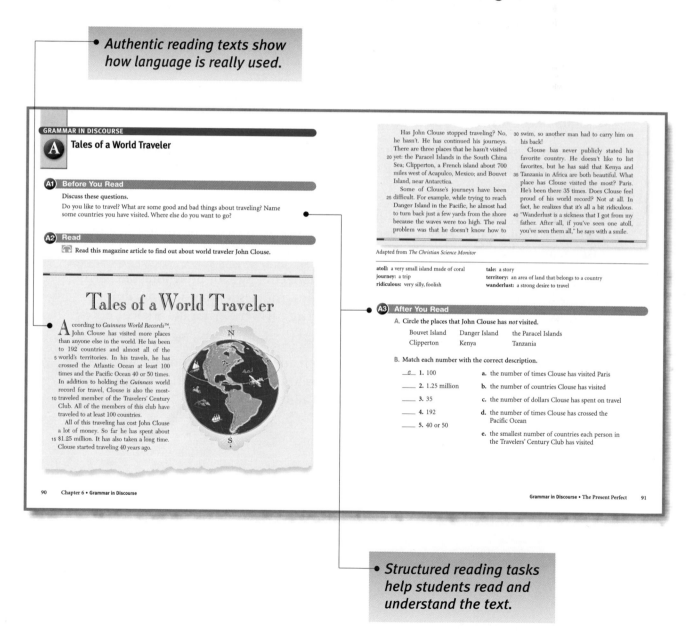

GRAMMAR IN DISCOURSE

A Tales of a World Traveler

A1 Before You Read

Discuss these questions.

Do you like to travel? What are some good and bad things about traveling? Name some countries you have visited. Where else do you want to go?

A2 Read

Read this magazine article to find out about world traveler John Clouse.

Tales of a World Traveler

According to *Guinness World Records*™, John Clouse has visited more places than anyone else in the world. He has been to 192 countries and almost all of the 5 world's territories. In his travels, he has crossed the Atlantic Ocean at least 100 times and the Pacific Ocean 40 or 50 times. In addition to holding the *Guinness* world record for travel, Clouse is also the most-10 traveled member of the Travelers' Century Club. All of the members of this club have traveled to at least 100 countries.

All of this traveling has cost John Clouse a lot of money. So far he has spent about 15 $1.25 million. It has also taken a long time. Clouse started traveling 40 years ago.

Has John Clouse stopped traveling? No, he hasn't. He has continued his journeys. There are three places that he hasn't visited 20 yet: the Paracel Islands in the South China Sea; Clipperton, a French island about 700 miles west of Acapulco, Mexico; and Bouvet Island, near Antarctica.

Some of Clouse's journeys have been 25 difficult. For example, while trying to reach Danger Island in the Pacific, he almost had to turn back just a few yards from the shore because the waves were too high. The real problem was that he doesn't know how to 30 swim, so another man had to carry him on his back!

Clouse has never publicly stated his favorite country. He doesn't like to list favorites, but he has said that Kenya and 35 Tanzania in Africa are both beautiful. What place has Clouse visited the most? Paris. He's been there 35 times. Does Clouse feel proud of his world record? Not at all. In fact, he realizes that it's all a bit ridiculous. 40 "Wanderlust is a sickness that I got from my father. After all, if you've seen one atoll, you've seen them all," he says with a smile.

Adapted from *The Christian Science Monitor*

atoll: a very small island made of coral
journey: a trip
ridiculous: very silly, foolish

tale: a story
territory: an area of land that belongs to a country
wanderlust: a strong desire to travel

A3 After You Read

A. Circle the places that John Clouse has *not* visited.

Bouvet Island	Danger Island	the Paracel Islands
Clipperton	Kenya	Tanzania

B. Match each number with the correct description.

__e__ 1. 100   a. the number of times Clouse has visited Paris

____ 2. 1.25 million   b. the number of countries Clouse has visited

____ 3. 35   c. the number of dollars Clouse has spent on travel

____ 4. 192   d. the number of times Clouse has crossed the Pacific Ocean

____ 5. 40 or 50   e. the smallest number of countries each person in the Travelers' Century Club has visited

90   Chapter 6 • Grammar in Discourse

Grammar in Discourse • The Present Perfect   91

• *Structured reading tasks help students read and understand the text.*

The **Form** section(s) provides clear presentation of the target structure, detailed notes, and thorough practice exercises.

• *Inductive **Examining Form** exercises encourage students to think about how to form the target structure.*

FORM

B The Present Perfect

Examining Form

Look at the sentences and complete the tasks below. Then discuss your answers and read the Form charts to check them.

1a. He has crossed the Atlantic many times. **2a.** They flew to Paris last night.
1b. He crossed the Atlantic in 1999. **2b.** They have flown to Paris many times.

1. Which two sentences are in the simple past? Which two sentences are in the present perfect? How many words are necessary to form the present perfect?

2. Underline the verb forms that follow *has* and *have*. These are past participles. Which form resembles the simple past? Which form is irregular?

3. Look back at the article on page 90. Find five examples of the present perfect.

Affirmative Statements

SUBJECT	HAVE/HAS	PAST PARTICIPLE	
I	have		
You			
He She It	has	traveled flown	to Paris.
We			
You	have		
They			

CONTRACTIONS			
I've			
She's		traveled	to Paris.
They've			

Negative Statements

SUBJECT	HAVE/HAS	NOT	PAST PARTICIPLE	
I	have			
You				
He She It	has	not	traveled flown	to Paris.
We				
You	have			
They				

CONTRACTIONS			
I	haven't		
She	hasn't	traveled	to Paris.
They	haven't		

Yes/No Questions

HAVE/HAS	SUBJECT	PAST PARTICIPLE	
Have	you		
Has	it	traveled flown	to Paris?
Have	they		

Short Answers

YES	SUBJECT	HAVE/HAS	NO	SUBJECT	HAVE/HAS + NOT
	I	have.		I	haven't.
Yes,	he	has.	No,	he	hasn't.
	they	have.		they	haven't.

Information Questions

WH- WORD	HAVE/HAS	SUBJECT	PAST PARTICIPLE	
Who What	have	you	seen?	
Why	has	she		
How long	have	they	been	in the hospital?

WH- WORD (SUBJECT)	HAS	PAST PARTICIPLE	
Who	has	traveled	to Paris?
What		happened?	

• The past participle of a regular verb has the same form as the simple past (verb + *-d/-ed*). See Appendices 4 and 5 for the spelling and pronunciation of verbs ending in *-ed*.
• Irregular verbs have special past participle forms. See Appendix 6 for a list of irregular verbs and their past participles.

B4 Completing Conversations with the Present Perfect

A. Complete these conversations with the words in parentheses and the present perfect. Use contractions where possible.

Conversation 1

Silvio: How long _____*have*_____ you _____*lived*_____ (live) here?
  1   2

Victor: Five years. _____ you _____ (be) here long?
      3   4

Silvio: No, I _____ (not). I _____ only
      5   6
_____ (be) here for six months.
      7

Conversation 2

Gina: Hi, Julie. I _____ (not/see) you for a long time.
      1

Julie: Hi, Gina. I think it _____ (be) almost three years since we last
      2
met. How _____ your family _____ (be)?
      3   4

Gina: Oh, there _____ (be) a lot of changes. My older brother, Chris,
      5
_____ (get) married, and Tony and his wife, Marta,
      6
_____ (have) two children.
      7

B. Practice the conversations in part A with a partner.

B5 Building Sentences

A. Build eight logical sentences: four in the present perfect and four in the simple past. Punctuate your sentences correctly.

Present Perfect: *She has been a good friend.*   Simple Past: *She went to a restaurant.*

		been	for a long time
she	have	waited	to a restaurant
they	has	learned	a good friend
		went	English

B. Rewrite your sentences as negative statements.

• *Clear and detailed **Form Charts** make learning the grammar easy.*

• *A wealth of exercises provide practice in manipulating the form.*

The **Meaning and Use** section(s) offers clear and comprehensive explanations of how the target structure is used, and exercises to practice using it appropriately.

• Inductive **Examining Meaning and Use** exercises encourage students to analyze how we use the target structure.

MEANING AND USE 1

C Continuing Time Up to Now

C1 Listening for Meaning and Use ▶ Note 1

🔊 Listen to each sentence. Is the speaker talking about a past situation that continues to the present, or a situation that began and ended in the past? Check (✓) the correct column.

MEANING AND USE 2

D Indefinite Past Time

Examining Meaning and Use

Read the sentences and answer the questions below. Then discuss your answers and read the Meaning and Use Notes to check them.

1a. I've flown in an airplane.
1b. I flew to Rome last month.

2a. There have been many car accidents on this road.
2b. There was an accident here yesterday.

1. Which sentences talk about an indefinite (not exact) time in the past? Which form of the verb is used in these sentences?

2. Which sentences mention a definite (exact) time in the past? Which form of the verb is used in these sentences?

Meaning and Use Notes

Indefinite Past Time

1A Use the present perfect to talk about actions or states that happened at an indefinite (not exact) time in the past.

A: Have you met Bob?
B: Yes, I've met him. He's really nice.

1B Actions or states in the present perfect can happen once or repeatedly.

He's visited Hawaii once.
I've tried three times to pass my driver's license exam.

1C Do not use the present perfect with time expressions that express a definite (exact) time in the past. When you mention the definite time an event happened, use the simple past.

I went to Europe in 1999.
*I've gone to Europe in 1999. (INCORRECT)

100   Chapter 6 • Meaning and Use 2

Using _Ever_ with Indefinite Past Time

2 The adverb _ever_ means "at any time." Use _ever_ in present perfect questions to ask if an action took place at any time in the past.

A: Have you ever seen a ghost?
B: Yes, I have. OR
No, I haven't.

⚠ We usually do not use _ever_ in present perfect affirmative statements.
I have seen a ghost.
* I have ever seen a ghost. (INCORRECT)

D1 Listening for Meaning and Use ▶ Notes 1A, 1C

🔊 Listen to each sentence. Does it refer to a definite time in the past or an indefinite time in the past? Check (✓) the correct column.

	DEFINITE TIME IN THE PAST	INDEFINITE TIME IN THE PAST
1.		✓

D3 Asking Questions About Indefinite Past Time ▶ Notes 1A, 2

Write two _Yes/No_ questions for each of these situations. Use the present perfect.

1. Your friends have traveled a lot. You want to find out about their trips.

   Have you ever been to Egypt? Have you seen the pyramids?

2. You are thinking about buying a used car. You meet a woman who is trying to sell her car.

3. You want to hire a babysitter. You are interviewing a teenager for the job.

4. You are looking for a new roommate. Someone comes to see your apartment.

5. Your friend, Lee, has moved to a new town. You want to find out about his experiences.

D4 Describing Progress ▶ Notes 1A, 1B

Paul has made a list of things to do before he moves to his new apartment. Look at the list and make statements about his progress so far.

He's called the moving company.
He hasn't vacuumed the apartment.

TO DO
✓ Call the moving company
   Vacuum apartment
✓ Disconnect telephone
   Pack all clothes
   Throw away trash
   Contact the post office
✓ Call mom and give her new address
   Clean oven
   Leave key with superintendent

Meaning and Use 2 • The Present Perfect   103

• Succinct explanations and authentic examples illustrate the various meanings and uses of the structure.

• Practice exercises enable students to use the structure appropriately and fluently.

The **Review** section allows students to demonstrate their mastery of all aspects of the structure. It can be used for further practice or as a test.

• *Thinking About Meaning and Use* exercises consolidate students' understanding of all aspects of the structure.

• *Editing* exercises teach students to correct their own writing.

E Combining Form, Meaning, and Use

E1 Thinking About Meaning and Use

Choose the best answer to complete each conversation. Then discuss your answers in small groups.

1. **A:** He visited Sweden four years ago.

   B: _____
   a. Where is he staying?
   (b.) Did he have a good time?

2. **A:** Emily has worked for the school for a long time.

   B: _____
   a. Is she going to retire soon?
   b. Why did she leave?

3. **A:** I've already cooked dinner.

   B: _____
   a. Can I help you?
   b. What did you cook?

4. **A:** It has rained only once this month.

   B: _____
   a. Does it usually rain more?
   b. Has it rained a lot?

5. **A:** We've been here for half an hour, and a waiter still hasn't come to our table.

   B: _____
   a. I'm sorry. I'll try to find your waiter.
   b. How long have you been here?

6. **A:** I haven't been to Europe yet.

   B: _____
   a. Do you want to go sometime?
   b. When did you go?

7. **A:** Have you ever flown a plane?

   B: _____
   a. No, I didn't.
   b. No, not yet.

8. **A:** So far I've spent $100 on course books.

   B: _____
   a. Do you think you'll need to buy more?
   b. You're lucky you don't need any more.

E2 Editing

Find the errors in this paragraph and correct them. Use the simple present, the simple past, and the present perfect.

Rita and Bob ~~have been~~ are the most-traveled people I know. They went almost everywhere. Rita has been a photographer, and Bob has been a travel writer, so they often travel for work. They been to many

KENYA
THIS SIGN IS ON THE EQUATOR
EQUATOR

▶ Beyond the Classroom

Searching for Authentic Examples

Find examples of English grammar in everyday life. Look in an English-language encyclopedia or on the Internet for information about someone's life. Choose a person who is still alive. What has he or she done or accomplished? Find three sentences in the present perfect and bring them to class. Why is the present perfect used instead of the simple past? Discuss your findings with your classmates.

Writing

Follow the steps below to write a paragraph about someone you admire.

1. Write about someone who is still alive. Think about your subject and make notes about what you want to say. Use these questions to help you.
   • Who do you admire?
   • What has the person done? For example, has he or she worked somewhere special or helped other people?
   • Where has the person lived and worked?
   • How has the person influenced you?

2. Write a first draft. Use the present perfect, simple past, and simple present where appropriate.

3. Read your work carefully and circle grammar, spelling, and punctuation errors. Work with a partner to decide how to fix your errors and improve the content.

4. Rewrite your draft.

   I admire my Uncle Tomás. He is a doctor. He has worked with poor people since he graduated from college twenty years ago. . . .

• *Beyond the Classroom* activities offer creative suggestions for further practice in new contexts.

Special Sections appear throughout the chapters, with clear explanations, authentic examples, and follow-up exercises.

• Pronunciation Notes *show students how to pronounce selected forms of the target language.*

• Beyond the Sentence *sections show how structures function differently in extended discourse.*

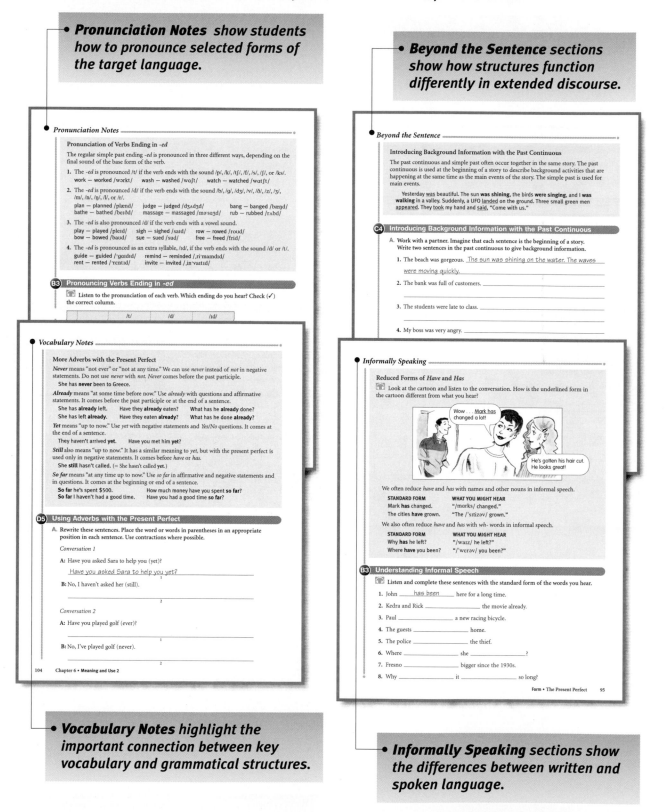

• Pronunciation Notes

Pronunciation of Verbs Ending in -ed

The regular simple past ending *-ed* is pronounced in three different ways, depending on the final sound of the base form of the verb.

1. The *-ed* is pronounced /t/ if the verb ends with the sound /p/, /k/, /tʃ/, /f/, /s/, /ʃ/, or /ks/.
   work — worked /wɑrkt/   wash — washed /wɑʃt/   watch — watched /wɑtʃt/

2. The *-ed* is pronounced /d/ if the verb ends with the sound /b/, /g/, /dʒ/, /v/, /ð/, /z/, /ʒ/, /m/, /n/, /ŋ/, /l/, or /r/.
   plan — planned /plænd/   judge — judged /dʒʌdʒd/
   bathe — bathed /beɪðd/   massage — massaged /məsɑʒd/   bang — banged /bæŋd/
                                                              rub — rubbed /rʌbd/

3. The *-ed* is also pronounced /d/ if the verb ends with a vowel sound.
   play — played /pleɪd/   sigh — sighed /saɪd/   row — rowed /roʊd/
   bow — bowed /baʊd/   sue — sued /sud/   free — freed /frid/

4. The *-ed* is pronounced as an extra syllable, /ɪd/, if the verb ends with the sound /d/ or /t/.
   guide — guided /ˈgaɪdɪd/   remind — reminded /rɪˈmaɪndɪd/
   rent — rented /ˈrɛntɪd/   invite — invited /ɪnˈvaɪtɪd/

B3) Pronouncing Verbs Ending in -ed

🎧 Listen to the pronunciation of each verb. Which ending do you hear? Check (✓) the correct column.

	/t/	/d/	/ɪd/

• Vocabulary Notes

More Adverbs with the Present Perfect

Never means "not ever" or "not at any time." We can use *never* instead of *not* in negative statements. Do not use *never* with *not*. Never comes before the past participle.
   She has **never** been to Greece.

Already means "at some time before now." Use *already* with questions and affirmative statements. It comes before the past participle or at the end of a sentence.
   She has **already** left.   Have they **already** eaten?   What has he **already** done?
   She has left **already**.   Have they eaten **already**?   What has he done **already**?

Yet means "up to now." Use *yet* with negative statements and *Yes/No* questions. It comes at the end of a sentence.
   They haven't arrived **yet**.   Have you met him **yet**?

Still also means "up to now." It has a similar meaning to *yet*, but with the present perfect is used only in negative statements. It comes before *have* or *has*.
   She **still** hasn't called. (= She hasn't called yet.)

So far means "at any time up to now." Use *so far* in affirmative and negative statements and in questions. It comes at the beginning or end of a sentence.
   So far he's spent $500.   How much money have you spent **so far**?
   So far I haven't had a good time.   Have you had a good time **so far**?

D5) Using Adverbs with the Present Perfect

A. Rewrite these sentences. Place the word or words in parentheses in an appropriate position in each sentence. Use contractions where possible.

Conversation 1

A: Have you asked Sara to help you (yet)?

   Have you asked Sara to help you yet?
   ―――――――――――――――――――――――――1

B: No, I haven't asked her (still).

   ―――――――――――――――――――――――――2

Conversation 2

A: Have you played golf (ever)?

   ―――――――――――――――――――――――――1

B: No, I've played golf (never).

   ―――――――――――――――――――――――――2

104   Chapter 6 • Meaning and Use 2

• Beyond the Sentence

Introducing Background Information with the Past Continuous

The past continuous and simple past often occur together in the same story. The past continuous is used at the beginning of a story to describe background activities that are happening at the same time as the main events of the story. The simple past is used for main events.

   Yesterday <u>was</u> beautiful. The sun **was shining**, the birds **were singing**, and I **was walking** in a valley. Suddenly, a UFO <u>landed</u> on the ground. Three small green men <u>appeared</u>. They <u>took</u> my hand and <u>said</u>, "Come with us."

C4) Introducing Background Information with the Past Continuous

A. Work with a partner. Imagine that each sentence is the beginning of a story. Write two sentences in the past continuous to give background information.

1. The beach was gorgeous. The sun was shining on the water. The waves were moving quickly.

2. The bank was full of customers. ―――――――――――――

3. The students were late to class. ―――――――――――――

4. My boss was very angry. ―――――――――――――

• Informally Speaking

Reduced Forms of *Have* and *Has*

🎧 Look at the cartoon and listen to the conversation. How is the underlined form in the cartoon different from what you hear?

Wow . . . <u>Mark has</u> changed a lot!

He's gotten his hair cut. He looks great!

We often reduce *have* and *has* with names and other nouns in informal speech.

STANDARD FORM	WHAT YOU MIGHT HEAR
Mark **has** changed.	"/mɑrks/ changed."
The cities **have** grown.	"The /ˈsɪtiəv/ grown."

We also often reduce *have* and *has* with *wh-* words in informal speech.

STANDARD FORM	WHAT YOU MIGHT HEAR
Why **has** he left?	"/waɪz/ he left?"
Where **have** you been?	"/ˈwɛrəv/ you been?"

B3) Understanding Informal Speech

🎧 Listen and complete these sentences with the standard form of the words you hear.

1. John __has been__ here for a long time.
2. Kedra and Rick ―――――― the movie already.
3. Paul ―――――― a new racing bicycle.
4. The guests ―――――― home.
5. The police ―――――― the thief.
6. Where ―――――― she ――――――?
7. Fresno ―――――― bigger since the 1930s.
8. Why ―――――― it ―――――― so long?

Form • The Present Perfect   95

• Vocabulary Notes *highlight the important connection between key vocabulary and grammatical structures.*

• Informally Speaking *sections show the differences between written and spoken language.*

The Present

The Simple Present

A Mysterious Island

A1 Before You Read

Discuss these questions.

What do you think about when you imagine an island? Do you imagine warm weather or cold weather? Can you name any islands that are countries?

A2 Read

 Read this geography quiz to find out more about Iceland.

QUIZ

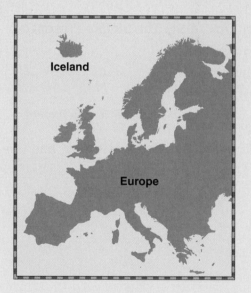

ICELAND IS A TRULY UNIQUE ISLAND—
in fact, it's like nowhere else on Earth.
The interior of this island nation contains
incredible contrasts. It has tundras, huge
5 glaciers, volcanoes, and waterfalls.

Read these amazing facts about Iceland.
Then guess the answers to the questions.
Check your guesses on page 5.

1

Swimsuit maker Speedo® <u>sells</u> a very large
10 number of bathing suits in Iceland. Is it
warm here all year?

2

The island's climate is cool, but most people
don't pay much money for heat. Energy is
very cheap and it doesn't cause pollution.
15 What kind of energy do Icelanders use?

3

Icelanders <u>eat</u> fresh fruit and vegetables
all year, but they rarely buy them from
other countries. Where do they get them?

4

Icelanders like to play golf all night during
20 the summer. How do they see the ball?

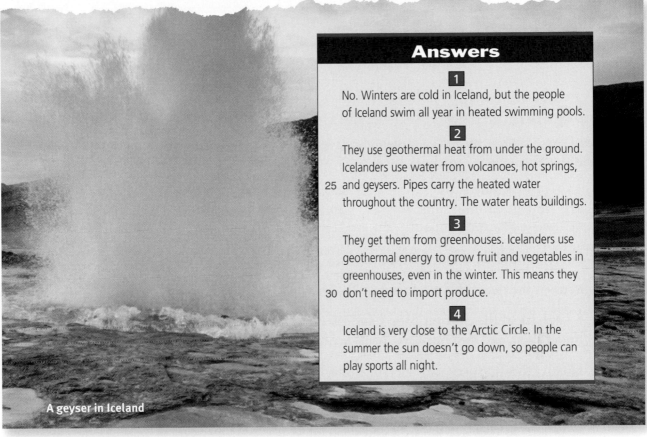

Answers

1

No. Winters are cold in Iceland, but the people of Iceland swim all year in heated swimming pools.

2

They use geothermal heat from under the ground. Icelanders use water from volcanoes, hot springs, 25 and geysers. Pipes carry the heated water throughout the country. The water heats buildings.

3

They get them from greenhouses. Icelanders use geothermal energy to grow fruit and vegetables in greenhouses, even in the winter. This means they 30 don't need to import produce.

4

Iceland is very close to the Arctic Circle. In the summer the sun doesn't go down, so people can play sports all night.

A geyser in Iceland

Adapted from *The Christian Science Monitor*

---

climate: the typical weather conditions of a place
geyser: a hot spring that shoots water into the air
glacier: a large body of ice that moves slowly over land
greenhouse: a glass building used for growing plants

produce: foods such as fruit and vegetables
tundra: a large, flat area of frozen land without trees
volcano: a mountain from which hot melted rock, gas, smoke, and ash can escape from a hole in its top

A3 After You Read

Write *T* for true or *F* for false for each statement.

__F__ **1.** Iceland is warm in the winter.

_____ **2.** Icelanders use geothermal energy.

_____ **3.** Geothermal energy comes from the sun.

_____ **4.** Icelanders heat their houses with oil.

_____ **5.** Icelanders don't grow fresh fruit.

_____ **6.** The sun shines all night in Iceland in the summer.

B The Simple Present

Examining Form

Read these sentences and complete the tasks below. Then discuss your answers and read the Form charts to check them.

1a. I <u>sell</u> bathing suits.   **2a.** You <u>don't buy</u> fruit.
1b. He <u>sells</u> bathing suits.   **2b.** She <u>doesn't buy</u> fruit.
1c. We <u>sell</u> bathing suits.   **2c.** They <u>don't buy</u> fruit.

1. Look at the affirmative verb forms in 1a–1c. What is different about the form in 1b?

2. Look at the negative verb forms in 2a–2c. What is different about the form in 2b?

3. Look back at the quiz on page 4 and the answers on page 5. Two affirmative forms are underlined, and two negative forms are circled. Find two more examples of each form.

4. Look at the questions below. Which is a *Yes/No* question? Which is an information question? How are they different? How are they the same?

   a. Does it snow in the winter?
   b. Where do they get the fruit and vegetables?

\	Affirmative Statements		
SUBJECT	**BASE FORM OF VERB or BASE FORM OF VERB + -S/-ES**		
I	eat		
You			
He She It	eats		fresh fruit.
We	eat		
You			
They			

\	Negative Statements		
SUBJECT	**DO/DOES + NOT**	**BASE FORM OF VERB**	
I	do not don't		
You			
He She It	does not doesn't	eat	fresh fruit.
We	do not don't		
You			
They			

Yes/No Questions

DO/DOES	SUBJECT	BASE FORM OF VERB	
Do	you		
Does	she	**eat**	fresh fruit?
Do	they		

Short Answers

YES	SUBJECT	DO/DOES	NO	SUBJECT	DO/DOES + NOT
	I	**do.**		I	**don't.**
Yes,	she	**does.**	**No,**	she	**doesn't.**
	they	**do.**		they	**don't.**

Information Questions

WH- WORD	DO/DOES	SUBJECT	BASE FORM OF VERB	
Who	**do**	you	**teach**	on Tuesdays?
What	**does**	he	**eat?**	
When				
Where	**do**	they	**travel**	in the winter?
Why				
How				

WH- WORD (SUBJECT)		BASE FORM OF VERB + -S/-ES	
Who		**works**	on Tuesdays?
What		**happens**	there?

- In affirmative statements, add *-s* or *-es* to the base form of the verb when the subject is third-person singular (*he, she,* or *it*). See Appendices 1 and 2 for the spelling and pronunciation of verbs ending in *-s* and *-es*.
- Use *does* in negative statements and questions when the subject is third-person singular. For all other persons, use *do*.

  She **doesn't play** golf.   I **don't play** golf.

  Does he **play** golf?   **Do** they **play** golf?

⚠️ Do not use *do* or *does* in information questions when *who* or *what* is the subject.

  Who **lives** here?   *Who does live here. (INCORRECT)

- *Have* and *be* are irregular in the simple present.

  I **have** a problem.   She **has** a red car.   We **have** dinner at 6:00.

  I **am** busy.   He **is** a musician.   They **are** home.

⚠️ Do not use *do/does* in negative statements or in questions with *be*.

  You **aren't** late.   **Is** he ready?

🎧 Listen to this paragraph. Write the verb forms you hear.

Many people in Hawaii ____live____ in two different worlds—the world of
                              1
traditional Hawaiian culture and the world of modern American culture. Keenan

Kanaeholo _____ a typical Hawaiian. He _____ on the island of
                  2   3
Oahu. Like many Hawaiians, Keenan _____ two languages. At home he and
                                          4
his family _____ English. They _____ to each other in Hawaiian.
                  5   6
Keenan _____ in a large hotel. At work he _____ English. Keenan's
              7   8
wife, Emeha, _____ in the hotel. She _____ at an elementary school.
                    9   10
Both Keenan and Emeha _____ to dance. They _____ to discos on
                              11   12
the weekends. Emeha also _____ the hula, but Keenan _____ .
                                13   14

Complete this paragraph with the correct form of the verbs in parentheses. Use
contractions where possible.

An okapi ___looks___ (look) like the child of
                1
a zebra and a giraffe, but it _____ (not/be).
                                    2
It _____ (have) stripes like a zebra, and it
        3
_____ (have) a body like a giraffe. The
      4
okapi's stripes _____ (hide) it from its
                        5
enemies. The okapi _____ (be) a relative
                          6
of the giraffe, but it _____ (not/have)
                              7
a long neck. It _____ (not/need) one
                      8
to find food because it _____ (eat) fruit
                                9

and leaves near the ground. Okapis _____ (play) in a strange way. They
                                          10
_____ (put) their heads down, _____ (move) their tails, and
      11   12
_____ (run) in circles. Okapis _____ (live) only in Central Africa
      13   14
and _____ (be) very rare.
          15

Pronunciation Notes

Pronunciation of Verbs Ending in -s or -es

The letters -s or -es at the end of third-person singular verbs are pronounced in three different ways, depending on the final sound of the base form of the verb.

1. The -s or -es is pronounced /s/ if the base form of the verb ends with the sound /p/, /t/, /k/, or /f/.

    stop – stops /staps/   like – likes /laɪks/   laugh – laughs /læfs/

2. The -s or -es is pronounced /z/ if the base form of the verb ends with the sound /b/, /d/, /g/, /v/, /ð/, /m/, /n/, /ŋ/, /l/, /r/, or a vowel sound.

    leave – leaves /livz/   run – runs /rʌnz/   go – goes /gouz/

3. The -es is pronounced /ɪz/ if the base form of the verb ends with the sound /s/, /z/, /ʃ/, /ʒ/, /tʃ/, /dʒ/, or /ks/. This adds an extra syllable to the word.

    notice – notices /ˈnouṭəsɪz/   buzz – buzzes /ˈbʌzɪz/   watch – watches /ˈwatʃɪz/

B3 Pronouncing Verbs Ending in -s or -es

A. 🎧 Listen to the pronunciation of each verb. What ending do you hear? Check (✓) the correct column.

		/s/	/z/	/ɪz/
1.	lives		✓	
2.	practices			
3.	works			
4.	closes			
5.	arranges			
6.	tells			

B. Work with a partner. Take turns reading these sentences aloud. Be sure to pronounce the verb endings correctly.

1. Pablo lives in San Diego.

2. The team practices every day.

3. The computer works just fine.

4. My mother closes the window at night.

5. Tony arranges all the meetings.

6. Sara tells everyone's secrets.

B4 Forming *Yes/No* Questions

A. Use these words and phrases to form *Yes/No* questions. Punctuate your sentences correctly.

1. study/do/a lot/you <u>Do you study a lot?</u>

2. teacher/does/your/speak/language/your _____

3. have/do/homework/you/a lot of _____

4. a/do/use/you/dictionary _____

5. speak/you/do/English/of/class/outside _____

6. your/computers/school/does/have _____

B. Work with a partner. Take turns asking and answering the questions in part A.

A: Do you study a lot?
B: Yes, I do. OR *No, I don't.*

B5 Changing Statements into Questions

A. Write an information question about each underlined word or phrase.

1. <u>Water</u> freezes at 32° Fahrenheit. <u>What freezes at 32° Fahrenheit?</u>

2. <u>Kim</u> has a test today. _____

3. A power plant makes <u>electricity</u>. _____

4. Niagara Falls is <u>in North America</u>. _____

5. <u>Dan</u> drives Lee to school every day. _____

6. Dan drives <u>Lee</u> to school every day. _____

7. It is hot in Chicago <u>in the summer</u>. _____

8. The eucalyptus tree is from <u>Australia</u>. _____

B. In your notebook, write a *Yes/No* question about each sentence in part A.

Does water freeze at 32° Fahrenheit?

The Simple Present

Examining Meaning and Use

Read the sentences and answer the questions below. Then discuss your answers and read the Meaning and Use Notes to check them.

    a. Thailand has three seasons: a hot season, a cold season, and a rainy season.
    b. Maria doesn't like her new roommate.
    c. My teacher always arrives at school before class starts.

1. Which sentence talks about a repeated activity?

2. Which sentence talks about factual information that you can find in a book?

3. Which sentence talks about a feeling?

Meaning and Use Notes

Repeated Activities

1   Use the simple present to talk about activities that happen repeatedly (again and again). These events can be personal habits or routines (for example, activities at home or at work), or scheduled events.

Habits or Routines	*Scheduled Events*
I always **eat** cereal for breakfast.	School **starts** at 8:00 and **finishes** at 3:00.
He **takes** the bus to work every day.	The club **meets** in the library every Friday.

Factual Information

2   Use the simple present to talk about factual information, such as general truths, scientific facts, or definitions.

General Truths	*Definitions*
Doctors **study** for many years.	The word *brilliant* **means** "very intelligent."
Scientific Facts	
Iceland **has** more than 100 volcanoes.	

(Continued on page 12)

States or Conditions

3 Use the simple present with stative verbs (verbs that do not express action) to talk about states or conditions, such as physical descriptions, feelings, relationships, knowledge, beliefs, or possession. Some common stative verbs are *be, have, seem, like, want, know, understand, mean, believe, own,* and *belong.* See Appendix 7 for a list of common stative verbs.

He **is** tall and **has** dark hair.   She **knows** the answer.

She **seems** angry.   I don't **understand.**

You **like** sports.   I **believe** you.

They **want** a new car.   We **belong** to the soccer club.

Adverbs of Frequency with the Simple Present

4 Use adverbs of frequency with the simple present to express how often something happens. Adverbs of frequency usually come before the main verb, but after the verb *be.*

She **always** has ballet from 3:00 to 6:00 P.M.

The cafeteria food is **usually** bad.

My mother **often** cooks for us.

It **sometimes** rains here in the summer.

My brother and I **seldom** fight.

He **never** cleans his room.

C1 Listening for Meaning and Use

► Notes 1, 2

Listen to each statement. Is the speaker describing a personal routine or a general truth? Check (✓) the correct column.

	PERSONAL ROUTINE	GENERAL TRUTH
1.		✓
2.		
3.		
4.		
5.		
6.		

C2 Talking About Routines

▶ Notes 1, 4

A. Read these statements. Check (✓) the ones that are true for you.

_____ **1.** I always wash the dishes after dinner.

_____ **2.** I often ride the bus in the morning.

_____ **3.** My friends sometimes visit me on Saturdays.

_____ **4.** I often get up at 7:00 A.M.

_____ **5.** I usually recycle newspapers.

_____ **6.** I never go to bed before midnight.

_____ **7.** My friends and I sometimes study together in the evenings.

_____ **8.** I never stay home on Saturday nights.

B. Work with a partner. Look at the statements in part A that you did not check. Take turns talking about them.

A: *I don't always wash the dishes after dinner. I sometimes leave them for the next day.*
B: *I seldom ride the bus in the morning. I have a car.*

C3 Asking for Definitions

▶ Note 2

A. Work with a partner. How much do you remember from the quiz about Iceland on page 4? Take turns asking and answering questions about the meaning of these words. If you don't remember the meaning of a word, look at the definitions on page 5.

1. tundra

    A: *What does the word* tundra *mean?*
    B: *The word* tundra *means "a large, flat area of frozen land."*

2. glacier

3. greenhouse

4. climate

5. geyser

6. volcano

B. Look back at the quiz on page 4. Find a word that is new to you and ask your partner what it means. If your partner doesn't know, look in a dictionary.

A. Complete this paragraph with the correct form of the verbs in parentheses.

Bobsledding ____is____ (be) a dangerous sport. A bobsled
1

_____ (weigh) about 600 pounds and _____ (carry) four people.
2   3

Each person on a bobsled team _____ (have) an important job. First,
4

all four people _____ (move) the sled back and forth. When it
5

_____ (start) to move, they _____ (push) it very hard, and the pilot
6   7

_____ (jump) into the bobsled to steer. Then, the person on each side
8

_____ (jump) in. The brakeman _____ (stay) at the back and
9   10

_____ (push) for a few more seconds. Then he or she _____ (get)
11   12

in, too. The bobsled _____ (be) very fast. It _____ (go) up to
13   14

90 miles per hour.

B. Describe another sport. In your notebook, write five or six facts about
the sport, using the simple present.

Ice hockey is a popular sport in cold places like Canada
and the northeastern United States. This game has two
teams of players. The players wear ice skates and play on an
ice-skating rink. . . .

D Combining Form, Meaning, and Use

D1 Thinking About Meaning and Use

Look at these topics. Check (✓) the ones you can discuss or write about with the simple present. Then discuss your answers in small groups.

_✓_ **1.** Traditions in your country

_____ **2.** Your childhood

_____ **3.** A party you went to last night

_____ **4.** The geography of a country

_____ **5.** The life of a 19ᵗʰ-century politician

_____ **6.** A vacation you took

_____ **7.** How a machine works

_____ **8.** Your best friend's personality

D2 Editing

Find the errors in this paragraph and correct them.

    Which large American city are on three islands? New York City! New York is on

Manhattan Island, Long Island, and Staten Island. Most people thinks of Manhattan

when they think of New York City. This is because Manhattan have the tall buildings that

New York is famous for. Sometimes people travel from Staten Island to Manhattan by

boat. However, most people in New York not use boats to go from one part of the city to

another. Large bridges connects the islands. Trains and cars also uses long tunnels under

the water to move between the islands. In fact, New Yorkers usually forget that they lives

on an island.

▶ Beyond the Classroom

Searching for Authentic Examples

Find examples of English grammar in everyday life. Look for advertisements in English-language newspapers and magazines or on the Internet. Find five examples of the simple present and bring them to class. Try to find examples with different meanings and uses. Discuss your findings with your classmates.

Speaking

Follow these steps to prepare an oral report about an unusual animal like the okapi on page 8.

1. Do research at the library or on the Internet for information about an unusual animal.

2. Take notes. Answer these questions, and write five or six facts about the animal. Use the simple present.
   - What is the animal?
   - What does it look like?
   - Where does it live?
   - What interesting or unusual habits does it have?

3. Try to find a photo of the animal.

4. Bring your notes and photo to class. Use the information in your notes to tell your classmates about the animal.

◀

Imperatives

Do's and Don'ts with Bears

A1 Before You Read

Discuss these questions.

Do you like to walk in the woods? Are there wild animals in the woods in your area? Are they dangerous?

A2 Read

 Read the leaflet on the following page to find out about what to do if you see a bear.

A3 After You Read

Write *T* for true or *F* for false for each statement.

__F__ **1.** Bears often attack cars.

_____ **2.** If a bear attacks you, you should run.

_____ **3.** Bears attack when they feel threatened.

_____ **4.** Bears are great tree climbers.

_____ **5.** Garbage attracts bears because they think it is food.

_____ **6.** Bears are slow and weak.

Do's and Don'ts with Bears

About 250 black bears live in Black Bear Mountain Park. If you run into a bear in the park, it is important to know what to do.

5 🐾Talk loudly, sing, or clap as you walk through the woods. Bears don't like surprises. Singing or clapping will probably frighten the bears off before you even see them.

🐾Don't hike through the woods at night. 10 Bears are most active at nighttime.

🐾If you are in a car and see a bear, stay inside. Close the windows. Most bears will not attack a car, so you are safest inside. Don't get out to take a photograph.

15 🐾If you are outside and see a bear, stay calm. Stand still and don't run. Slowly move backward. Bears are nervous animals. They are more likely to attack you if they feel threatened.

20 🐾If a bear attacks you, don't fight. Lie still and be quiet. Maybe the bear will lose interest and wander off.

🐾Do not climb a tree to get away from a bear. Bears are great tree climbers!

25 🐾Do not keep food or cosmetics in your tent. Put them in a bag and hang them in a tree that is at least 100 yards from your tent. Bears like anything that resembles food. Remove food, cosmetics, and 30 toothpaste from your tent so you won't attract their attention.

🐾Burn food waste. Bears cannot tell the difference between food and garbage. They will go after both.

35 Remember bears are dangerous animals. They are very fast and very strong. Be safe. Don't be sorry!

---

attract: to cause someone or something to feel interest
do's and don'ts: rules about what you should and should not do in a situation
resemble: to be like or to look like

run into: meet by chance
wander off: to walk away from a place

B Imperatives

Examining Form

Read the sentences and complete the tasks below. Then discuss your answers and read the Form charts to check them.

a. Bears are dangerous animals.   **c.** Most bears do not attack cars.
b. Do not climb a tree.   **d.** Lie still and be quiet.

1. Underline the verbs. Circle the subjects. Which sentences do not seem to have a subject? These are imperatives.

2. Look back at the leaflet on page 19. Find five imperatives.

Affirmative Imperatives	
BASE FORM OF VERB	
Open	your books.
Drive	carefully.
Be	here at six.

Negative Imperatives		
DO + NOT	BASE FORM OF VERB	
Do not **Don't**	**open**	your books.
	leave	yet.
	be	late.

- The subject of an imperative is *you* (singular or plural), even though we don't usually say or write the subject.
- The imperative has the same form whether we talk to one person or more than one.
  Teacher to Student: **Sit** down, please.   *Teacher to Class:* **Sit** down, please.
- In spoken English, *don't* is more common than *do not* in negative imperatives.

B1 Listening for Form

🎧 Listen to these sentences. Write the verb forms you hear.

1. <u>Don't leave.</u> It's early.

2. _____ right at the corner.

3. _____ in the kitchen.

4. _____ home before dinner.

5. _____ angry with me, please.

6. Please _____ off the light.

B2 Forming Sentences with Imperatives

Use these words and phrases to form sentences with affirmative and negative imperatives. Punctuate your sentences correctly.

1. take/you/your/with/book _Take your book with you._

2. notebook/leave/your/home/at/don't _____

3. tomorrow/be/for/test/ready/the _____

4. questions/to/the/answer/all/try _____

5. not/the/during/talk/test/do _____

B3 Working on Affirmative and Negative Imperatives

A. Read the tips below. Check (✓) the ones that you think are bad advice.

✓ 1. Don't write English definitions for new words.

_____ 2. Keep a vocabulary notebook.

_____ 3. Don't try to use new words in conversation.

_____ 4. Look up every new word you read.

_____ 5. Try to guess the meaning of new words.

_____ 6. Write a translation of every new word.

B. Now change the bad advice to good advice. Compare answers with a partner.

Write English definitions for new words.

B4 Building Sentences

Build ten imperative and simple present sentences. Use a word or phrase from each column, or from the second and third columns only. Punctuate your sentences correctly.

Imperative: *Listen to him!*   Simple Present: *She goes to class.*

	goes	to class
she	listen	gum
don't	speak	late
they	chew	to him
	is	Korean

Imperatives

Examining Meaning and Use

Read the sentences and answer the questions below. Then discuss your answers and read the Meaning and Use Notes to check them.

    a. <u>Walk to the corner and turn left.</u> The post office is right there.
    b. <u>Watch out!</u> There's ice on the road.
    c. Are you getting coffee now? <u>Buy me a coffee, too, please.</u>
    d. <u>Talk to the teacher.</u> She can help you.

1. Which underlined sentence gives advice?

2. Which underlined sentence makes a request?

3. Which underlined sentence gives directions?

4. Which underlined sentence gives a warning?

Meaning and Use Notes

> ### Common Uses of Imperatives
>
> **1A** An imperative tells someone to do something. Common uses include:
>
> | | |
> |---:|:---|
> | *Giving Commands:* | **Stop** the car! |
> | *Giving Advice:* | **Don't worry** about it. |
> | *Making Requests:* | Please **come** home early. |
> | *Giving Directions:* | **Turn** left. **Walk** three blocks. |
> | *Giving Instructions:* | First, **peel** the potatoes. Then, **boil** the water. |
> | *Giving Warnings:* | **Be** careful! The floor is wet. |
> | *Making Offers:* | Here. **Have** another piece of cake, Gina. |
>
> ---
>
> **1B** Although we usually leave out the subject *you* (singular or plural), it is understood as the subject of an imperative.
>
> | *Boss to Employee* | *Boss to Several Employees* |
> |:---|:---|
> | **Come** to my office, please. | **Come** to my office, please. |

2A Use *please* to make an imperative sound more polite or less authoritative. We often use imperatives with *please* in formal situations when we speak to strangers or to people in authority. In less formal situations, especially with friends and family members, *please* is often used to soften the tone of an imperative. If *please* comes at the end of a sentence, we put a comma before it.

Train Conductor to Passenger   *Child to Parent*

<u>Please</u> **watch** your step.   Mom, **hand** me a towel, <u>please</u>. I spilled my drink.

2B You can also make an imperative sound more polite by using polite forms such as *sir, ma'am,* or *miss.* In written English, the polite form of address is separated from the rest of the sentence with a comma.

<u>Sir</u>, **watch** your step!   **Stay** calm, <u>ma'am</u>. Help is on the way.

Using *You* or Names in Imperatives

3 Although we usually leave out the subject *you,* we sometimes use it to make it clear who we are speaking to. We can also add the person's name with or without *you* as the stated subject.

A Roommate to Two Other Roommates

<u>You</u> **sweep** the hall, <u>you</u> **vacuum** the living room, and I'll clean the bathroom.
<u>Maria</u>, <u>you</u> **sweep** the hall. <u>Bill</u>, <u>you</u> **vacuum** the rug. I'll clean the bathroom.

C1 **Listening for Meaning and Use**   ► Notes 1–3

 Listen to each conversation. Who are the speakers? Choose the correct answer.

1. **a.** a boss and an employee
   b. two co-workers
   c. two strangers

2. **a.** a teacher and a student
   b. two family members
   c. two strangers

3. **a.** two strangers
   b. two friends
   c. two family members

4. **a.** two family members
   b. two strangers
   c. a boss and an employee

5. **a.** a boss and an employee
   b. two family members
   c. two strangers

6. **a.** a teacher and a student
   b. two friends
   c. two strangers

Look at the pictures. Match the warnings and commands to the pictures.

Stop! Police!   Please put your seat belt on.   Watch out for the ball!

Look out!   Don't step on the truck!   Sit down and be quiet.

1. Look out!

4. _____

2. _____

5. _____

3. _____

6. _____

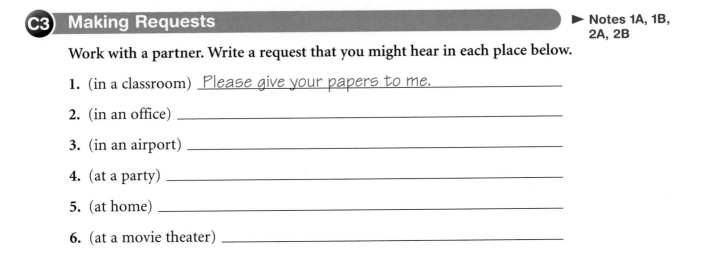

C3 Making Requests ▶ Notes 1A, 1B, 2A, 2B

Work with a partner. Write a request that you might hear in each place below.

1. (in a classroom) _Please give your papers to me._

2. (in an office) _____

3. (in an airport) _____

4. (at a party) _____

5. (at home) _____

6. (at a movie theater) _____

C4 Giving Advice ▶ Notes 1A, 1B

Read each problem. In your notebook, write two sentences of advice: one with an affirmative imperative and one with a negative imperative. Then compare answers with a partner.

1. The light doesn't work.

   Don't touch the lightbulb. Turn the light off first.

2. My son is sick.

3. The gas tank is almost empty.

4. I can't sleep at night.

5. I don't have many friends.

6. I have a headache.

C5 Giving Instructions ▶ Notes 1A, 1B, 2A

Work with a partner. You are leaving on vacation, and a friend is going to stay in your apartment. Take turns telling your friend what to do while you are away. Use affirmative and negative imperatives.

| cat | lights | newspaper | rent | voice mail |
| dog | mail | plants | trash | windows |

Don't forget to feed the cat.
Please walk the dog twice a day.

A. Write an appropriate affirmative or negative imperative sentence for each situation.

1. Your friend is new in town. Tell him how to go to the post office.

   <u>Go down three blocks and turn left at the traffic light.</u>

2. You are a bus driver. A man is getting off the bus. Tell him to watch his step.

   _____

3. You are going on vacation with some friends. Your mother is worried. Reassure her.

   _____

4. You are a salesperson. Tell your customer to sign the credit card receipt.

   _____

5. You want your roommates to help you clean the apartment. Give each person a chore.

   _____

6. You dropped a glass on the floor. Warn your roommate.

   _____

7. Josh, a close friend, is visiting your home. Offer him something to eat.

   _____

8. Your uncle looks very tired. Give him some advice.

   _____

9. You are going out to dinner with some co-workers. Tell them to wait for you in the lobby.

   _____

10. You are crossing a busy street with your cousin. Give her a warning.

    _____

B. Would you use *you* in any of the situations in part A? Why or why not? Discuss your ideas with a partner.

D Combining Form, Meaning, and Use

D1 Thinking About Meaning and Use

Read what each person says. Is the imperative appropriate for the situation? If it is not appropriate, rewrite it. Then discuss your answers with a partner.

1. (an army sergeant to a soldier) Please get up. It's 5:00 A.M.

   Get up! It's 5:00 A.M.

2. (a cook to his assistant) Bake the chicken at 375° for one hour.

   _____

3. (one stranger to another on the street) Please look out! A car is coming!

   _____

4. (a young girl to her grandmother) Sit down!

   _____

5. (a bank robber to a bank teller) Please give me all of your money.

   _____

6. (an adult to a child) Turn off the television, sir.

   _____

D2 Editing

Some of these sentences have errors. Find the errors and correct them.

1. You don't worrying about your memory. _Don't worry_

2. Be not noisy!

3. Don't to listen to her.

4. Megan, closes the door, please.

5. Study the vocabulary for tomorrow's test.

6. Leave not now!

▶ Beyond the Classroom

Searching for Authentic Examples

Find examples of grammar in everyday life. Look for imperatives in how-to articles or advice columns in an English-language magazine or on the Internet. You can also look at the English-language section of an instruction manual for a computer, DVD player, or other home appliance. Write down five examples and bring them to class. Discuss your findings with your classmates.

Speaking

Find a recipe for your favorite food in an English-language cookbook or on the Internet. Bring it to class. Work with a partner. Take turns telling each other how to prepare your recipes. Use imperatives where possible.

My favorite recipe is my mother's chocolate cake. First, beat two eggs in a bowl. Then, add a cup of milk and stir well. Next, . . .

The Present Continuous

A ## Long-Distance Messenger

 A1 **Before You Read**

Discuss these questions.

Do you think there is life on other planets? Is it a good idea to look for life on other planets? Why or why not?

 A2 **Read**

🎧 Read the magazine article on the following page to discover the two different purposes of a famous spacecraft.

A3 **After You Read**

Write *T* for true or *F* for false for each statement.

__T__ **1.** *Voyager* is a spacecraft.

_____ **2.** *Voyager* is traveling through space.

_____ **3.** *Voyager* is coming back to Earth right now.

_____ **4.** People aren't traveling on *Voyager*.

_____ **5.** *Voyager* isn't carrying pictures.

_____ **6.** *Voyager* is carrying live animals.

LONG-DISTANCE MESSENGER

Voyager I is a spacecraft that left Earth in 1977. Its purpose was to explore our solar system. Scientists expected to receive information about other planets
5 from *Voyager* for ten to fifteen years. They were very wrong. They are still receiving messages from *Voyager* today. *Voyager* is currently moving away from Earth at a speed of 39,000 miles per
10 hour (62,904 kilometers per hour). Now it is so far away that its messages take almost ten hours to travel to Earth. After all this time, these messages are still giving scientists important information
15 about our solar system.

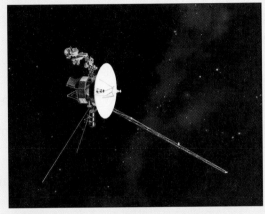

Voyager I

Voyager has another important job. It is a messenger from our planet to other planets. *Voyager* is not carrying any astronauts, but it is carrying more than
20 100 pictures of life on Earth and greetings in over 50 languages. It also has examples of animal sounds, different kinds of music, the sound of a mother kissing a baby, and messages from world
25 leaders. In addition, it is carrying pictures of humans and a map that shows Earth's location.

Scientists say that *Voyager* will send messages until the year 2020. Perhaps
30 one day someone from another planet will find the spacecraft and learn about our planet.

---

astronaut: a person who travels in a spacecraft

greetings: words that you say when you see or meet someone

messenger: a person or thing that brings information

solar system: the Sun and the planets that move around it

spacecraft: a vehicle that can travel in space

voyager: somebody or something that travels

B The Present Continuous

Examining Form

Read the sentences and complete the tasks below. Then discuss your answers and read the Form charts to check them.

    a. *Voyager* is a messenger from Earth.   **b.** It is carrying pictures of humans.

1. Underline the verbs. Which is simple present? Which is present continuous?

2. How many words are necessary to form the present continuous? What ending is added to the base form of the verb?

3. Look back at the article on page 31. Find three examples of the present continuous.

Affirmative Statements			
SUBJECT	**BE**	**BASE FORM OF VERB + -ING**	
I	am		
You	are		
He She It	is	working	today.
We	are		
You			
They			

CONTRACTIONS		
I'm		
You're	working	today.
He's		
They're		

Negative Statements				
SUBJECT	**BE**	**NOT**	**BASE FORM OF VERB + -ING**	
I	am			
You	are			
He She It	is	not	working	today.
We	are			
You				
They				

CONTRACTIONS		
I'm not		
You're not You aren't		
He's not He isn't	working	today.
They're not They aren't		

Yes/No Questions

BE	SUBJECT	BASE FORM OF VERB + *-ING*	
Are	you		
Is	it	**working**	now?
Are	they		

Short Answers

YES	SUBJECT	BE		NO	SUBJECT + BE + NOT
	I	**am.**			**I'm not.**
Yes,	it	**is.**		No,	it **isn't.**
	they	**are.**			they **aren't.**

Information Questions

WH- WORD	BE	SUBJECT	BASE FORM OF VERB + *-ING*
How	**am**	I	**doing?**
Who			**calling?**
What	**are**	you	**studying?**
Where	**is**	he	**working?**
Why	**are**	they	**shouting?**

WH- WORD (SUBJECT)	BE		BASE FORM OF VERB + *-ING*
Who			**laughing?**
What	**is**		**happening?**

- See Appendix 3 for the spelling of verbs ending in *-ing*.
- See Appendix 16 for more contractions with *be*.
- ⚠ Do not use contractions in affirmative short answers.
     Yes, I **am.**
     *Yes, I'm. (INCORRECT)
- ⚠ Do not use a subject pronoun in information questions when *who* or *what* is the subject.
     What is happening?
     *What is it happening? (INCORRECT)

🎧 Listen to each sentence. Choose the verb form you hear.

1. a. is living
    b. isn't living
    c. are living
    (d.) aren't living

2. a. am trying
    b. am not trying
    c. are trying
    d. are not trying

3. a. is meeting
    b. is not meeting
    c. are meeting
    d. are not meeting

4. a. am sleeping
    b. am not sleeping
    c. is sleeping
    d. is not sleeping

5. a. is working
    b. isn't working
    c. are working
    d. aren't working

6. a. am cooking
    b. am not cooking
    c. are cooking
    d. aren't cooking

B2 **Forming Statements and *Yes/No* Questions**

A. Form sentences in the present continuous from these words and phrases. Use contractions where possible, and punctuate your sentences correctly.

1. in Canada/Maria and Hector/live

    Maria and Hector are living in Canada.

2. Hector/in a factory/work

    _____

3. not/Maria/in a factory/work

    _____

4. she/Spanish/teach

    _____

5. English/Hector/at night/study

    _____

6. not/live/they/in an apartment

    _____

7. rent/a small house/they

_____

8. learn/Maria and Hector/about life in Canada

_____

B. Work with a partner. Take turns asking and answering _Yes/No_ questions about the sentences in part A.

A: Are Maria and Hector living in Canada?
B: Yes, they are. OR
A: Are Maria and Hector living in the United States?
B: No, they're not. They're living in Canada.

B3 **Writing Information Questions**

Write an information question about each underlined word or phrase.

1. The rice is burning!

 What is burning?_____

2. Carol is talking on the telephone.

_____

3. Ben is reading the newspaper.

_____

4. Eric is studying at the library.

_____

5. Their children are playing a game.

_____

6. The children are yelling because they're excited.

_____

7. He's feeling sad today.

_____

8. They're doing their homework now.

_____

C The Present Continuous

Examining Meaning and Use

Read the sentences and answer the questions below. Then discuss your answers and read the Meaning and Use Notes to check them.

    a. The earth's climate is becoming warmer.
    b. I'm eating dinner now. Can I call you back?
    c. I'm taking a computer programming course this semester.

1. Which sentence describes an activity that is happening at the exact moment the speaker is talking?

2. Which sentence describes an activity that is in progress, but not happening at the exact moment the speaker is talking?

3. Which sentence describes a changing situation?

Meaning and Use Notes

> ### Activities in Progress
>
> **1A** Use the present continuous for activities that are in progress (or happening) at the exact moment the speaker is talking. You can use time expressions such as *now* or *right now* to emphasize that an action is happening currently (and may end soon).
>
> *Activities in Progress at This Exact Moment*
> Look! It**'s snowing**!
> She**'s making** dinner <u>now</u>.
> Steve can't come to the phone <u>right now</u>. He**'s taking** a bath.
>
> **1B** Use the present continuous for activities that are in progress, but not happening at the exact moment the speaker is talking. You can use time expressions such as *this week* or *these days* to show when the action is happening.
>
> *Activities in Progress, but Not Happening at This Exact Moment*
> I**'m looking** for a cheap car. Do you have any ideas?
> I**'m painting** my house <u>this week</u>. It**'s taking** a long time.

1C Use the present continuous for changing situations.

Changing Situations
My grades **are improving** this semester.
Computers **are getting** cheaper all the time.

Stative Verbs and the Present Continuous

2A Many stative verbs are not generally used in the present continuous. They are usually used in the simple present. Some of these verbs are *know, mean, own, seem,* and *understand.* See Appendix 7 for a list of more stative verbs.

Simple Present	*Present Continuous*
Do you **know** the answer?	*Are you knowing the answer? (INCORRECT)
What **does** *solar system* **mean**?	*What is *solar system* meaning? (INCORRECT)
We **don't own** a car.	*We're not owning a car. (INCORRECT)

2B Some stative verbs can be used in the present continuous, but they are used as action verbs and have a different meaning from their simple present meaning. Some of these verbs are *have, look, see, taste, think,* and *weigh.*

Simple Present	*Present Continuous*
They **have** a large house. (They own a large house.)	They**'re having** a good time. (They're experiencing a good time.)
Mark **looks** very unhappy. (Mark seems unhappy.)	Mark **is looking** for his car keys. (Mark is searching for his car keys.)
I **see** Lisa. She's behind Bob. (I'm looking at Lisa.)	I**'m seeing** Lisa. (I'm dating Lisa.)
The soup **tastes** salty. (The soup has a salty taste.)	The chef **is tasting** the soup. (The chef is trying the soup.)
I **think** that's a great idea. (I believe that's a great idea.)	I**'m thinking** about Lisa. I like her a lot. (Lisa is in my thoughts right now.)
The package **weighs** two pounds. (Its weight is two pounds.)	The postal worker **is weighing** the package. (The postal worker is using a scale.)

2C Stative verbs that refer to physical conditions can occur in the simple present or present continuous with no difference in meaning. Some of these verbs are *ache, feel,* and *hurt.*

Simple Present	*Present Continuous*
I **don't feel** well.	I**'m not feeling** well.
My throat **hurts**.	My throat **is hurting**.

C1 Listening for Meaning and Use

► Note 1A

🎧 Listen to the announcements. Where would you hear each one?

in an airport   on an airplane   on a train

in a store   on a ship   on television or the radio

1. <u>on an airplane</u>   3. _____   5. _____

2. _____   4. _____   6. _____

C2 Understanding Meaning and Use

► Notes 1A–1C

Read each conversation and look at the underlined verb form. Is the statement that follows true or false? Write *T* for true or *F* for false. Then discuss your answers with a partner.

1. **Carlos:** Thanks for the ride, Marta. You seem really tired. Are you OK?
   Marta: Well, I'<u>m working</u> a lot of extra hours these days. I guess I am pretty tired.

   __F__ Marta is working in the office right now.

2. **Dan:** I need to find a cheap apartment, and it's not easy.
   Lee: I know. Rents here <u>are becoming</u> more expensive every year.

   _____ The cost of renting an apartment is changing.

3. **Amy:** How's school this semester?
   Emily: Great! I'<u>m studying</u> physics, and I really like it.

   _____ Emily is studying physics at this exact moment.

4. **Nesha:** Please answer the phone, Nicole.
   Nicole: I'm sorry. I can't. I'<u>m helping</u> a customer.

   _____ Nicole is helping a customer right now.

5. **Steve:** How's your new puppy?
   Jenny: Don't ask! She'<u>s ruining</u> everything in my apartment.

   _____ The puppy is ruining everything these days.

6. **Minhee:** What's wrong, Hanna? You don't look happy.
   Hanna: I'<u>m getting</u> a cold.

   _____ Hanna woke up with a bad cold.

Look at the pictures. How are they different? In your notebook, write as many sentences as you can. Use the verbs below and the present continuous. (You can use some verbs more than once.)

chase   enter   help   look   run   shout   wait   walk

In picture 1, the police officer is helping the woman.
In picture 2, he isn't helping the woman. He's chasing a thief.

1.

2.

Vocabulary Notes

Adverbs and Time Expressions with the Present Continuous

Still and the Present Continuous *Still* is an adverb that is often used with the present continuous. *Still* emphasizes that the activity or state is in progress. It often suggests surprise that the activity or state has not ended. Place *still* after *be* in affirmative statements, before *be* in negative statements, and after the subject in questions.

AFFIRMATIVE STATEMENT	**NEGATIVE STATEMENT**
He is **still** living with his parents.	He **still** isn't living on his own.

YES/NO **QUESTION**	**INFORMATION QUESTION**
Is he **still** living with his parents?	Why is he **still** living with his parents?

Time Expressions with the Present Continuous Time expressions are also commonly used with the present continuous. Some time expressions refer to an exact moment in the present. These include *now, right now,* and *at the moment.*

Others refer to a longer time period that includes the present moment. These include *this morning, this afternoon, this evening, this week, this month, this semester, this year, these days,* and *nowadays.*

Time expressions can occur at the beginning or end of a sentence.

EXACT MOMENT	**LONGER TIME PERIOD**
Now I'm making dinner.	She's working hard **this morning**.
He's sleeping **right now**.	**This week** I'm doing research at the library.
He's taking a shower **at the moment**.	She's feeling much better **these days**.

C4 Using Adverbs and Time Expressions with the Present Continuous

In your notebook, write sentences about yourself and people you know. Use the present continuous and these subjects and time expressions.

1. I/right now

   I am studying English right now.

2. My best friend/these days

3. Some of my friends/still

4. My English class/right now

5. My family/nowadays

6. I/still

7. I/this year

8. My neighbor/still

Look at the pictures. In your notebook, use these words and phrases to write sentences about the people's jobs and what they are doing now.

1. Tom/drive a taxi/watch TV
   Tom drives a taxi. Now he's watching TV.

4. Greg/teach math/play the violin

2. Celia/teach ballet/shop for food

5. David/cook in a restaurant/fish

3. Linda and Kendra /wait on tables/go to the movies

6. Ed and Reiko/work in a hospital/bowl

A. Complete this conversation with the correct form of the verbs in parentheses. Use the simple present or present continuous. More than one answer is sometimes possible.

Doctor: What _____seems_____ (seem) to be the problem?
₁

Rita: I _____ (not/know). My head _____ (hurt),
₂ ₃
and my stomach _____ (ache).
₄

Doctor: You _____ (look) pale. I _____ (think) it's
₅ ₆
probably the flu.

Rita: Oh, no! I _____ (have) a hard time at work right now. I can't
₇
get sick now!

Doctor: I _____ (think) about your health right now, not your work.
₈

B. Practice the conversation in Part A with a partner.

Read each pair of sentences and look at the underlined verbs. Do the verbs have different meanings or the same meaning? Write *D* for different or *S* for same. Discuss your answers in small groups.

__D__ **1. a.** You <u>look</u> really nice today.
  b. We<u>'re looking</u> at some photos right now.

_____ **2. a.** I <u>weigh</u> 150 pounds.
  b. The clerk <u>is weighing</u> the bananas.

_____ **3. a.** I need to go home because I don't <u>feel</u> well.
  b. Paul says that he<u>'s not feeling</u> well.

_____ **4. a.** I <u>see</u> the boys. There they are!
  b. I<u>'m seeing</u> Jake. He's wonderful!

_____ **5. a.** Nicole <u>is thinking</u> about moving.
  b. I <u>don't think</u> that's a good plan.

_____ **6. a.** They<u>'re having</u> a good time at the party.
  b. We <u>have</u> a new puppy.

D Combining Form, Meaning, and Use

Thinking About Meaning and Use

Choose the best answer to complete each conversation. Then discuss your answers in small groups.

1. **A:** Stop her! She ____!

   B: What's the matter?
   a. leaves
   (b.) is leaving
   c. leave

2. **A:** ____ you ____ hard these days?

   B: Yes, I'm really tired every night.
   a. Are/working
   b. Do/work
   c. Are/work

3. **A:** ____ you ____ their car?

   B: I'm not sure. Is it that green Ford?
   a. Do/see
   b. Are/seeing
   c. Is/see

4. **A:** Why ____ he ____ German?

   B: He's not studying enough.
   a. does/fail
   b. is/failing
   c. does/failing

5. **A:** How ____ the soup ____?

   B: It's delicious.
   a. is/tasting
   b. is/taste
   c. does/taste

6. **A:** What ____?

   B: My parents. I'm worried about them.
   a. do you think
   b. do you think about
   c. are you thinking about

7. **A:** This package is really heavy.

   B: How much ____ it ____?
   a. is/weigh
   b. does/weigh
   c. is/weighing

8. **A:** Where's Maria?

   B: She's busy now. She ____ the baby.
   a. feeds
   b. feeding
   c. is feeding

Find the errors in this letter and correct them.

Dear Donna,

    I love Sunrise Inn. It ~~is having~~ ^{has} a very restful atmosphere. Right now I sit under a large tree in the garden. I don't worrying about anything. The sun shining, a cool breeze blows, and birds singing. I have a wonderful vacation!

    What do you do these days? Are you work hard? Is Ted still being angry at you? Are you have good weather?

    Write and tell me your news.

    Myles

▶ Beyond the Classroom

Searching for Authentic Examples

Find examples of English grammar in everyday life. Listen to an English-language news report for uses of the present continuous. Write down three examples and bring them to class. Why do you think the reporter used the present continuous? Discuss your findings with your classmates.

Writing

Follow the steps below to write a paragraph about what you are doing these days at school, at work, or in your free time.

1. Write a list of activities that you are doing these days, such as studying English, reading newspapers, working in an office, exercising, etc.

2. Write a first draft. Use the present continuous where appropriate.

3. Read your work carefully and circle grammar, spelling, and punctuation errors. Work with a partner to decide how to fix your errors and improve the content.

4. Rewrite your draft.

    These days I'm studying a lot for my English exams. I'm also cooking a lot of Italian food at home. . . .

The Past

PART

2

The Simple Past

The Decade That Made a Difference

A1 Before You Read

Discuss these questions.

What do you know about the 1960s? What were some important events? Do you have a good opinion or a bad opinion about this decade?

A2 Read

 Read the book excerpt on the following page to find out about the 1960s.

A3 After You Read

Write *T* for true and *F* for false for each statement.

__F__ **1.** Before the 1960s all Americans questioned their country's values.

_____ **2.** John F. Kennedy led the Civil Rights movement during the 1960s.

_____ **3.** The Vietnam War occurred during the 1960s.

_____ **4.** All young people agreed with the war in Vietnam.

_____ **5.** Hippies agreed with their parents' ideas about life.

_____ **6.** Relationships between men and women were different after the 1960s.

Woodstock music festival, 1969

THE DECADE THAT MADE A DIFFERENCE

Many people who grew up during the 1960s think it was a very special time. Before the 1960s most Americans used to believe that the American way was the
5 best. People respected the law, trusted their leaders, and did not use to question American values. All that changed in the 1960s.

The 1960s was the decade that made
10 a difference. John F. Kennedy became president; Martin Luther King, Jr., led the Civil Rights movement; and women's groups fought for equal rights. It was an exciting time to be young: the Beatles
15 wrote their songs, and many young Americans flocked to the famous three-

A 1960s peace protest

day Woodstock music festival. But the 1960s was also the time of the Vietnam War. Many young people were very angry with the government. They protested against the war because they did not want to fight.

20 The youth rebellion of the 1960s went beyond politics. It questioned many of the values of American society. This was the time of the "hippies." The hippies were young people who had long hair, wore strange, colorful clothes, and believed in peace. They were not interested in money, and they did not agree with many of their parents' ideas about life.

25 Many things changed in the 1960s. Some of them, such as hairstyles and clothing, were not very important. Others, such as laws about the rights of African Americans and the relationship between men and women, were very significant. And there is certainly no doubt about one thing: when the 1960s ended, the United States was different, and the world was, too.

Civil Rights movement: a series of political and social actions to gain equal rights for African Americans

decade: a period of ten years (for example, 1960–1969)

protest: to express strong public disagreement

rebellion: organized fighting or protest against a government or other authority

significant: important

value: a belief about what is right or wrong

B The Simple Past

Examining Form

Read the sentences and complete the tasks below. Then discuss your answers and read the Form charts to check them.

   a. The youth rebellion questioned the values of American society.
   b. Young people protested against the war.
   c. The hippies believed in peace.

1. Underline the verbs.

2. All of these verbs are regular verbs in the simple past. How do we form the simple past of regular verbs?

3. Look back at the excerpt on page 49. Find the simple past of the irregular verbs below. How are they different from the verbs in sentences a, b, and c?

   make   lead   write   go

Affirmative Statements		
SUBJECT	BASE FORM OF VERB + -D/-ED or IRREGULAR FORM	
I		
You		
He She It	arrived worked left	yesterday.
We		
You		
They		

Negative Statements			
SUBJECT	DID + NOT	BASE FORM OF VERB	
I			
You			
He She It	did not didn't	arrive work leave	yesterday.
We			
You			
They			

Yes/No Questions

DID	SUBJECT	BASE FORM OF VERB	
	you	**arrive**	
Did	he	**work**	yesterday?
	they	**leave**	

Short Answers

YES	SUBJECT	DID		NO	SUBJECT	DID + NOT
	I				I	
Yes,	he	**did.**		**No,**	he	**didn't.**
	they				they	

Information Questions

WH- WORD	DID	SUBJECT	BASE FORM OF VERB	
Who		you	**see**	
What		he	**do**	
Where		she	**go**	
When	**did**	we	**study**	yesterday?
Why		you	**leave**	
How		they	**feel**	

WH- WORD (SUBJECT)			VERB + -D/-ED or IRREGULAR FORM	
Who			**left**	
What			**happened**	yesterday?

- To form the simple past of most regular verbs, add *-ed* to the base form. If the base form of a regular verb ends in *e,* add *-d.* See Appendices 4 and 5 for the spelling and pronunciation of verbs ending in *-ed.*
- Some verbs are irregular in the simple past. See Appendix 6 for a list of irregular verbs and their simple past forms.

⚠️ Do not use *did* in information questions when *who* or *what* is the subject.

    What happened yesterday?

- The verb *be* has two irregular simple past forms: *was* and *were.*

    I **was** at the concert.   You **were** at the mall.
    He **was** a musician.   They **were** home.

⚠️ Do not use *did* in negative statements or questions with *was/were.*

    I **wasn't there.**   Why **was** she late?
    We **weren't** angry.   **Were you at the concert?**

Listening for Form

🎧 Listen to these sentences. Write the simple past verb forms you hear.

1. Dan ___invited___ us to the movies.

2. They _____ to the hockey game.

3. She _____ 20 dollars on the street.

4. They _____ the store at nine.

5. I _____ to work by car every day last week.

6. He _____ baseball for the New York Mets.

7. You _____ a haircut! It looks great!

8. We _____ chocolate cake at the restaurant.

B2 **Working on Regular Verb Forms**

Complete this paragraph with the simple past form of the verbs below.

believe   carry   listen   live   protest   study   support   want

I was a college student in the 1960s. I

___studied___ history at a university in Chicago.
       1

I _____ in an apartment near the
       2

university with four classmates. Like many other

students, I _____ against the war in
              3

Vietnam. My friends and I _____ signs
                             4

that said "Peace." We all _____ in peace
                            5

and freedom. We _____ to change the
                   6

world. We also _____ the Civil Rights
                  7

movement and _____ to speeches by its
                 8

leader, Martin Luther King, Jr.

Martin Luther King, Jr., 1963

Pronunciation Notes

Pronunciation of Verbs Ending in *-ed*

The regular simple past ending *-ed* is pronounced in three different ways, depending on the final sound of the base form of the verb.

1. The *-ed* is pronounced /t/ if the verb ends with the sound /p/, /k/, /tʃ/, /f/, /s/, /ʃ/, or /ks/.

   work — worked /wərkt/   wash — washed /wɑʃt/   watch — watched /wɑtʃt/

2. The *-ed* is pronounced /d/ if the verb ends with the sound /b/, /g/, /dʒ/, /v/, /ð/, /z/, /ʒ/, /m/, /n/, /ŋ/, /l/, or /r/.

   plan — planned /plænd/   judge — judged /dʒʌdʒd/   bang — banged /bæŋd/
   bathe — bathed /beɪðd/   massage — massaged /məˈsɑʒd/   rub — rubbed /rʌbd/

3. The *-ed* is also pronounced /d/ if the verb ends with a vowel sound.

   play — played /pleɪd/   sigh — sighed /saɪd/   row — rowed /roʊd/
   bow — bowed /baʊd/   sue — sued /sud/   free — freed /frid/

4. The *-ed* is pronounced as an extra syllable, /ɪd/, if the verb ends with the sound /d/ or /t/.

   guide — guided /ˈgaɪdɪd/   remind — reminded /ˌriˈmaɪndɪd/
   rent — rented /ˈrɛntɪd/   invite — invited /ˌɪnˈvaɪtɪd/

B3) Pronouncing Verbs Ending in *-ed*

🎧 Listen to the pronunciation of each verb. Which ending do you hear? Check (✓) the correct column.

		/t/	/d/	/ɪd/
1.	waited			✓
2.	walked			
3.	rained			
4.	played			
5.	coughed			
6.	decided			
7.	jumped			
8.	answered			

A. Read about the first airplane flight by Wilbur and Orville Wright. Complete the paragraph with the verbs in parentheses and the simple past.

The first airplane flight

___took___ (take) place in
    1

Kitty Hawk, North Carolina,

on December 17, 1903. Orville

Wright _____ (lie) face
              2

down in the middle of the

airplane, and his brother, Wilbur

Wright, _____ (run) alongside it. Near the end of the runway, the plane
              3

_____ (rise) smoothly into the air. It _____ (fly) for several seconds, but
        4   5

then it _____ (fall) to the ground. This 12-second flight _____ (make)
              6   7

history, but no one _____ (pay) attention to the Wright brothers at first.
                          8

However, after they _____ (give) many public demonstrations of their flying
                          9

machine, the Wright brothers _____ (become) famous.
                                    10

B. In your notebook, write three *Yes/No* and three *Wh-* questions about the paragraph in part A.

Did the first airplane flight take place in North Carolina?
OR
Where did the first airplane flight take place?

C. Work with a partner. Take turns asking and answering your questions in part B.

A: Did the first airplane flight take place in North Carolina?
B: Yes, it did.
OR
A: Where did the first airplane flight take place?
B: In North Carolina.

Building *Yes/No* Questions in the Simple Past

Build eight logical *Yes/No* questions. Use a word or phrase from each column.
Punctuate your sentences correctly.

Did it rain yesterday?

did was were	it the party the test Maria you the children they your team	rain yesterday first nervous fun win leave difficult start on time

B6 **Working on *Yes/No* Questions and Short Answers in the Simple Past**

A. Complete this conversation with *did, didn't, was, wasn't, were,* or *weren't.*

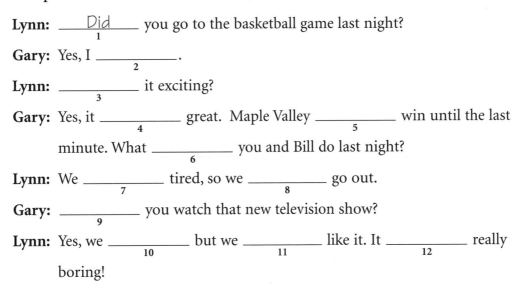

Lynn: ____Did____ you go to the basketball game last night?
 1

Gary: Yes, I _____.
 2

Lynn: _____ it exciting?
 3

Gary: Yes, it _____ great. Maple Valley _____ win until the last
 4 5

minute. What _____ you and Bill do last night?
 6

Lynn: We _____ tired, so we _____ go out.
 7 8

Gary: _____ you watch that new television show?
 9

Lynn: Yes, we _____ but we _____ like it. It _____ really
 10 11 12

boring!

B. Practice the conversation in part A with a partner.

Informally Speaking

Reduced Form of *Did You*

 Look at the cartoon and listen to the conversation. How is the underlined form in the cartoon different from what you hear?

> Did you forget my birthday? It was Saturday.

> Oh, no! I'm really sorry!

Did you is often pronounced /ˈdɪdʒə/ in informal speech.

STANDARD FORM	WHAT YOU MIGHT HEAR
Did you work yesterday?	"/ˈdɪdʒə/ work yesterday?"
Did you eat yet?	"/ˈdɪdʒə/ eat yet?"

B7 Understanding Informal Speech

Listen and write the standard form of the words you hear.

1. **A:** <u>Did you go</u> to the party?

          ₁
   B: Yes, I did.

   A: _____ a good time?

               ₂
   B: Yes, but today I'm very tired.

2. **A:** _____ lunch yet?

          ₁
   B: Yes, I did.

   A: What _____?

               ₂
   B: A burger and fries.

3. **A:** _____ home last night?

          ₁
   B: No, I went to a movie.

   A: _____ it?

          ₂
   B: No, it wasn't very good.

4. **A:** Why _____ so late?

               ₁
   B: My boss needed help on a report.

   A: _____ it?

          ₂
   B: Yes, it wasn't difficult.

The Simple Past

Examining Meaning and Use

Read the sentences and answer the questions below. Then discuss your answers and read the Meaning and Use Notes to check them.

    a. I walk a mile every day.
    b. During my childhood we lived in Morocco.
    c. I went to Jake's party last night.

Which sentence talks about the present? Which sentences talk about situations that started and ended in the past? Which sentence talks about a situation that happened a short time ago? a long time ago?

Meaning and Use Notes

> ### Actions or States Completed in the Past
>
> **1A** Use the simple past for actions or states that started and ended in the past. Use time expressions to describe the time period.
>
> | | |
> |---|---|
> | I **lived** in Boston in <u>1999</u>. | They **played** baseball <u>on Saturdays</u>. |
> | We **went** shopping <u>yesterday</u>. | The garden **was** beautiful <u>last year</u>. |
>
> **1B** The actions or states can happen in the recent past (a short time ago) or the distant past (a long time ago).
>
> | *Recent Past* | *Distant Past* |
> |---|---|
> | He **called** five minutes ago. | They **got married** in 1973. |
> | She **felt** tired yesterday. | He **was** very sick ten years ago. |
>
> **1C** The actions or states can last for a long or short period of time.
>
> | *Long Period of Time* | *Short Period of Time* |
> |---|---|
> | I **worked** there for many years. | It **rained** hard all afternoon. |
> | She **was** ill for six months. | He **seemed** happy to see me. |
>
> **1D** The actions or states can happen once or repeatedly.
>
> | *Happened Once* | *Happened Repeatedly* |
> |---|---|
> | I **graduated** on June 5, 1999. | He always **studied** hard before a test. |

A. 🎧 Listen to each conversation. Listen carefully for the phrases in the chart. Is the second speaker talking about the recent past or the distant past? Check (✓) the correct column.

		RECENT PAST	DISTANT PAST
1.	grandmother died	✓	
2.	walked to school		
3.	saw Kedra		
4.	bought the dress		
5.	took part in protests		
6.	studied French		

B. 🎧 Listen again. Is the second speaker referring to a situation that happened once or repeatedly? Check (✓) the correct column.

		HAPPENED ONCE	HAPPENED REPEATEDLY
1.	grandmother died	✓	
2.	walked to school		
3.	saw Kedra		
4.	bought the dress		
5.	took part in protests		
6.	studied French		

C2 Making Excuses ▶ Notes 1A–1D

A. You were supposed to meet your friend for lunch yesterday, but you didn't. Use these words and phrases to make excuses.

1. go/the wrong restaurant

   I'm sorry. I went to the wrong restaurant.

2. forget/the name of the restaurant

3. have/an important meeting at work

4. my car/run out of gas

5. my watch/stop

6. have/a terrible headache

B. Now think of three more excuses. Use your imagination.

Work with a partner. Look at the pictures and guess what happened. Use *maybe* or *perhaps* and the simple past to make two sentences for each picture.

1.

Maybe she didn't study for the test.
Perhaps she forgot about the test.

4.

2.

5.

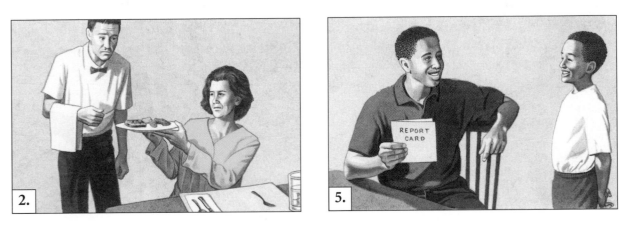

3.

6.

Vocabulary Notes

Time Expressions with the Simple Past

Time expressions are commonly used with the simple past. These words and phrases often refer to an exact point in time in the past or to a past time period. Time expressions can occur at the beginning or end of a sentence.

yesterday	I saw Silvio **yesterday**.
the day before yesterday	We didn't go to school **the day before yesterday**.
this morning/afternoon	**This morning** she stayed home.
last night/week/month/year	Where did they go **last month**?
recently	Did you move **recently**?
a few/several/many years ago	**A few years ago** he lost his job.
a long time ago/a while ago	Rick graduated **a long time ago**.

C4 Using Time Expressions with the Simple Past

A. In your notebook, write sentences about yourself in the simple past with these time expressions and the phrases below. You can use a time expression more than once.

a while ago	recently	this . . .
last . . .	the day before yesterday	yesterday

1. write a letter

   I wrote a letter last night.

2. wash the dishes

3. talk to a friend on the telephone

4. eat in a restaurant

5. speak English outside of class

6. go to a movie

7. receive an e-mail

8. take a vacation

B. Work with a partner. Take turns asking and answering information questions about the sentences you wrote in part A.

A: When was the last time you wrote a letter?
B: I wrote a letter last night.

Beyond the Sentence

Using Time Expressions with Tense Changes

In stories and descriptions, we often use the simple past and the simple present to contrast situations in the past and present. We use time expressions to clarify the change of tenses.

Compare the paragraphs below. The paragraphs on the left are confusing because they do not use time expressions to show the change from the past to the present or the present to the past. The paragraphs on the right are clear because they use time expressions to clarify the tense change in each paragraph.

WITHOUT TIME EXPRESSIONS	WITH TIME EXPRESSIONS
Sally **walked** home in the rain. She **feels** sick and **doesn't want** to go to work.	Sally **walked** home in the rain <u>yesterday</u>. <u>Now</u> she **feels** sick and **doesn't want** to go to work.
I always **walk** my dog. It **was** cold, and he **didn't want** to go outside. So we **stayed** in.	I always **walk** my dog <u>in the morning</u>. <u>This morning</u> it **was** cold, and he **didn't want** to go outside. So we **stayed** in.

C5 Using Time Expressions with Tense Changes

Complete these sentences with one of the time expressions below. There is more than one correct answer for each sentence.

last night	now	recently	these days
last week	nowadays	the day before yesterday	this morning

1. My parents rarely leave home, but _____recently_____ they decided to visit Washington, D.C.

2. The movie I saw last week scared me to death. _____ I'm afraid to stay home alone.

3. My dog and cat are good friends. _____ I found them playing together in my apartment.

4. My neighbors are very noisy. They often keep me up until late at night. _____ I finally called the police.

5. I was on my college swim team last year. However, _____ I don't have time for sports. I have too much homework.

6. I celebrated my birthday _____, and Jim didn't even send me a card.

D Used To

Examining Form

Read the sentences and complete the tasks below. Then discuss your answers and
read the Form charts to check them.

   a. He didn't use to visit his parents so often.
   b. Did she use to like the class?
   c. We used to swim every morning.
   d. Where did you use to live?

1. Underline *used to* or *use to* in each sentence. Circle all the examples of *did* or *didn't*.

2. When do we use the form *used to*? When do we use the form *use to*?

Affirmative Statements			
SUBJECT	*USED TO*	**BASE FORM OF VERB**	
I			
You			
He She It	used to	arrive	late.
We			
You			
They			

Negative Statements				
SUBJECT	*DID + NOT*	*USE TO*	**BASE FORM OF VERB**	
I				
You				
He She It	did not didn't	use to	arrive	late.
We				
You				
They				

Yes/No Questions				
DID	**SUBJECT**	*USE TO*	**BASE FORM OF VERB**	
Did	you he they	use to	arrive	late?

Short Answers					
YES	**SUBJECT**	*DID*	*NO*	**SUBJECT**	*DID + NOT*
Yes,	I he they	did.	No,	I he they	didn't.

Information Questions

WH- WORD	DID	SUBJECT	USE TO	BASE FORM OF VERB	
Why		you		**arrive**	early?
When	**did**	she	**use to**	**protest**	against the government?
Where		they		**live**	in Chicago?

WH- WORD (SUBJECT)			USED TO	BASE FORM OF VERB	
Who			**used to**	**live**	across the street?
What				**happen**	on New Year's Eve?

- Use *used to* in affirmative statements.
- Use *use to* in negative statements with *didn't*, in *Yes/No* questions, and in information questions with *did*.
- The forms *used to* and *use to* have the same pronunciation: /ˈyustu/.

⚠ Do not use *did* in information questions when *who* or *what* is the subject. Use *used to* with these questions.

    Who used to take you to school?

    *Who did used to take you to school? (INCORRECT)

D1 Listening for Form

🎧 Listen to each sentence. Which form of *used to* does the speaker use? Check (✓) the correct column.

	USED TO	DIDN'T USE TO	DID . . . USE TO
1.	✓		
2.			
3.			
4.			
5.			
6.			
7.			
8.			

D2) Rewriting Statements and Questions with *Used To*

Rewrite these simple past sentences and questions with the correct form of *used to*.

1. They walked to the park every Sunday.

   They used to walk to the park every Sunday.

2. Were you in the army?

   _____

3. I didn't go to the movies very often.

   _____

4. He wasn't a good student in high school.

   _____

5. Did your family rent a beach house every summer?

   _____

6. We visited our parents on weekends.

   _____

D3) Completing Conversations with *Used To*

Complete these conversations with the words in parentheses and the correct form of *used to*. Then practice the conversations with a partner.

Conversation 1

A: Where ___did you use to live___ (you/live)?
                                 1

B: In Chicago. _____ (we/have) an apartment on Lake Shore Drive.
                            2

Conversation 2

A: _____ (Satomi/date) Hiro?
           1

B: No, she didn't, but _____ (they/be) good friends.
                                     2

Conversation 3

A: _____ (I/not/like) Kevin.
           1

B: Yeah. _____ (he/not/be) nice to me, but now we are good friends.
                     2

The Habitual Past with *Used To*

Examining Meaning and Use

Read the sentences and answer the questions below. Then discuss your answers and read the Meaning and Use Notes to check them.

1a. We used to walk five miles to school.
1b. One morning the bus didn't come, and we walked five miles to school.

2a. Mary used to swim. Now she ice skates.
2b. Mary swam every day. She enjoyed it very much.

1. Look at 1a and 1b. Which one refers to a repeated action in the past?

2. Look at 2a and 2b. Which suggests that Mary's present situation is different from the past? Which doesn't suggest anything about Mary's present situation?

Meaning and Use Notes

> **Comparing the Past and the Present**
>
> **1A** *Used to* suggests that a habit or situation was true in the past, but is not true now. Use *used to* for repeated (or habitual) actions or states that started and finished in the past. Do not use it for actions or states that happened only once. Adverbs of frequency and other time expressions with *used to* emphasize the repeated actions or states.
>
> We <u>often</u> **used to visit** my grandparents <u>during summer vacation</u>. We don't <u>anymore</u>.
> **Did** you **use to travel** a lot for work?
> She **used to be** unfriendly. She <u>never</u> smiled.
> This city **didn't use to have** a subway system <u>in the old days</u>.
>
> ---
>
> **1B** You can use the simple present with time expressions to say how a present situation is different from the past.
>
> I often **used to watch** TV after school. <u>Now</u> I <u>don't have</u> time to do that.
> In the 1930s people **used to get** their news from newspapers or the radio. <u>These days</u> most people <u>get</u> their news from TV or the Internet.

E1) Listening for Meaning and Use

🎧 Listen to each statement. Choose the sentence that best follows it.

1. **(a.)** Now I'm married and have a son.
   b. I enjoyed having a lot of people in the house.

2. **a.** We added two rooms last year.
   b. Now there isn't enough room.

3. **a.** Now we don't talk to each other.
   b. Now we see each other every day.

4. **a.** We always ate in restaurants together.
   b. Now we eat out twice a week.

5. **a.** Now they don't want to go.
   b. They always complained about their teachers.

6. **a.** I always did everything myself.
   b. We cleaned together every Saturday.

7. **a.** He always cries when he sees one.
   b. Now he's studying to be a vet.

8. **a.** But we changed our minds.
   b. But we decided to have six.

E2) Comparing the Past and the Present

Work with a partner. Look at these facts about the past. How is the present different? Write two sentences for each fact. In the first, rewrite the fact using the correct form of *used to*. In the second, use the simple present with a time expression and the word or phrase in parentheses.

1. Few people had cars. (many)

   In the past few people used to have cars. Now many people have cars.

2. Women didn't work outside the home. (have jobs)

3. Most people didn't go to college. (many)

4. Supermarkets didn't stay open late. (24 hours)

5. People didn't move away from their families. (live far away)

6. Most people got married very young. (many/in their thirties)

E3) Remembering Your Past

Work with a partner. Talk about your past habits and routines. Use *used to* and other simple past verbs.

A: I used to play basketball after school with my friends. We always had a lot of fun together, but we were extremely competitive.
B: I used to travel . . .

Combining Form, Meaning, and Use

F1 Thinking About Meaning and Use

Choose the best answer to complete each conversation. Then discuss your answers in small groups.

1. **A:** Did you go to school yesterday?

   B: _____
   - **a.** Yes, I go today.
   - **b.** No, I was sick.

2. **A:** I went to the soccer game last night.

   B: _____
   - **a.** Who won?
   - **b.** Is it fun?

3. **A:** When I was young, I used to climb trees.

   B: _____
   - **a.** Did you climb trees?
   - **b.** Did you ever fall out of one?

4. **A:** Julie finished law school last year.

   B: _____
   - **a.** Is she still in school?
   - **b.** Did she enjoy it?

5. **A:** It rained here last night.

   B: Really? _____
   - **a.** It didn't rain here.
   - **b.** It isn't raining here.

6. **A:** She didn't use to live alone.

   B: _____
   - **a.** Did she like living with other people?
   - **b.** Did she like living alone?

F2 Editing

Some of these sentences have errors. Find the errors and correct them.

1. I used to graduate from high school in 1997.   *graduated* (used to graduate crossed out)

2. We didn't needed any help.

3. Ana taked the cake to Miguel.

4. Where did they went?

5. He failed his driving test three times!

6. Who give you a present?

7. When left he?

8. You didn't answer my question.

9. The test were on Saturday.

10. What did happened here?

▶ Beyond the Classroom

Searching for Authentic Examples

Find examples of English grammar in everyday life. Look in an English-language newspaper or on the Internet for news stories written in the simple past. Find three examples of regular verbs and three examples of irregular verbs. Bring them to class. When is the simple past used? Does the article include any forms of *used to*? If so, why? Discuss your findings with your classmates.

Writing

Follow the steps below to write a paragraph about a famous person from the past.

1. Choose a famous person from the 1960s or another time in history. Do research in the library or on the Internet to find information about the person. Make notes about what you want to say.

2. Write a first draft. Use the simple past, *used to*, and time expressions where appropriate.

3. Read your work carefully and circle grammar, spelling, and punctuation errors. Work with a partner to decide how to fix the errors and improve the content.

4. Rewrite your draft.

   Jackie Robinson was a great sports hero. He was the first African American in major-league baseball in the United States. African Americans didn't use to play professional baseball with white players. . . .

The Past Continuous and Past Time Clauses

A Galveston's Killer Hurricane

A1 Before You Read

Discuss these questions.

Do you have bad storms where you live? Do they cause a lot of damage? What do people in your city or town do to prepare for bad weather?

A2 Read

 Read this excerpt from a history textbook to find out about how much damage occurred during the worst storm in U.S. history.

Galveston's Killer Hurricane

The worst weather disaster in the history of the United States was a hurricane that hit the city of Galveston on September 8, 1900.
5 Galveston is on an island near the Texas coast. At that time it was the richest city in Texas, and about 38,000 people <u>were living</u> there.

On the morning of Tuesday,
10 September 6, 1900, the head of the Galveston weather station, Isaac Cline, received a telegram about a storm. It was moving

Galveston before the hurricane

north over Cuba and coming toward Galveston. Cline didn't worry when he got
15 the news. Galveston often had bad storms. However, by the next afternoon Cline became concerned. The wind was getting stronger, the ocean waves were getting larger, and the tide was much higher than normal.

On the morning of September 8, Cline began to tell people to leave the island. However, few people listened. Most of them just went to friends' and relatives'
20 houses away from the water. By 4:00 that afternoon, the storm was much worse.

The tide was getting higher and higher when a four-foot wave went through the town. A twenty-foot wave followed it.

Cline was at his house with a lot of other people. While the storm was going on, he was making careful notes of the water's height around his house. Suddenly, a huge
25 wave hit the house and it collapsed. Everyone went into the water. For the next three hours they floated on the waves. "While we were drifting," he later wrote, "we had to protect ourselves from pieces of wood and other objects that were flying around."

Galveston after the hurricane

After the storm ended, the city was in ruins. More than 7,000
30 people were dead. The storm also destroyed more than 3,600 buildings. As a result, the people of Galveston built a seawall. It was 3 miles long, 17 feet high, and
35 16 feet thick.

Today the people of Galveston depend on weather satellites and other technology to give them hurricane warnings, but they still
40 talk about the great hurricane of 1900.

---

collapse: to suddenly fall down
concerned: worried
disaster: an event that causes a lot of damage
drift: to be carried along by moving water

satellite: a man-made object that travels around the Earth and sends back information
tide: the regular rise and fall of the level of the ocean

 After You Read

Answer these questions in your notebook.

1. What happened on September 8, 1900?

2. Where is Galveston?

3. What did most of the people of Galveston do before the storm hit?

4. Why did Isaac Cline's house collapse?

5. What did the people of Galveston do to protect themselves from other storms?

The Past Continuous

Examining Form

Look back at the excerpt on page 70 and complete the tasks below. Then discuss your answers and read the Form charts to check them.

1. An example of the past continuous is underlined. Find four more examples.

2. How many words are necessary to form the past continuous? What two forms of the verb *be* are used? What ending is added to the base form of the verb?

Affirmative Statements

SUBJECT	WAS/WERE	BASE FORM OF VERB + -ING	
I	was		
You	were		
He She It	was	living	there.
We			
You	were		
They			

Negative Statements

SUBJECT	WAS/WERE + NOT	BASE FORM OF VERB + -ING	
I	was not wasn't		
You	were not weren't		
He She It	was not wasn't	living	there.
We			
You	were not weren't		
They			

Yes/No Questions

WAS/WERE	SUBJECT	BASE FORM OF VERB + -ING	
Were	you		
Was	he	living	there?
Were	they		

Short Answers

YES	SUBJECT	WAS		NO	SUBJECT	WAS/WERE + NOT
	I				I	
Yes,	he	was.		No,	he	wasn't.
	they	were.			they	weren't.

Information Questions

WH- WORD	WAS/WERE	SUBJECT	BASE FORM OF VERB + -ING
Who	were	you	watching?
What	was	she	
When	were	they	traveling?
Where			
Why			
How			

WH- WORD (SUBJECT)	WAS/WERE		BASE FORM OF VERB + -ING
Who	was		leaving?
What			happening?

- See Appendix 3 for the spelling of verbs ending in *-ing*.

⚠ Do not use a subject pronoun when *who* or *what* is the subject of an information question.
   What was happening?
   *What was it happening? (INCORRECT)

B1) Listening for Form

🎧 Listen to these sentences. Choose the verb forms you hear.

1. **a.** are living
   (b.) were living
   c. was living

2. **a.** wasn't raining
   b. was raining
   c. isn't raining

3. **a.** were leaving
   b. weren't leaving
   c. are leaving

4. **a.** aren't going
   b. were going
   c. weren't going

5. **a.** are . . . going
   b. were . . . going
   c. was . . . going

6. **a.** was . . . crying
   b. is . . . crying
   c. wasn't . . . crying

A. Look at the picture. Write sentences about what the people were doing at Kevin's house last night.

1. Paulo and Dan _were playing music._____

2. Alex _____

3. Myles and Reiko _____

4. Kevin _____

5. Kalin and Kim _____

6. Nicole and her dog, Sparks, _____

B. Work with a partner. Take turns asking and answering *Yes/No* questions about the people in the picture.

A: *Was Paulo playing the guitar?*
B: *No, he wasn't. He was playing the drums.*

B3 Forming Information Questions in the Past Continuous

In your notebook, form information questions from these words and phrases. Punctuate your sentences correctly.

1. four o'clock/happening/what/was/yesterday afternoon/at

   What was happening at four o'clock yesterday afternoon?

2. feeling/how/your/was/grandfather/last night

3. the/this morning/leading/meeting/who/was

4. was/what/Mr. Gonzalez/last semester/teaching

5. you/living/five years ago/were/where

6. Dan and Ben/were/on Saturday/fighting/why

B4 Asking and Answering Information Questions in the Past Continuous

Work with a partner. Take turns asking and answering questions with these time expressions and the past continuous.

1. two hours ago

   A: What were you doing two hours ago?
   B: I was making dinner.

2. at three o'clock yesterday afternoon

3. last night at midnight

4. at seven o'clock this morning

5. at six o'clock yesterday evening

6. ten minutes ago

B5 Building Past Continuous and Simple Past Sentences

Build as many logical sentences as you can in the past continuous or simple past. Use a word or phrase from each column. Punctuate your sentences correctly.

Past Continuous: *Carlos was sleeping.*   Simple Past: *Carlos had a cold.*

Carlos	was	sleeping
you	had	call
Ana and Rose	didn't	studying
	weren't	a cold
		early

The Past Continuous

Examining Meaning and Use

Read the sentences and answer the questions below. Then discuss your answers and read the Meaning and Use Notes to check them.

    a. This morning I walked the dog and then I took a shower.
    b. At seven o'clock this morning, I was walking the dog and my sister was taking a shower.

1. Which sentence shows two past activities in progress at the same time?

2. Which sentence shows two completed past activities?

Meaning and Use Notes

> ### Activities in Progress in the Past
>
> **1A**   Use the past continuous to talk about activities that were in progress (happening) at a specific time in the past. This may be an exact moment in the past or a longer period of time in the past.
>
> It **wasn't raining** <u>at lunchtime</u>. It **was snowing**.
> You **were acting** strangely <u>last night</u>.
> I **was studying** at Tokyo University <u>in 2001</u>.
>
> ---
>
> **1B**   The past continuous is often used to talk about several activities that were in progress at the same time.
>
> <u>At six o'clock</u> she **was making** a phone call, and we **were eating** dinner.
>
> ---
>
> **1C**   The past continuous expresses an ongoing past activity that may or may not be completed. In contrast, the simple past usually expresses a completed past activity.
>
> | *Past Continuous* | *Simple Past* |
> |---|---|
> | At 5:45 Greg **was making** dinner in the kitchen. (He was in the middle of making dinner.) | At 5:45 Greg was in the kitchen. He **made** dinner. Then he washed the dishes. (He completed dinner preparations.) |

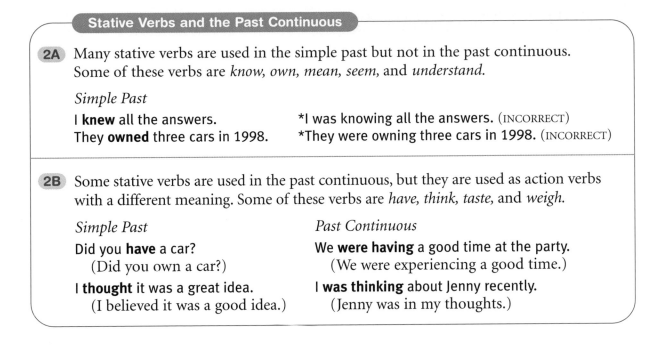

Stative Verbs and the Past Continuous

2A Many stative verbs are used in the simple past but not in the past continuous. Some of these verbs are *know, own, mean, seem,* and *understand.*

Simple Past

I **knew** all the answers.   *I was knowing all the answers. (INCORRECT)
They **owned** three cars in 1998.   *They were owning three cars in 1998. (INCORRECT)

2B Some stative verbs are used in the past continuous, but they are used as action verbs with a different meaning. Some of these verbs are *have, think, taste,* and *weigh.*

Simple Past

Did you **have** a car?
    (Did you own a car?)

I **thought** it was a great idea.
    (I believed it was a good idea.)

Past Continuous

We **were having** a good time at the party.
    (We were experiencing a good time.)

I **was thinking** about Jenny recently.
    (Jenny was in my thoughts.)

C1 Listening for Meaning and Use   ▶ Notes 1A–1C

🎧 Listen to each statement. Look at the phrases in the chart. Is the speaker talking about an ongoing past activity or a completed past activity? Check (✓) the correct column.

		ONGOING	COMPLETED
1.	live in Japan		✓
2.	write a book		
3.	paint the house		
4.	fix the air conditioner		
5.	write a paper		
6.	take flying lessons		

C2 Describing Activities in Progress at the Same Time   ▶ Notes 1A–C

Think about a time when you arrived late for an event. In your notebook, write about what was happening when you arrived. Then read your description to the class.

I arrived at the soccer game late. My favorite team was winning. The crowd was standing and everyone was cheering. . . .

C3 Describing Past Situations

► Notes 1A–C,
2A, 2B

A. Complete these conversations with the correct form of the verbs in parentheses. Use the past continuous or the simple past where appropriate.

Conversation 1

Chris: Where were you during the summer of 1997?

Matt: I ___was traveling___ (travel) around the United States.

                1

Chris: How? By plane?

Matt: No, by car. I _____ (own) a car then.

                     2

Conversation 2

Paul: _____ you _____ (know) Takeshi

        1   2

before this year?

Eric: Not very well. I _____ (arrive) at school in the middle

                  3

of the year. Takeshi _____ (take) several courses at that

                  4

time, but we _____ (not/be) in the same classes.

                  5

Conversation 3

Josh: You _____ (miss) the turn! Now we're on the

                  1

wrong road.

Amy: Oops. I'm sorry. I _____ (not/pay) attention. I

                  2

_____ (think) about something else.

    3

Conversation 4

Celia: I _____ (see) Susan at the library yesterday

          1

Maria: What _____ she _____ (do) there?

          2   3

Celia: She _____ (look) for information for her English project.

          4

B. Practice the conversations in part A with a partner.

Beyond the Sentence

> ### Introducing Background Information with the Past Continuous
>
> The past continuous and simple past often occur together in the same story. The past continuous is used at the beginning of a story to describe background activities that are happening at the same time as the main events of the story. The simple past is used for main events.
>
> Yesterday <u>was</u> beautiful. The sun **was shining**, the birds **were singing**, and I **was walking** in a valley. Suddenly, a UFO <u>landed</u> on the ground. Three small green men <u>appeared</u>. They <u>took</u> my hand and <u>said</u>, "Come with us."

C4 Introducing Background Information with the Past Continuous

A. Work with a partner. Imagine that each sentence is the beginning of a story. Write two sentences in the past continuous to give background information.

1. The beach was gorgeous. <u>The sun was shining on the water. The waves were moving quickly.</u>

2. The bank was full of customers. _____

   _____

3. The students were late to class. _____

   _____

4. My boss was very angry. _____

   _____

5. The cafeteria was crowded and noisy. _____

   _____

6. The sky looked cloudy and dark. _____

   _____

B. Complete one of the story beginnings in part A. Use the past continuous to add more background information, and use the simple past for main events.

> The beach was gorgeous. The sun was shining on the water. The waves were moving quickly. Suddenly, a swimmer yelled for help. A lifeguard dove into the water. . . .

D Past Time Clauses

Examining Form

Read the sentences and complete the tasks below. Then discuss your answers and read the Form charts to check them.

    a. At that time, Galveston was the richest city in Texas.
    b. Cline didn't worry when he got the news.
    c. After the storm ended, the city was in ruins.

1. Underline the verbs. Which sentences have two verbs?

2. Look at the sentences with two verbs. Each verb is part of a clause. There is a main clause and a past time clause. A past time clause begins with a word such as *before, when, while,* or *after*. Circle the past time clauses.

Sentences with Past Time Clauses

	PAST TIME CLAUSE		MAIN CLAUSE	
	SUBJECT	**VERB**	**SUBJECT**	**VERB**
Before	**the storm**	**hit,**	everyone	was sleeping.
When	**the house**	**collapsed,**	I	was eating dinner.
While	**I**	**was sleeping,**	the phone	rang.
After	**the play**	**ended,**	everyone	clapped.

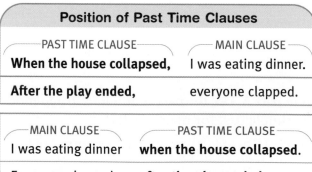

Position of Past Time Clauses

PAST TIME CLAUSE	MAIN CLAUSE
When the house collapsed,	I was eating dinner.
After the play ended,	everyone clapped.

MAIN CLAUSE	PAST TIME CLAUSE
I was eating dinner	**when the house collapsed.**
Everyone clapped	**after the play ended.**

Overview

- A clause is a group of words that has a subject and a verb.
- A main clause can stand alone as a complete sentence.
- A dependent clause cannot stand alone and must be used with a main clause.

Past Time Clauses

- Past time clauses are dependent clauses. They begin with words such as *before, when, while,* and *after*.
- The verbs in a past time clause and main clause can be in the simple past or in the past continuous.
- A past time clause can come before or after the main clause with no change in meaning. If the past time clause comes first, it is separated from the main clause by a comma.

D1 Listening for Form

 Listen to these sentences. Write the past time clauses you hear.

1. Some people left town _before the storm began_ .

2. The weather forecaster warned us about the storm _____ .

3. _____ , the tornado hit the house.

4. _____ , we went into the basement.

5. The river overflowed _____ .

6. The sky was beautiful _____ .

D2 Forming Sentences with Past Time Clauses

Match the clauses to make logical sentences. Pay attention to punctuation.

__f__ 1. He went to bed   **a.** several people were still outside.

____ 2. When the storm hit,   **b.** while I was waiting for the train.

____ 3. After we visited Chicago,   **c.** he made a speech.

____ 4. I made a phone call   **d.** when he was taking her picture.

____ 5. Before Steve gave Alan the award,   **e.** we went to Cleveland.

____ 6. She closed her eyes   **f.** before I came home.

D3 Practicing Punctuation with Past Time Clauses

Read this paragraph. Underline the time clauses. Add commas where necessary.

A terrible storm hit last night <u>while my friend was staying at my house.</u> All the lights went out when lightning struck the house. While I was looking for matches I tripped over a rug. I heard a knock on the door. I went to the door and answered it. A strange man was standing outside. He was wearing a hood. The wind was blowing the trees back and forth while the storm was raging. When I saw the stranger I became nervous. Then, when he began to speak I recognized his voice. It was my friend's father.

D4 Changing the Position of Past Time Clauses

Change the order of the clauses in these sentences. Add or delete commas where necessary.

1. Alex saw Maria when he went to the laundromat.

   <u>When Alex went to the laundromat, he saw Maria.</u>

2. While Reiko was swimming, she got a cramp in her leg.

   _____

3. When my sister woke up this morning, she ate pizza for breakfast.

   _____

4. It started to rain while I was driving to work.

   _____

5. Eva became a ballet dancer after she finished high school.

   _____

E Past Time Clauses

Examining Meaning and Use

Read the sentences and complete the tasks below. Then discuss your answers and read the Meaning and Use Notes to check them.

    a. I was taking a nap when the mailman knocked on the door.
    b. I put on suntan lotion before I went to the beach.
    c. We were playing soccer while Josh was studying for an exam.

1. Which sentence shows that two events were happening at exactly the same time?

2. Which sentence shows that one event interrupted the other?

3. Which sentence shows that one event happened after the other?

Meaning and Use Notes

Simultaneous Events

1 Sentences with past time clauses describe the order in which two past events occurred. When the verbs in both the time clause and the main clause are in the past continuous, the events were simultaneous (happening at exactly the same time). *When* or *while* introduces the time clause.

Past Continuous	*Past Continuous*
When I was sleeping,	the children <u>were watching</u> TV.
I <u>was sleeping</u>	**while the children were watching TV.**

Interrupted Events

2 When one verb is in the simple past and the other is in the past continuous, it shows that one event interrupted the other. The event in the past continuous started first and was interrupted by the simple past event. *When* or *while* begins the time clause, which uses the past continuous.

Past Continuous (First Event)	*Simple Past (Second Event)*
When I was sleeping,	the telephone rang.
While I was sleeping,	the telephone rang.

(Continued on page 84)

3 When the verbs in both the time clause and the main clause are in the simple past, one event happened after the other (in sequence). *Before, when,* or *after* introduces the time clause and indicates the order of events.

Simple Past (First Event)	*Simple Past (Second Event)*
I <u>walked</u> past my sister	**before I recognized her.**
When the phone rang,	I <u>answered</u> it.
After he gave me the diploma,	I <u>shook</u> his hand.

E1 Listening for Meaning and Use ▶ Notes 1–3

 Listen to each conversation. Is the second speaker talking about simultaneous events, an interrupted event, or events in sequence? Check (✓) the correct column.

	SIMULTANEOUS	INTERRUPTED	IN SEQUENCE
1.		✓	
2.			
3.			
4.			
5.			
6.			

E2 Understanding Time Clauses ▶ Notes 2, 3

Work with a partner. Discuss why these sentences are not logical. Then change the time clause in each sentence to make it logical.

1. Before Carlos threw the ball, I caught it.

   A: Sentence 1 isn't logical. You can't catch a ball before someone throws it.
   B: It should be "After Carlos threw the ball, I caught it."

2. While Ben found his car keys, he drove away.

3. When the sun came up, it was very dark.

4. Everyone danced before the band started to play.

5. After we went swimming, they filled the pool with water.

Writing About Events in Sequence ▶ Note 3

Read each situation. Then complete each sentence with a clause in the simple past.

1. Silvio and Maria bought a new house last month.

   Before they bought the house, _they saved a lot of money._

   When they saw the house for the first time, _____

   After they moved in, _____

2. Megan went to a great party last night.

   Before she went to the party, _____

   When she arrived at the party, _____

   After she left the party, _____

3. Paul traveled to Europe last summer for his vacation.

   Before _____

   When _____

   After _____

E4 **Expressing Simultaneous, Interrupted, and Sequential Events** ▶ Notes 1–3

Complete the time clauses. Use the simple past or the past continuous.

1. Donna and I made dinner together last night. While Donna was

   chopping the vegetables, _I was baking a cake for dessert._

2. We were watching the movie when _____

3. I'm sorry I didn't answer the phone this morning. It rang while _____

   _____

4. Last night while I was watching TV, _____

5. At first Lauren wasn't a good student. After _____

   _____, her grades improved.

6. Why did you leave the party so early? We had a great time! After you left,

   _____

F Combining Form, Meaning, and Use

F1 Thinking About Meaning and Use

Read each sentence and answer the questions that follow with *Yes, No,* or *It's not clear.* Then discuss your answers with a partner.

1. We ran out of the building when the fire alarm started to ring.

   _____Yes_____ **a.** Were they in the building before the fire alarm started to ring?

   _____No_____ **b.** After the fire alarm rang, did they stay in the building for a long time?

2. Lynn was sleeping while Holly was cleaning the house.

   _____ **a.** Did Lynn help Holly clean the house?

   _____ **b.** Did Lynn fall asleep before Holly started cleaning the house?

3. Lisa saw Jake this morning. He was walking down the street with his dog.

   _____ **a.** Did Lisa walk down the street with Jake?

   _____ **b.** Did Jake continue walking after Lisa saw him?

4. Gina was afraid. It was raining very hard, and the wind was blowing.

   _____ **a.** Did the wind and the rain make Gina afraid?

   _____ **b.** Was Gina afraid before the storm started?

5. Jake was working on the roof when he fell off.

   _____ **a.** Did he hurt himself badly?

   _____ **b.** Did he work after he fell?

6. When he left the house, he wasn't carrying his umbrella.

   _____ **a.** Did he take his umbrella with him?

   _____ **b.** Was it raining when he left the house?

7. The fire started after we left the building.

_____ a. Were we in danger?

_____ b. Did we start the fire?

8. She was unlocking the door when she heard a loud noise.

_____ a. Did she hear the noise before she unlocked the door?

_____ b. Did she hear the noise at the same time as she was unlocking the door?

9. Don was waiting in the car while Helen was arguing with the store manager.

_____ a. Did Don go into the store?

_____ b. Did Don and Helen both argue with the manager?

10. Mike left before the end of the game.

_____ a. Did Mike see the end of the game?

_____ b. Did the game end after Mike left?

F2 Editing

Some of these sentences have errors. Find the errors and correct them.

1. I feel terrible. I ~~was breaking~~ *broke* my favorite necklace when I put it on this morning.

2. I'm so sorry about your mug. I was dropping it.

3. They were owning a house before they had children.

4. It snowing when we went to school.

5. While we were shopping, they were cleaning the house.

6. After he was throwing the ball, it hit the window.

7. What did he say to you while you watched the movie?

8. Where were you going when I was seeing you yesterday?

9. She was reading after she fell asleep.

10. He hit his head when he had the car accident.

▶ Beyond the Classroom

Searching for Authentic Examples

Find examples of English grammar in everyday life. Look in an article in an English-language newspaper or on the Internet for examples of the past continuous and past time clauses. Write down three examples of each and bring them to class. Why was the past continuous used? Why was the simple past used? Discuss your findings with your classmates.

Writing

Follow the steps below to write a paragraph about a hurricane, flood, or other natural disaster.

1. Do research in the library or on the Internet about a natural disaster. Take notes. Use these questions to help you.

   • What, if anything, did people do to prepare for the disaster?

   • What did they do when the disaster struck?

   • What damage occurred during the disaster?

   • What happened after the disaster?

2. Write a first draft. Use the simple past, the past continuous, and past time clauses where appropriate.

3. Reread your work carefully and circle grammar, spelling, and punctuation errors. Work with a partner to decide how to fix your errors and improve the content.

4. Rewrite your draft.

   A terrible earthquake hit my country last year. When it hit, people were working at their jobs and children were studying at school. It seemed like a normal day. . . .

The Present Perfect

A Tales of a World Traveler

Discuss these questions.

Do you like to travel? What are some good and bad things about traveling? Name some countries you have visited. Where else do you want to go?

 Read this magazine article to find out about world traveler John Clouse.

Tales of a World Traveler

According to *Guinness World Records*™, John Clouse has visited more places than anyone else in the world. He has been to 192 countries and almost all of the 5 world's territories. In his travels, he has crossed the Atlantic Ocean at least 100 times and the Pacific Ocean 40 or 50 times. In addition to holding the *Guinness* world record for travel, Clouse is also the most-10 traveled member of the Travelers' Century Club. All of the members of this club have traveled to at least 100 countries.

All of this traveling has cost John Clouse a lot of money. So far he has spent about 15 $1.25 million. It has also taken a long time. Clouse started traveling 40 years ago.

Has John Clouse stopped traveling? No, he hasn't. He has continued his journeys. There are three places that he hasn't visited 20 yet: the Paracel Islands in the South China Sea; Clipperton, a French island about 700 miles west of Acapulco, Mexico; and Bouvet Island, near Antarctica.

Some of Clouse's journeys have been 25 difficult. For example, while trying to reach Danger Island in the Pacific, he almost had to turn back just a few yards from the shore because the waves were too high. The real problem was that he doesn't know how to 30 swim, so another man had to carry him on his back!

Clouse has never publicly stated his favorite country. He doesn't like to list favorites, but he has said that Kenya and 35 Tanzania in Africa are both beautiful. What place has Clouse visited the most? Paris. He's been there 35 times. Does Clouse feel proud of his world record? Not at all. In fact, he realizes that it's all a bit ridiculous. 40 "Wanderlust is a sickness that I got from my father. After all, if you've seen one atoll, you've seen them all," he says with a smile.

Adapted from *The Christian Science Monitor*

atoll: a very small island made of coral
journey: a trip
ridiculous: very silly, foolish

tale: a story
territory: an area of land that belongs to a country
wanderlust: a strong desire to travel

 After You Read

A. Circle the places that John Clouse has *not* visited.

Bouvet Island	Danger Island	the Paracel Islands
Clipperton	Kenya	Tanzania

B. Match each number with the correct description.

__e__ **1.** 100

_____ **2.** 1.25 million

_____ **3.** 35

_____ **4.** 192

_____ **5.** 40 or 50

a. the number of times Clouse has visited Paris

b. the number of countries Clouse has visited

c. the number of dollars Clouse has spent on travel

d. the number of times Clouse has crossed the Pacific Ocean

e. the smallest number of countries each person in the Travelers' Century Club has visited

B The Present Perfect

Examining Form

Look at the sentences and complete the tasks below. Then discuss your answers and read the Form charts to check them.

1a. He has crossed the Atlantic many times.
1b. He crossed the Atlantic in 1999.

2a. They flew to Paris last night.
2b. They have flown to Paris many times.

1. Which two sentences are in the simple past? Which two sentences are in the present perfect? How many words are necessary to form the present perfect?

2. Underline the verb forms that follow *has* and *have*. These are past participles. Which form resembles the simple past? Which form is irregular?

3. Look back at the article on page 90. Find five examples of the present perfect.

<table>
<tr><th colspan="4">Affirmative Statements</th></tr>
<tr><th>SUBJECT</th><th>HAVE/HAS</th><th>PAST PARTICIPLE</th><th></th></tr>
<tr><td>I</td><td rowspan="2">have</td><td rowspan="4">traveled
flown</td><td rowspan="4">to Paris.</td></tr>
<tr><td>You</td></tr>
<tr><td>He
She
It</td><td>has</td></tr>
<tr><td>We</td><td rowspan="3">have</td></tr>
<tr><td>You</td></tr>
<tr><td>They</td></tr>
</table>

<table>
<tr><th colspan="5">Negative Statements</th></tr>
<tr><th>SUBJECT</th><th>HAVE/HAS</th><th>NOT</th><th>PAST PARTICIPLE</th><th></th></tr>
<tr><td>I</td><td rowspan="2">have</td><td rowspan="4">not</td><td rowspan="4">traveled
flown</td><td rowspan="4">to Paris.</td></tr>
<tr><td>You</td></tr>
<tr><td>He
She
It</td><td>has</td></tr>
<tr><td>We</td><td rowspan="3">have</td></tr>
<tr><td>You</td></tr>
<tr><td>They</td></tr>
</table>

<table>
<tr><th colspan="3">CONTRACTIONS</th></tr>
<tr><td>I've</td><td rowspan="3">traveled</td><td rowspan="3">to Paris.</td></tr>
<tr><td>She's</td></tr>
<tr><td>They've</td></tr>
</table>

<table>
<tr><th colspan="4">CONTRACTIONS</th></tr>
<tr><td>I</td><td>haven't</td><td rowspan="3">traveled</td><td rowspan="3">to Paris.</td></tr>
<tr><td>She</td><td>hasn't</td></tr>
<tr><td>They</td><td>haven't</td></tr>
</table>

Yes/No Questions

HAVE/HAS	SUBJECT	PAST PARTICIPLE	
Have	you		
Has	it	traveled flown	to Paris?
Have	they		

Short Answers

YES	SUBJECT	HAVE/HAS	NO	SUBJECT	HAVE/HAS + NOT
	I	have.		I	haven't.
Yes,	he	has.	No,	he	hasn't.
	they	have.		they	haven't.

Information Questions

WH- WORD	HAVE/HAS	SUBJECT	PAST PARTICIPLE	
Who	have	you	seen?	
What				
Why	has	she	been	in the hospital?
How long	have	they		

WH- WORD (SUBJECT)	HAS		PAST PARTICIPLE	
Who	has		traveled	to Paris?
What			happened?	

- The past participle of a regular verb has the same form as the simple past (verb + -d/-ed). See Appendices 4 and 5 for the spelling and pronunciation of verbs ending in -ed.
- Irregular verbs have special past participle forms. See Appendix 6 for a list of irregular verbs and their past participles.

⚠ Do not confuse the contraction of *is* with the contraction of *has* in the present perfect.

> He**'s traveling** a lot = He is traveling a lot.
>
> He**'s traveled** a lot = He has traveled a lot.

- See Appendix 16 for more contractions with *have.*

⚠ Do not use a subject pronoun in information questions when the *wh-* word is the subject.

> **What** has happened?
>
> *What has it happened? (INCORRECT)

B1 Listening for Form

🎧 Listen to these sentences. Write the present perfect verb forms you hear. You will hear both contracted and full forms.

1. I ____have worked____ here for three years.

2. We _____ Yuji since August.

3. I'm sorry. Mr. O'Neill _____ for the day.

4. Our class _____ the exam yet.

5. It _____ every day this week!

6. Don't leave yet. You _____ your breakfast.

B2 Working on Irregular Past Verb Forms

Complete the chart. See Appendix 6 if you need help.

	BASE FORM	SIMPLE PAST	PAST PARTICIPLE
1.	know	knew	known
2.		got	
3.			taken
4.		bought	
5.	leave		
6.			cost
7.		showed	
8.	be		
9.			gone
10.	eat		
11.			made
12.		did	
13.		saw	
14.			thought
15.		grew	
16.			spent

Informally Speaking

Reduced Forms of *Have* and *Has*

🎧 Look at the cartoon and listen to the conversation. How is the underlined form in the cartoon different from what you hear?

Wow . . . <u>Mark has</u> changed a lot!

He's gotten his hair cut. He looks great!

We often reduce *have* and *has* with names and other nouns in informal speech.

STANDARD FORM	WHAT YOU MIGHT HEAR
Mark **has** changed.	"/mɑrks/ changed."
The cities **have** grown.	"The /ˈsɪtizəv/ grown."

We also often reduce *have* and *has* with *wh-* words in informal speech.

STANDARD FORM	WHAT YOU MIGHT HEAR
Why **has** he left?	"/waɪz/ he left?"
Where **have** you been?	"/ˈwɛrəv/ you been?"

B3 Understanding Informal Speech

🎧 Listen and complete these sentences with the standard form of the words you hear.

1. John _____has been_____ here for a long time.

2. Kedra and Rick _____ the movie already.

3. Paul _____ a new racing bicycle.

4. The guests _____ home.

5. The police _____ the thief.

6. Where _____ she _____?

7. Fresno _____ bigger since the 1930s.

8. Why _____ it _____ so long?

B4 Completing Conversations with the Present Perfect

A. Complete these conversations with the words in parentheses and the present perfect. Use contractions where possible.

Conversation 1

Silvio: How long _____have_____ you _____lived_____ (live) here?
                              1   2

Victor: Five years. _____ you _____ (be) here long?
                              3   4

Silvio: No, I _____ (not). I _____ only
                       5   6

_____ (be) here for six months.
      7

Conversation 2

Gina: Hi, Julie. I _____ (not/see) you for a long time.
                              1

Julie: Hi, Gina. I think it _____ (be) almost three years since we last
                                      2

met. How _____ your family _____ (be)?
                3   4

Gina: Oh, there _____ (be) a lot of changes. My older brother, Chris,
                            5

_____ (get) married, and Tony and his wife, Marta,
      6

_____ (have) two children.
      7

B. Practice the conversations in part A with a partner.

B5 Building Sentences

A. Build eight logical sentences: four in the present perfect and four in the simple past. Punctuate your sentences correctly.

Present Perfect: *She has been a good friend.*   Simple Past: *She went to a restaurant.*

		been	for a long time
she	have	waited	to a restaurant
they	has	learned	a good friend
		went	English

B. Rewrite your sentences as negative statements.

Continuing Time Up to Now

Examining Meaning and Use

Read the sentences and answer the questions below. Then discuss your answers and read the Meaning and Use Notes to check them.

1a. Hiro has lived in New York since 1989.   **2a.** Rosa has been a teacher for ten years.
1b. Hiro lived in Chicago for three years.   **2b.** Rosa was a nurse for one year.

1. Which sentences show situations that began and ended in the past? Which show situations that began in the past and have continued up to the present time?

2. Which sentences use the present perfect? Which use the simple past?

Meaning and Use Notes

> **Continuing Time Up to Now**
>
> **1**   The present perfect connects the past with the present. Use the present perfect for actions or states that began in the past and have continued up to the present time. These actions or states may continue into the future.
>
> He**'s worked** here for five years.   She**'s lived** in the same town since 2001.

> **For and Since**
>
> Sentences expressing continuing time up to now often use *for* and *since*.
>
> **2A**   *For* + a length of time tells how long an action or state has continued up to the present time.
>
> I've worked here **for** <u>a long time</u>.   I've lived here **for** <u>ten years</u>.
>
> **2B**   *Since* + a point in time tells when an action or state began.
>
> I've worked here **since** <u>2000</u>.   I've been here **since** <u>Tuesday</u>.
>
> *Since* can also introduce a time clause. When it does, the verb in the time clause is usually in the simple past.
>
> I've lived here **since** <u>I was 20</u>.   I've worked here **since** <u>I left home</u>.

C1 Listening for Meaning and Use

🎧 Listen to each sentence. Is the speaker talking about a past situation that continues to the present, or a situation that began and ended in the past? Check (✓) the correct column.

	PAST SITUATION THAT CONTINUES TO THE PRESENT	SITUATION THAT BEGAN AND ENDED IN PAST
1.	✓	
2.		
3.		
4.		
5.		
6.		
7.		
8.		

C2 Contrasting *For* and *Since*

A. Complete these sentences with *for* or *since*.

1. Alex has climbed mountains ___since___ he was 15 years old.

2. They've been out of town _____ Saturday.

3. My boss has been in a meeting _____ a long time.

4. He has worked in Brazil _____ last September.

5. That restaurant has been closed _____ a week now.

6. I've known Matt _____ we were in high school.

7. They've studied French _____ a few months.

8. Lisa has lived in New York _____ ten years.

9. Keiko has liked Takeshi _____ she met him.

10. We've been here _____ half an hour.

B. Use these words and phrases to write sentences. Use the present perfect with *for* or *since*.

1. Sue/live/Rome/1999

    <u>Sue has lived in Rome since 1999.</u>

2. Betty/work/at Happy Systems/ten years

    _____

3. Paul/study/French/two semesters

    _____

4. I/be married/to Kalin/last August

    _____

5. Liz and Sara/know/Celia/many years

    _____

 Talking About How Long ▶ Notes 1, 2

A. Work with a partner. Look at the timeline. Use the phrases below and the present perfect to ask and answer questions about Gary's life. Use contractions where possible.

| be a U.S. citizen | have a business | live in the U.S. |
| be married | know his best friend | own a house |

A: How long has he been a U.S. citizen?
B: He's been a U.S. citizen since 2003. OR *He's been a U.S. citizen for . . . years.*

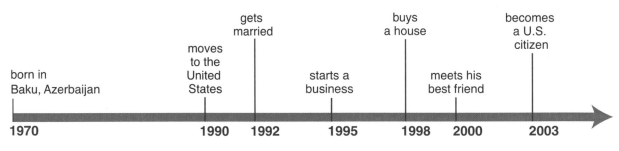

B. Make a list of questions about your partner's life. Use the present perfect with *for* and *since*. Take turns asking and answering each other's questions. Use contractions where possible.

A: How long have you studied English?   *B: How long have you lived in this city?*
B: I've studied English for five years.   *A: I've lived here since 2002.*

D Indefinite Past Time

Examining Meaning and Use

Read the sentences and answer the questions below. Then discuss your answers and read the Meaning and Use Notes to check them.

1a. I've flown in an airplane.
1b. I flew to Rome last month.

2a. There have been many car accidents on this road.
2b. There was an accident here yesterday.

1. Which sentences talk about an indefinite (not exact) time in the past? Which form of the verb is used in these sentences?

2. Which sentences mention a definite (exact) time in the past? Which form of the verb is used in these sentences?

Meaning and Use Notes

> **Indefinite Past Time**
>
> **1A** Use the present perfect to talk about actions or states that happened at an indefinite (not exact) time in the past.
>
> A: Have you met Bob?
> B: Yes, I've met him. He's really nice.
>
> ---
>
> **1B** Actions or states in the present perfect can happen once or repeatedly.
>
> He's visited Hawaii once.
> I've tried three times to pass my driver's license exam.
>
> ---
>
> **1C** Do not use the present perfect with time expressions that express a definite (exact) time in the past. When you mention the definite time an event happened, use the simple past.
>
> I went to Europe in 1999.
> *I've gone to Europe in 1999. (INCORRECT)

2 The adverb *ever* means "at any time." Use *ever* in present perfect questions to ask if an action took place at any time in the past.

A: **Have** you **ever seen** a ghost?
B: Yes, I have. OR
No, I haven't.

⚠ We usually do not use *ever* in present perfect affirmative statements.

I **have seen** a ghost.

* I have ever seen a ghost. (INCORRECT)

D1 **Listening for Meaning and Use** ▶ Notes 1A, 1C

 Listen to each sentence. Does it refer to a definite time in the past or an indefinite time in the past? Check (✓) the correct column.

	DEFINITE TIME IN THE PAST	INDEFINITE TIME IN THE PAST
1.		✓
2.		
3.		
4.		
5.		
6.		
7.		
8.		
9.		
10.		

A. Each of these situations begins with a sentence about the indefinite past. Complete the second sentence with an example expressing the definite past.

1. I've met a lot of famous people. For example, last year I _spoke to_
   Madonna in an elevator at the Plaza Hotel.

2. I've met some interesting people since I moved here. For example, this year
   I _____

3. My friend has done a lot of crazy things. Last month _____
   _____

4. My parents have helped me a lot. When I was younger, they _____
   _____

5. I had a difficult professor a while ago. For example, once _____
   _____

B. Now write sentences about an indefinite time in the past. Use the present perfect to introduce each situation.

1. _My parents have traveled a lot_. Last summer they went to California
   and Oregon, and they visited Florida and Arizona in October.

2. _____. He worked in a restaurant for
   one year, he sold cars for six months, and he worked as a bank teller for
   only one month!

3. _____. She danced in a Broadway
   musical last December, and she sang in another show in Chicago this year.

4. _____. This morning I cleaned the
   house, washed the clothes, and even worked in the garden!

5. _____. They lived in Venezuela for two
   years, they stayed in Mexico for six months, they lived in Seattle for one
   year, and now they live in Tucson, Arizona.

Conversation 3

A: Has she bought the tickets (yet)?

_____
1

B: No. She's made the reservations (already), but I don't think that she has paid

for the tickets (yet).

_____
2

Conversation 4

A: How's the fund drive going? Have you raised any money (yet)?

_____
1

B: Yes. We've raised $2,000 (so far). We haven't finished (still).

_____
2

Conversation 5

A: Has Rick left (yet)?

_____
1

B: Yes, he has left (already).

_____
2

Conversation 6

A: Have you made any friends at school (yet)?

_____
1

B: No, I've been too busy (so far).

_____
2

B. Practice the conversations in part A with a partner.

E Combining Form, Meaning, and Use

E1 Thinking About Meaning and Use

Choose the best answer to complete each conversation. Then discuss your answers in small groups.

1. **A:** He visited Sweden four years ago.

   B: _____
   a. Where is he staying?
   b. Did he have a good time?   *(b circled)*

2. **A:** Emily has worked for the school for a long time.

   B: _____
   a. Is she going to retire soon?
   b. Why did she leave?

3. **A:** I've already cooked dinner.

   B: _____
   a. Can I help you?
   b. What did you cook?

4. **A:** It has rained only once this month.

   B: _____
   a. Does it usually rain more?
   b. Has it rained a lot?

5. **A:** We've been here for half an hour, and a waiter still hasn't come to our table.

   B: _____
   a. I'm sorry. I'll try to find your waiter.
   b. How long have you been here?

6. A: I haven't been to Europe yet.

   B: _____

       a. Do you want to go sometime?

       b. When did you go?

7. A: Have you ever flown a plane?

   B: _____

       a. No, I didn't.

       b. No, not yet.

8. A: So far I've spent $100 on course books.

   B: _____

       a. Do you think you'll need to buy more?

       b. You're lucky you don't need any more.

E2 Editing

Find the errors in this paragraph and correct them. Use the simple present, the simple past, and the present perfect.

    Rita and Bob ~~have been~~ _are_ the most-traveled people I know. They went almost everywhere. Rita has been a photographer, and Bob has been a travel writer, so they often travel for work. They been to many countries, such as Nepal and India. They have also travel to Turkey, Greece, and Bulgaria. They have see some places yet, though. For example, they still haven't visited New Zealand. This year they've been already away from home a total of three months, and it has been only June. In January Rita has gone to Kenya while Bob has toured Indonesia. Then they both have traveled to Argentina and Norway. Right now they're at home. They were here for two weeks already. Two weeks at home is like a vacation for Rita and Bob.

▶ Beyond the Classroom

Searching for Authentic Examples

Find examples of English grammar in everyday life. Look in an English-language encyclopedia or on the Internet for information about someone's life. Choose a person who is still alive. What has he or she done or accomplished? Find three sentences in the present perfect and bring them to class. Why is the present perfect used instead of the simple past? Discuss your findings with your classmates.

Writing

Follow the steps below to write a paragraph about someone you admire.

1. Write about someone who is still alive. Think about your subject and make notes about what you want to say. Use these questions to help you.

   - Who do you admire?
   - What has the person done? For example, has he or she worked somewhere special or helped other people?
   - Where has the person lived and worked?
   - How has the person influenced you?

2. Write a first draft. Use the present perfect, simple past, and simple present where appropriate.

3. Read your work carefully and circle grammar, spelling, and punctuation errors. Work with a partner to decide how to fix your errors and improve the content.

4. Rewrite your draft.

   I admire my Uncle Tomás. He is a doctor. He has worked with poor people since he graduated from college twenty years ago. . . .

The Future

Future Time:
Be Going To, Will, and the Present Continuous

A The Election

A1 Before You Read

Discuss these questions.

Are you interested in politics? Do you vote? Why or why not?

A2 Read

 Read this feature article from a local newspaper to find out about four people's opinions of candidates in an election for governor.

THE ELECTION

With the election for governor just a week away, our *Public View* reporter asked people at Westlake Mall the following question: Who are you going to vote for and why?

I'm voting for Greta Monroe. She's the best
5 candidate. She's honest, hardworking, and intelligent. Just think, we <u>are going to have</u> our first woman
10 governor! I am sure that she'll do a great job. For one thing, she's fair. She wants to help poor people, but she isn't going to raise taxes for the rest of us. She's also very interested in education, and that's
15 important to me.

Diane Marshall, 67
retired teacher

I'm not voting. I used to vote in every election and nothing changed. I'm not going
20 to waste my time anymore. In fact, I am leaving for Chicago the day before the election, so I'm not even going to be here. Besides, I'm sure
25 Overmeyer is going to win. He's not a politician; he's a businessman. He started his own company and now it's one of the state's largest employers. All the business people will vote for him. The others don't
30 have a chance.

Richard Chen, 26
accountant

I'm undecided. I'm not voting for Monroe, that's for sure. So I still have to decide between either 35 Overmeyer or Kelly. Overmeyer has made a lot of promises, but will he keep them? He says that he is going to help bring jobs to the state. But how is he going to 40 do that? And what kind of jobs will they be? Are they going to be jobs for skilled workers at good salaries, or will they be minimum wage jobs for teenagers? And Kelly? Well, I'm not sure about him, either. He's done a good 45 job as mayor, but running a state is a lot more difficult than running a city.

Steve Corum, 38
unemployed mechanic

I'm new here and I don't know enough about the candidates 50 to make a decision. People say that Kelly will probably raise taxes, Monroe won't be able to do the job, and Overmeyer will 55 only help businesses. I've received a lot of information in the mail about all three. I'm going to sit down this weekend and read it. I hope I can make a decision after that.

Marcy Willis, 28
chef

---

governor: the head of a state government

candidate: a person who people can vote for in an election

running: managing, directing

mayor: the head of a city government

skilled: trained

minimum wage: the lowest amount an employer can pay a worker for an hour's work

A3 **After You Read**

Look at the questions in the chart. Check (✓) the correct column.

	WHICH CANDIDATE . . .	MONROE	OVERMEYER	KELLY
1.	isn't going to raise taxes?	✓		
2.	is a woman?			
3.	runs a large company?			
4.	promises to bring jobs to the state?			
5.	is a mayor?			
6.	wants to raise taxes?			

B The Future with *Be Going To* and the Present Continuous

Examining Form

Look back at the article on page 112 and complete the tasks below. Then discuss your answers and read the Form charts to check them.

1. An example of *be going to* + verb is underlined. Find three more affirmative examples.

2. What form of *be going to* is used with *we*? with *he*? with *I*?

3. An example of the present continuous as future (*be* + verb + *-ing*) is circled. Find one more affirmative example.

THE FUTURE WITH *BE GOING TO*

Affirmative Statements				
SUBJECT	BE	GOING TO	BASE FORM OF VERB	
I	am			
You	are			
He She It	is	going to	help	later.
We				
You	are			
They				

Negative Statements					
SUBJECT	BE	NOT	GOING TO	BASE FORM OF VERB	
I	am				
You	are				
He She It	is	not	going to	help	later.
We					
You	are				
They					

Yes/No Questions				
BE	SUBJECT	GOING TO	BASE FORM OF VERB	
Are	you			
Is	she	going to	help	later?
Are	they			

Short Answers					
YES	SUBJECT	BE	NO	SUBJECT + BE + NOT	
	I	am.		I'm not.	
Yes,	she	is.	No,	she isn't.	
	they	are.		they aren't.	

Information Questions

WH- WORD	BE	SUBJECT	GOING TO	BASE FORM OF VERB	
Who	**are**	you		**call**	later?
What	**is**	she	**going to**	**do**	tomorrow?
When	**are**	they		**study**	at the library?

WH- WORD (SUBJECT)	BE		GOING TO	BASE FORM OF VERB	
Who	**is**		**going to**	**win**	the election?
What				**happen**	next?

- See Appendix 16 for contractions with *be*.
- ⚠ Do not use contractions with affirmative short answers.
  - Yes, I **am**.   *Yes, I'm. (INCORRECT)

——— THE PRESENT CONTINUOUS AS FUTURE ———

Affirmative Statements

SUBJECT	BE	BASE FORM OF VERB + -ING	
She	**is**	**helping**	later.

Negative Statements

SUBJECT	BE	NOT	BASE FORM OF VERB + -ING	
She	**is**	**not**	**helping**	later.

Yes/No Questions

BE	SUBJECT	BASE FORM OF VERB + -ING	
Are	they	**helping**	later?

Information Questions

WH- WORD	BE	SUBJECT	BASE FORM OF VERB + -ING	
When	**are**	they	**helping**?	later?

- See Chapter 3 for more information on the present continuous.

A. 🎧 Listen to these sentences. Write the subjects and future verb forms you hear.

1. _She's going to start_ school next year.

2. _____ home tonight. The airline canceled our flight.

3. Where _____ tonight?

4. Take your umbrella. _____.

5. _____ TV tonight?

6. They hate that hotel so _____ there again.

7. _____ on vacation tomorrow.

8. _____ to the office next week. I'm on vacation.

9. Study hard, or _____ the test.

10. I'm really excited. _____ on a business trip to Brazil next month.

B. Work with a partner. Look at each sentence again. Which future form is used: *be going to* or the present continuous as future?

B2 Working on *Be Going To*

Complete these sentences with the correct forms of *be going to* and the words in parentheses. Use contractions where possible.

1. Soo-jin _is going to study_ (study) in the United States next year.

2. She and her classmates _____ (take) language exams in December.

3. She _____ (not/apply) to many schools – just a few in Boston.

4. She knows that it _____ (be) difficult to study abroad.

5. Her parents aren't worried, because she _____ (not/be) alone.

6. She _____ (stay) with relatives there.

7. She _____ (live) with her aunt and uncle.

8. Soo-jin and her relatives are very close so they _____ (enjoy) living together.

Building Present Continuous Sentences

Build six logical sentences with the present continuous as future. Use a word or phrase from each column. Punctuate your sentences correctly.

I am taking a test tomorrow.

I	am	giving	a test	next summer
my friends	is	taking	to Europe	tomorrow
our teacher	are	going	to a restaurant	tonight

B4 **Forming Questions with** *Be Going To*

Complete each conversation with a *Yes/No* question or information question. Use *be going to* and the words and phrases in parentheses.

1. **A:** Is he going to study tonight? _____ (study/tonight)

   B: Yes, he is.

2. **A:** _____ (call/tomorrow)

   B: No, they aren't.

3. **A:** _____ (graduate/this semester)

   B: No, I'm not.

4. **A:** _____ (move/to Canada)

   B: No, I'm not.

5. **A:** _____ (he/study/tonight)

   B: In the library.

6. **A:** _____ (they/call)

   B: Tonight.

7. **A:** _____ (you/graduate)

   B: Next semester.

8. **A:** _____ (you/move)

   B: To Japan.

Informally Speaking

Reduced Form of *Going To*

Look at the cartoon and listen to the conversation. How are the underlined forms in the cartoon different from what you hear?

Going to is often pronounced /gənə/ in informal speech.

STANDARD FORM

They are **going to** call.

He is **going to** spend all the money.

I am **going to** stay home.

WHAT YOU MIGHT HEAR

"They're/gənə/call."

"He's/gənə/spend all the money."

"I'm/gənə/stay home."

B5 Understanding Informal Speech

Listen and write the standard form of the words you hear.

1. We _____are going to make_____ dinner soon.

2. I _____ to the beach.

3. We _____ him in Seattle.

4. Our class _____ next Wednesday.

5. The store _____ in five minutes.

6. Mark _____ at Lincoln University.

7. The children _____ happy about this.

8. They _____ the test tomorrow.

Be Going To and the Present Continuous as Future

Examining Meaning and Use

Read the sentences and answer the questions below. Then discuss your answers
and read the Meaning and Use Notes to check them.

    a. I'm going to buy my father a book for his birthday.
    b. I think we're going to have a storm tonight.
    c. We're taking a trip next month.

1. Which two sentences talk about an intention (something you're thinking about doing)
or a plan?

2. Which sentence makes a prediction (a guess about the future)?

Meaning and Use Notes

Intentions and Plans with *Be Going To* and the Present Continuous

1A Use *be going to* to talk about intentions or future plans.

> **I'm going to study** hard for the test.
> **I'm going to visit** Greece this summer.

> A: What **is** Josh **going to study** at college?
> B: He**'s going to study** chemistry.

1B You can also use the present continuous to talk about intentions or future plans.
A future time expression is usually used with the present continuous to show that
the sentence refers to the future (and not something happening right now). The
verbs *go, come, do,* and *have,* as well as verbs related to travel, are especially
common with the present continuous as future.

> When **are** you **coming** to see me?
> **I'm visiting** Greece <u>this summer</u>.
> My flight **is arriving** <u>in the afternoon</u>. My father **is meeting** me at the airport.

> A: What **are** you **doing** <u>tomorrow</u>?
> B: **I'm having** lunch with friends. Then we**'re going** to a movie.

(Continued on page 120)

1C The present continuous often refers to more definite plans than *be going to*. With *be going to*, the speaker often has not decided on the details.

Present Continuous as Future (Details Definite)

I**'m taking** a 3:00 flight to Chicago. In Chicago, I**'m changing** planes and **flying** on to Miami.

Be Going To *(Details Not Definite)*

A: I**'m going to buy** a car.
B: What kind **are** you **going to get?**
A: I don't know yet.

Predictions with *Be Going To*

2 Use *be going to* for predictions (guesses about the future), especially when there is evidence that something is just about to happen. The present continuous is not used to make predictions.

Be careful! That glass **is going to fall**!

It's cloudy. I think it**'s going to rain** tonight.

*It's cloudy. I think it's raining tonight. (INCORRECT)

C1 **Listening for Meaning and Use** ► Notes 1A, 1B, 2

 Listen to each sentence. Is the speaker talking about an intention or plan, or making a prediction? Check (✓) the correct column.

	INTENTION/PLAN	PREDICTION
1.		✓
2.		
3.		
4.		
5.		
6.		
7.		
8.		

Work with a partner. Look at the pictures and make two predictions about what is going to happen in each situation. Use *be going to*.

1.

I think she's going to take a trip.
I think she's going to travel to a cold place.

4.

2.

5.

3.

6.

Vocabulary Notes

Future Time Expressions

The future time expressions below are commonly used in sentences about the future.

TODAY/TONIGHT/TOMORROW	**THIS + TIME PERIOD**	**NEXT + TIME PERIOD**
today	this afternoon	next Sunday
tonight	this Sunday	next week
tomorrow	this week	next August
the day after tomorrow	this year	next month
tomorrow morning/afternoon/night	this spring	next year
They're arriving **tomorrow**.	I'm leaving **this week**.	**Next week** I'm visiting Ana.

IN + QUANTITY OF TIME	**THE + TIME PERIOD + AFTER NEXT**
in five minutes	the week after next
in a few days	the weekend after next
in a few weeks	the month after next
in a few months	the year after next
He's going to call **in a few hours**.	We're having a test **the week after next**.

C3 Using Future Time Expressions

Work with a partner. Take turns asking and answering questions with *when* and *be going to* or the present continuous as future. Use *be going to* for intentions and the present continuous as future for more definite plans. Use future time expressions in your answers.

1. you/study

   A: *When are you going to study?*
   B: *I'm going to study tonight.*
   OR
   A: *When are you studying?*
   B: *I'm studying this afternoon.*

2. your best friend/visit you

3. you/finish your homework

4. your friends/have a party

5. you/check your e-mail

6. your history teacher/give a test

7. your family/take a vacation

8. you/clean your apartment

A. Write sentences about what you intend or plan to do at the future times in parentheses. Use *be going to* for intentions and the present continuous as future for more definite plans.

1. (next weekend) <u>Next weekend I'm going to visit my parents.</u>

2. (the day after tomorrow) _____

3. (next spring) _____

4. (in six months) _____

5. (next year) _____

6. (in an hour) _____

B. Work with a partner. Ask your partner about his or her intentions or plans. Use future time expressions in your questions.

A: What are you doing next weekend?
B: I'm visiting my parents.

C5 Thinking About Intentions and Plans ▶ Notes 1A–1C

A. Think about these possible events. Check (✓) the events that you can plan.

<u>✓</u> 1. learn to drive a car

____ 2. have bad weather

____ 3. give a party

____ 4. go to college

____ 5. get sick

____ 6. have a car accident

____ 7. look for a job

____ 8. rob a bank

____ 9. have an eye exam

____ 10. get married

____ 11. win the lottery

____ 12. watch a movie

B. Work with a partner. Talk about the things you plan to do. You can use the events you checked in part A or others. Use *be going to* for intentions or the present continuous as future for more definite plans. Use future time expressions.

A: I'm going to learn to drive this summer. My brother is going to teach me.
B: I'm watching a movie with some friends tonight. My friend Silvia is renting a video, and everyone is coming to my house at 7:00.

A. Fill in the chart below with your schedule for the next week.

	MONDAY	**TUESDAY**	**WEDNESDAY**	**THURSDAY**	**FRIDAY**
8:00 A.M.					
9:00 A.M.					
10:00 A.M.					
11:00 A.M.					
12:00 P.M.					
1:00 P.M.					
2:00 P.M.					
3:00 P.M.					
4:00 P.M.					
5:00 P.M.					

B. Now work with three other students to find a time for a two-hour meeting, a lunch date, and a one-hour work-out at the gym. Use the present continuous as future and time expressions to talk about your future plans.

A: *When can we have the meeting?*
B: *I'm free next Tuesday at 9 A.M.*
C: *I'm not. I'm working all morning.*
D: *What are you doing next Thursday at one?*
C: *I'm not doing anything until three.*

D The Future with *Will*

Examining Form

Read the sentences and complete the tasks below. Then discuss your answers and read the Form charts to check them.

  a. I will decide in a few weeks.
  b. He will probably raise taxes.
  c. They will vote for him.
  d. Will Overmeyer keep his promises?

1. Underline *will* + verb in each sentence. Circle the subjects.

2. Does the form of *will* change with different subjects?

3. Does *will* go before or after the subject in a question?

Affirmative Statements

SUBJECT	WILL	BASE FORM OF VERB	
I			
You			
He She It	will	leave	tomorrow.
We			
You			
They			

CONTRACTIONS		
I'll		
She'll	leave	tomorrow.
They'll		

Negative Statements

SUBJECT	WILL	NOT	BASE FORM OF VERB	
I				
You				
He She It	will	not	leave	tomorrow.
We				
You				
They				

CONTRACTIONS			
I			
She	won't	leave	tomorrow.
They			

(Continued on page 126)

Yes/No Questions

WILL	SUBJECT	BASE FORM OF VERB	
Will	you she they	**leave**	tomorrow?

Short Answers

YES	SUBJECT	WILL	NO	SUBJECT	WILL + NOT
Yes,	I she they	**will.**	No,	I she they	**won't.**

Information Questions

WH- WORD	WILL	SUBJECT	BASE FORM OF VERB	
Who	will	he	**see**	at the wedding tomorrow?
What		they	**do**	later?

WH- WORD (SUBJECT)	WILL		BASE FORM OF VERB	
Who	will		**leave**	first?
What			**happen**	next?

- Use the same form of *will* with every subject. See Appendix 16 for contractions with *will*.
- Do not use contractions with affirmative short answers.
  - Yes, I **will.**   *Yes, I'll. (INCORRECT)

D1 **Listening for Form**

 Listen to each sentence. Which form is used to talk about the future: *be going to*, the present continuous, or *will*? Check (✓) the correct column.

	BE GOING TO	PRESENT CONTINUOUS	WILL
1.	✓		
2.			
3.			
4.			
5.			
6.			
7.			
8.			

Complete these conversations with the words in parentheses and *will* or *won't*. Use contractions where possible. Then practice the conversations with a partner.

Conversation 1

Susan: I don't believe all these predictions. In the next ten years

_____we won't have_____ (we/not/have) hydrogen-powered cars.
                1

Bob: Oh, I think _____ (we).
                        2

Conversation 2

Jenny: _____ (we/be) friends in five years?
                    1

Keiko: Of course, _____ (we/be) friends.
                        2

Conversation 3

Lauren: Take your jacket or _____ (you/be) cold.
                                1

Dan: No, _____ (I/not). It's not cold outside.
                    2

Conversation 4

Paul: _____ (I/do) my homework in the morning. I
                1

promise, Mom.

Mom: No, _____ (you/not). You're always too tired in the
                    2

morning. Do it now.

Conversation 5

Carol: _____ (I/never/learn) how to program this new VCR.
                    1

Betty: I have the same one. _____ (I/show) you.
                                2

Conversation 6

Robin: Do you think _____ (you/find) an apartment in
                        1

San Francisco?

Kedra: That's a good question. _____ (it/be) difficult.
                                    2

Maybe _____ (I/try) Oakland, too.
            3

D3 Asking *Yes/No* Questions with *Will*

A. Imagine that this is the first day of your new English class. You are feeling very nervous. Use these phrases to write *Yes/No* questions to ask your teacher. Use *will* in your questions.

1. (get homework every night) <u>Will we get homework every night?</u>

2. (have a final exam) _____

3. (get grades for class participation) _____

4. (use a textbook) _____

5. (have a lot of tests) _____

6. (use the language lab) _____

B. Work with a partner. Think of two more questions to ask your teacher.

Will we use the Internet in class?

C. Take turns asking and answering the questions in parts A and B.

A: Will we get homework every night?
B: Yes, you will. It will help you a lot.

D4 Building Sentences

Build six logical information questions with *will*. Use each *wh-* word at least once. Remember that *wh-* (subject) questions do not need an item from the third column. Punctuate your sentences correctly.

What will you talk about at the meeting?

what when where who	will	dinner you your boss	talk about be go graduate	from college after class today at the meeting ready

Informally Speaking

Look at the cartoon and listen to the conversation. How are the underlined forms in the cartoon different from what you hear?

> Who will pick up the kids from school?

> I will. My boss will let me leave early.

Will is often contracted with nouns and *wh-* words in informal speech.

STANDARD FORM	WHAT YOU MIGHT HEAR
Jake will be late.	"/ˈdʒeɪkəl/ be late."
The **children will** be here soon.	"The /ˈtʃɪldrənəl/ be here."
How will you get to Boston?	"/ˈhaʊəl/ you get to Boston?"
Where will you live?	"/ˈwɛrəl/ you live?"

D5 Understanding Informal Speech

🎧 Listen and write the standard form of the words you hear.

1. <u>What will</u> you say to him tonight?

2. _____ Tony be home?

3. The _____ need paper and pencils for the test.

4. _____ help me carry these bags?

5. _____ help you with your homework.

6. After the test, the _____ grade our papers.

7. _____ get the job. He's so qualified.

8. The _____ be over at ten o'clock.

Will vs. *Be Going To*

Examining Meaning and Use

Read the conversations and answer the questions below. Then discuss your answers and read the Meaning and Use Notes to check them.

a.   **Waiter:** Our special today is chicken salad.
  Customer: I think I'll have a tuna sandwich instead, please.

b.   **Father:** I'm very angry with you.
  Daughter: I'm sorry. I'll never lie to you again.

c.   **Wife:** What time are your parents arriving?
  Husband: They'll probably be here by six.

1. In which conversation is the second person making a prediction?

2. In which conversation is the second person making a quick decision?

3. In which conversation is the second person making a promise?

Meaning and Use Notes

Predictions with *Will* and *Be Going To*

1A Use *will* or *be going to* to make predictions (guesses about the future). You can also use *probably* and other adverbs with *will* and *be going to* to express certainty or uncertainty.

Will	Be Going To
Electric cars **will become** popular in the next ten years.	Electric cars **are going to become** popular in the next ten years.
They**'ll** <u>probably</u> **win** the championship.	They**'re** <u>probably</u> **going to win** the championship.

1B With predictions, the meanings of *will* and *be going to* are not exactly the same. Use *be going to* when you are more certain that an event will happen because there is evidence. Do not use *will* in this situation.

She**'s going to have** a baby!

*She'll have a baby! (INCORRECT)

2 In statements with *I, will* and *be going to* have different meanings. *Will* is often used to express a quick decision made at the time of speaking (such as an offer to help). *Be going to,* however, shows that you have thought about something in advance. Do not use *be going to* for quick decisions.

Will *for Quick Decisions*

A: I don't have a fork.

B: **I'll ask** the waiter to bring you one.

A: Someone is at the door.

B: **I'll get** it.

Be Going To *for Advance Plans*

A: Do we have plastic forks for the party?

B: No. **I'm going to ask** Lisa to bring some.

A: Have you decided to buy the car?

B: Yes. **I'm going to get** it tomorrow.

3 In statements with *I, will* is often used to express a promise.

A: Chris, please clean your room.

B: **I'll do** it later, Mom. I promise.

E1 Listening for Meaning and Use ▶ Notes 1A, 1B, 2, 3

🎧 Listen to each sentence. Is the speaker making a promise, a prediction, or a quick decision? Check (✓) the correct column.

	PROMISE	PREDICTION	QUICK DECISION
1.		✓	
2.			
3.			
4.			
5.			
6.			

Contrasting *Be Going To* and *Will* ▶ Notes 1B, 2

Complete each conversation with the words in parentheses and the correct form of *be going to* or *will*. Use contractions where possible.

Conversation 1

A: ___Are you going___ (you/go) to Jake's party?
　　　　　　¹

B: I can't. _____ (I/visit) my grandmother this weekend.
　　　　　　　　　²

Conversation 2

A: Did you hear? _____ (Maria/have) a baby in February!
　　　　　　　　　¹

B: That's great news!

Conversation 3

A: Oh, there's the doorbell.

B: Don't worry. _____ (I/answer) it.
　　　　　　　　¹

Conversation 4

A: Maria, I have to ask you something important. _____ (you/marry) me?
　　　　　　　　　　　　　　　　　　　¹

B: Yes, of course, _____ (I), Luis.
　　　　　　　　　²

Making Quick Decisions ▶ Note 2

Complete each conversation with an offer of help. Use *will* and a contraction.

Conversation 1

A: My cat is stuck in the tree again! I'll never get him down.

B: ___Don't worry! I'll get him down for you.___

Conversation 2

A: I can't open the door. I'm carrying too many groceries.

B: _____

Conversation 3

A: Oh no! I don't have enough money to pay for dinner.

B: _____

Conversation 4

A: I'll never have time to clean this apartment before my mom comes over.

B: _____

Conversation 5

A: I lost my math notes and I need them to study for the quiz.

B: _____

E4 **Making Promises** ▶ Note 3

Read these situations. Write promises with *will* or *won't*.

1. Tony got bad grades this semester. His parents are angry. What does he promise them?

   I'll study much harder next semester.

2. Derek went away on vacation. He forgot to lock his house. Thieves came in and stole everything. What does he promise himself?

   _____

3. Pedro forgot his essay. What does he promise his professor?

   _____

4. Dr. Smith is about to give Sara an injection. What does he promise her?

   _____

5. Eve is on the telephone with the manager of the local telephone company. She hasn't paid her bill for three months. What does she promise?

   _____

E5 **Making Predictions** ▶ Note 1A

Work in small groups. Look at these topics. Make predictions using *be going to* and *will*. Then discuss your predictions with the rest of the class.

1. medicine

   Medical care is going to become more expensive, but more people will have health insurance.

2. space travel

3. war and peace

4. cars and planes

5. education

6. wealth and poverty

Combining Form, Meaning, and Use

F1 Thinking About Meaning and Use

Choose the best answer to complete each conversation. Then discuss your answers in small groups.

1. **A:** _____

   B: I'm getting up early, packing a lunch, and taking a bus to the beach.
   - **a.** What are you doing now?
   - **b.** What are you going to do tomorrow?

2. **A:** I don't need an umbrella. It's not raining.

   B: _____
   - **a.** But it's raining this afternoon.
   - **b.** But it's going to rain this afternoon.

3. **A:** Tomorrow's election is going to be close.

   B: _____
   - **a.** Yes, but I think O'Casey's winning.
   - **b.** Yes, but I think O'Casey will win.

4. **A:** Next Monday is Pat's birthday.

   B: _____
   - **a.** Yes. We're going to have a party for her.
   - **b.** Yes. We'll have a party for her.

5. **A:** This box is very heavy. I can't carry it any longer.

   B: _____
   - **a.** Don't worry. I'm going to carry it.
   - **b.** I'll carry it. You carry the lighter one.

6. A: We're going on a Caribbean cruise.

   B: _____

       a. Wow! You're having a great time.

       b. Wow! You're going to have a great time.

7. A: Does Lisa know whether she's going to have a boy or a girl?

   B: _____

       a. Yes, the doctor told her. She will have a boy.

       b. Yes, the doctor told her. She's going to have a boy.

8. A: Do you think electric cars will become more popular in the future?

   B: _____

       a. Yes, everyone will drive them.

       b. Yes, everyone is driving them.

F2   Editing

Some of these sentences have errors. Find the errors and correct them.

1. Betty ^is^ going to college this fall.

2. What she is going to study?

3. She is going to study cooking because she wants to be a chef.

4. Betty studying with some famous chefs next year.

5. Someday maybe Betty is being a famous chef, too.

6. Betty is also going to take some business classes.

7. After these classes she certainly wills know all about restaurant management.

8. Maybe in a few years Betty owns a restaurant.

9. What kind of food her restaurant will serve?

10. I predict it is serving Chinese.

▶ Beyond the Classroom

Searching for Authentic Examples

Find examples of English grammar in everyday life. Look in an English-language newspaper or on the Internet for articles about the future plans of the government or of a famous person. Find five examples of *will, be going to,* and the present continuous as future. Bring the examples to class. Which examples show predictions? advance plans? intentions? Why is *will, be going to,* or the present continuous used in each example? Discuss your findings with your classmates.

Speaking

Follow these steps for making a group presentation about your plans to solve a problem in your school or community.

1. Work with two or three other students outside of class. Think of a problem in your school or community.

2. Discuss the problem as a group. Makes notes about what the problem is, and how to fix it. Use these questions to help you.
   - What is the problem?
   - What are you or others going to do to fix the problem?
   - What results do you predict?

3. Use your notes to prepare your presentation. Be sure to use *be going to,* the present continuous as future, and *will* to talk about your plans and your predictions about the results.

4. Divide the presentation into three or four parts (one for each student in the group). Then present your plan to your classmates. At the end of the presentation, ask your classmates to ask questions and give their opinions about your plan.

   A lot of families in our neighborhood are not following the city's recycling laws. We are going to organize a campaign. First, we will . . .

Future Time Clauses and *If* Clauses

A What Will Happen in the Future?

A1 Before You Read

Discuss these questions.

Do you think about life in the future? What will be different in the future? Will the world be a better or worse place than it is today? Why?

A2 Read

 Read this magazine article to find out if your predictions about the future match one expert's predictions.

What Will Happen in the Future?

In the year 2010 we will continue the exploration of the planet Mars. The first interplanetary astronauts won't be humans, however. They will
5 be robots. Experts say these robots will be very different from the robots we usually see in movies. They won't have arms and legs. Instead, they will be like small armored vehicles. They
10 will explore the surface of the planet and they will perform scientific experiments. If the robots find water, humans will travel to Mars and create a colony.

15 **In the year 2015** people will live in "smart" houses. These houses will

Robots of the future probably won't look like this.

use less energy and will be more environmentally friendly than the houses of today. If a room is empty,
20 the lights and TV will go off. When the weather is cold, windows will shut automatically. They will open when the weather is hot. The windows will also change the energy of the sun into
25 electricity. Some people say that smart houses are not going to be very popular because we will prefer our traditional houses. Others say that smart houses will change our way of
30 life completely and everyone will love them.

In the year 2020 it will be possible for ordinary people to travel on supersonic planes such as the
35 Concorde. Today this kind of travel is extremely expensive. However, in the future it is going to be much cheaper. After prices go down, it will be possible for everyone to travel from Tokyo to
40 New York in just a few hours.

In the year 2025 we will build a space station on one of the moons of Jupiter. Some scientists believe that humans will travel into deep space
45 soon after that.

---

armored: covered in metal as protection from damage or attack

colony: a community of people living together in a new place

extremely: very

ordinary: like everyone else, not unusual

supersonic: traveling faster than sound

 A3 **After You Read**

Check (✓) the predictions that the writer makes in the article.

___✓___ 1. The first interplanetary astronauts will not be humans.

_____ 2. It is unlikely that robots will find water on Mars.

_____ 3. Humans will start a colony on Mars in the year 2010.

_____ 4. In 2015 smart houses will use energy from the sun.

_____ 5. People in smart houses will not need electricity.

_____ 6. In the year 2025 we will build a space station on one of the moons of Jupiter.

B Future Time Clauses and *If* Clauses

Examining Form

Read the sentences and complete the tasks below. Then discuss your answers and read the Form charts to check them.

    a. I'll see him before I leave.
    b. When they graduate, they're going to look for work.
    c. We're going to have dessert after we finish dinner.

1. Underline the main clause and circle the dependent clause in each sentence. What form of the verb is used in each main clause?

2. Look at each dependent clause. What is the first word? What form of the verb is used? These are future time clauses.

3. Look at this sentence. What is the first word of the dependent clause? This is an *if* clause.

    If I go to the store, I'll buy the groceries.

4. Look back at the article on page 138. Find two future time clauses and one *if* clause.

FUTURE TIME CLAUSES

FUTURE TIME CLAUSE	SUBJECT	VERB		MAIN CLAUSE
Before	I	**go**	to the movies,	**I'm going to do** my homework.
When	she	**gets**	to work,	she**'ll make** some phone calls.
After	we	**finish**	dinner,	we**'ll wash** the dishes.

MAIN CLAUSE	FUTURE TIME CLAUSE		SUBJECT	VERB	
I'm going to do my homework	**before**		I	**go**	to the movies.
She**'ll make** some phone calls	**when**		she	**gets**	to work.
We**'ll wash** the dishes	**after**		we	**finish**	dinner.

Overview

- A clause is a group of words that has a subject and a verb.
- A main clause can stand alone as a complete sentence.
- A dependent clause cannot stand alone and must be used with a main clause.

Future Time Clauses

- Future time clauses are dependent time clauses. They begin with words such as *before, when, while,* and *after.*
- A future time clause can come before or after the main clause with no change in meaning. If the future time clause comes first, then it is separated from the main clause by a comma.
- Use *will* or *be going to* in the main clause.
- The verb in the future time clause is in the simple present even though it has a future meaning.

⚠ Do not use *be going to* or *will* in the future time clause.

> After I **finish** my work, I'll watch TV.
> * After I will finish my work, I'll watch TV. (INCORRECT)

IF CLAUSES

		IF CLAUSE		(THEN)	MAIN CLAUSE
IF	**SUBJECT**	**VERB**		**(THEN)**	
	you	**exercise**	every day,		you**'ll feel** better.
If	it	**rains**	tomorrow	(then)	they**'ll cancel** the picnic.
	we	**don't score**	soon,		we**'re going to lose** the game.

MAIN CLAUSE		IF CLAUSE		
	IF	**SUBJECT**	**VERB**	
You**'ll feel** better		you	**exercise**	every day.
They**'ll cancel** the picnic	if	it	**rains**	tomorrow.
We**'re going to lose** the game		we	**don't score**	soon.

(Continued on page 142)

If Clauses

- *If* clauses are dependent clauses. They must be used with a main clause.
- An *if* clause can come before or after the main clause with no change in meaning. When the *if* clause comes first, it is separated from the main clause by a comma.
- When the *if* clause comes first, *then* can be added before the main clause with no change in meaning.
- Use *will* or *be going to* in the main clause.
- The verb in the *if* clause is in the simple present even though it has a future meaning.

⚠ Do not use *be going to* or *will* in the *if* clause.

   If I **finish** my work, I'll watch TV.

   * If I'll finish my work, I'll watch TV. (INCORRECT)

B1) Listening for Form

🎧 Listen to these sentences. Write the verb forms you hear.

1. When I _____*see*_____ Elena, I _'ll give_____ her the message.

2. We _____ more time if the test _____ very difficult.

3. Marcus and Maria _____ to Budapest after they _____ Prague.

4. She _____ us when she _____ here.

5. You _____ him if you _____ to the party.

6. If Matt _____ a loan from the bank, he _____ a new car.

B2) Building Sentences

Build five logical sentences with future time clauses and *if* clauses. Use a clause from each column. Use the correct form of the verbs in parentheses. Punctuate your sentences correctly.

After Megan finishes class, she'll have lunch.

after Megan (finish) class	we (get) a lot of money
before she (leave) the house	she (have) lunch
if we (win) the prize	you (pass) the test
if you (study) hard	she (call) you
when we (get) to the movies	we (save) you a seat

B3 **Working on Future Time Clauses and *If* Clauses**

A. Complete each sentence with a future time clause or a main clause. Use the words and phrases in parentheses and the correct punctuation.

1. When I get a job<u>, I'll buy a car.</u>   (I/buy/a car)

2. _____ (after/she/graduate) she's going to move to L.A.

3. After we save some money _____ (we/look/for a house)

4. _____ (they/visit/the Eiffel Tower) before they leave Paris.

B. Complete each sentence with an *if* clause or a main clause. Use the words and phrases in parentheses and the correct punctuation.

1. We'll take her out to dinner <u>if she visits.</u>   (if/she/visit)

2. _____ (I/call) if I hear any news.

3. If I feel better _____ (I/go/to work)

4. _____ (if/you/not/study) you won't do well on the test.

B4 **Completing Sentences with Future Time Clauses and *If* Clauses**

Complete this e-mail with the correct form of the verb in parentheses.

Emily,

We're planning a surprise party for Dan's birthday. Here are the plans.

Lauren <u>will bring</u> (bring) me their house key after Dan _____ (leave)
            1   2
for work on Friday. I _____ (decorate) before I _____ (go) to class.
                            3   4
I ordered a cake from the bakery. Stefan _____ (get) it when he
                                                5
_____ (go) shopping on Friday afternoon. We need your help. If Dan
      6
_____ (come) home right after work, we _____ (not/be) ready.
      7   8
Will you ask him to drive you home after work? If you _____ (ask) him to
                                                            9
take you home, he _____ (not/ be) suspicious. Then, when everyone
                        10
_____ (be) here, I _____ (call) you on your cell phone.
      11   12

Luisa

Using Future Time Clauses for Events in Sequence

Examining Meaning and Use

Read the sentences and complete the task below. Then discuss your answers and read the Meaning and Use Notes to check them.

    a. We'll give you the information when we get the results.
    b. Before you take the test, the teacher will review the homework.
    c. He'll need help after he comes home from the hospital.

Look at each sentence. Underline the event that happens first. Which word or words in each sentence tell you the order of the events?

Meaning and Use Notes

> **Future Events in Sequence**
>
> **1** Future time clauses show the time relationship between two events or situations in a sentence. When a time clause begins with *when* or *after*, the event in the time clause happens first. When a time clause begins with *before*, the event in the time clause happens second.
>
> | *First Event* | *Second Event* |
> |---|---|
> | **When I get home,** | I'll call you. |
> | **After they get married,** | they're going to move to California. |
> | I'm going to water the plants | **before I go on vacation.** |

C1 Listening for Meaning and Use
▶ Note 1

Listen to each sentence. Which event happens first and which happens second? Write *1* next to the first event and *2* next to the second.

1. __1__ I look for a job.   __2__ I graduate.

2. _____ He gets here.   _____ We make dinner.

3. _____ We go to the park.   _____ We go to the museum.

4. _____ I call you.   _____ They leave.

5. _____ I clean the house.   _____ I go shopping.

C2 **Talking About Two Future Events** ▶ **Note 1**

A. Complete these sentences with future time clauses or main clauses.

1. <u>When I finish school</u>, my family will be happy.

2. After I finish this English class, _____.

3. _____, I'll take a vacation.

4. I'll buy a new car _____.

5. _____, I'll speak English.

6. I'll be happy _____.

B. Work with a partner. In your notebook, write two main clauses and two future time clauses. Have your partner complete each one.

I'll call you _____.

When my friend visits me, _____.

C3 **Describing Future Events in Sequence** ▶ **Note 1**

Think about your day tomorrow. Write two sentences for each part of the day. Use future time clauses with *before, when,* and *after.*

1. (tomorrow morning)

   <u>I'll get up when my alarm rings.</u>

   _____

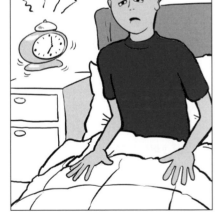

2. (tomorrow afternoon)

   _____

   _____

3. (tomorrow evening)

   _____

   _____

4. (tomorrow night)

   _____

   _____

D Expressing Future Possibility with *If* Clauses

Examining Meaning and Use

Read the sentences and complete the tasks below. Then discuss your answers and read the Meaning and Use Notes to check them.

1a. If you take some aspirin, you'll feel better.
1b. I'll take you out to dinner if you help me with the housework.

2a. If Ben leaves, call me.
2b. When Ben leaves, call me.

1. Look at 1a and 1b. Underline the *if* clauses. Circle the main clauses. Which clause in each sentence describes a possible situation? Which clause in each sentence describes a possible result of that situation?

2. Look at 1a and 1b again. Which sentence gives advice? Which sentence makes a promise?

3. Look at 2a and 2b. In which sentence is it more certain that Ben will leave?

Meaning and Use Notes

> **Cause-and-Effect Relationships**
>
> **1** Sentences with an *if* clause show a cause-and-effect relationship. The *if* clause introduces a possible situation (the cause). The main clause talks about the possible result (the effect) of that situation. The cause and effect can come in either order.
>
> | If *Clause (Cause)* | Main *Clause (Effect)* |
> |---|---|
> | **If she gets that job,** | her salary will increase. |
> | **If you press the red button,** | the elevator will stop. |
>
> | Main *Clause (Effect)* | If *Clause (Cause)* |
> |---|---|
> | Her salary will increase | **if she gets that job.** |
> | The elevator will stop | **if you press the red button.** |

Expressing Advice, Warnings, Promises, and Predictions

2 Sentences with an *if* clause and a main clause with *be going to* or *will* have several common uses:

Giving Advice:	If you rest now, you'll feel better later.
Giving a Warning:	If you don't tell the truth, you're going to be sorry.
Making a Promise:	If you elect me, I won't raise taxes.
Making a Prediction:	If he moves to the city, he won't be happy.

Possibility vs. Certainty

3 Use an *if* clause if you think something is possible but you are not sure it will happen. Use a future time clause with *when* if you are certain something will happen.

If *Clause (Possible)*	Future *Time Clause (Certain)*
If it goes on sale, I'll buy it.	**When it goes on sale,** I'll buy it.
I'll visit the Taj Mahal **if I go to India.**	I'll visit the Taj Mahal **when I go to India.**

D1 Listening for Meaning and Use ▶ Note 3

🎧 Listen to each conversation. Does the second speaker think the situation is possible or certain? Check (✓) the correct column.

	SITUATION	POSSIBLE	CERTAIN
1.	She and Amy will see a movie.	✓	
2.	He will go to the store.		
3.	It will snow this weekend.		
4.	He will go to Mexico.		
5.	Mark will ask Celia to marry him.		
6.	Jake will rent the apartment.		

D2 Giving Warnings

► Notes 1, 2

Complete each warning with an *if* clause or a main clause.

1. If you don't stop at a red light, _you'll get a ticket_____.

2. You'll burn your hand _____.

3. _____ if you don't pay your electric bill.

4. If you go swimming in cold weather, _____.

5. _____ if you don't eat breakfast.

6. _____ if you stay up all night.

7. You'll lose your job _____.

8. _____, you'll break your leg.

D3 Giving Advice

► Notes 1, 2

Write two pieces of advice for the person in each situation. Each piece of advice should include an *if* clause and a main clause.

1. Your friend is always late for school.

   a. _If you leave home on time, you won't be late for school._____

   b. _____

2. Your brother wants to go to a good university.

   a. _____

   b. _____

3. Your sister doesn't get along with a co-worker.

   a. _____

   b. _____

4. Your cousin wants to move to a new apartment, but he doesn't have much money.

   a. _____

   b. _____

Making Promises ► Notes 1, 2

Work with a partner. Read these situations. Take turns making promises. Each promise should include an *if* clause and a main clause. Switch roles after each situation.

1. **Student A:** You are a student. You need help with your English homework.
   Student B: You are the student's best friend.

   A: If you help me with my English homework, I'll help you with your math.
   B: I'll help you with your homework if you let me ride your motorcycle.

2. **Student A:** You are a teenager. You want to borrow the family car.
   Student B: You are the teenager's parent.

3. **Student A:** You are a driver. You were speeding.
   Student B: You are a police officer.

4. **Student A:** You are an employee. You are often late for work.
   Student B: You are the employee's boss.

D5 **Making Predictions** ► Notes 1, 2

Look at the picture. Write predictions about what will happen. Include an *if* clause and a main clause in each prediction.

If the man trips over the telephone cord, he'll fall.

E Combining Form, Meaning, and Use

E1 Thinking About Meaning and Use

Read each sentence and the statements that follow. Check (✓) the statement that
has the same meaning. Then discuss your answers in small groups.

1. After the children go to bed, we'll leave.

   _____ **a.** We'll leave, and then the children will go to bed.

   _✓_ **b.** The children will go to bed, and then we'll leave.

2. He'll come and get us when the program starts.

   _____ **a.** The program will start, and then he'll come and get us.

   _____ **b.** He'll come and get us, and then the program will start.

3. Before you graduate, you'll need another math course.

   _____ **a.** You can't graduate without another math course.

   _____ **b.** You'll graduate, and then you'll take another math course.

4. He'll leave before I leave.

   _____ **a.** I'll leave when he leaves.

   _____ **b.** He'll leave, and then I'll leave.

5. He'll be happy if he gets the job.

   _____ **a.** He'll get the job, and then he'll be happy.

   _____ **b.** It's possible that he'll get the job. If he does, he'll be happy.

6. We're going to buy a house when we get married.

   _____ **a.** We feel certain that we'll buy a house after we marry.

   _____ **b.** We don't feel certain that we'll get married and buy a house.

7. If the store is open, I'll buy some milk.

   _____ **a.** The store will be open, so I'll buy some milk.

   _____ **b.** Maybe the store will be open, and I'll buy some milk.

8. I'll help you when I finish making lunch.

   _____ **a.** I'll make lunch. Then I'll help you.

   _____ **b.** I'll help you. At the same time, I'll make lunch.

9. She'll cook dinner when her husband comes home.

   _____ **a.** Dinner will not be ready when he arrives.

   _____ **b.** Dinner will be ready when he arrives.

10. I'll see Ben if I go to the party.

   _____ **a.** I'm not certain that I'm going to the party.

   _____ **b.** Ben isn't certain that he's going to the party.

E2 Editing

Some of these sentences have errors. Find the errors and correct them. There may be more than one error in some sentences.

1. When I ~~will~~ see Debbie, I'll give her the book.

2. If I won't feel better soon, I'll go to the doctor.

3. If I get an A on the final, then I'll get an A for the course.

4. I'm going to check the prices on-line before I'm going to buy a camera.

5. We won't have time to see a movie after we go shopping.

6. He's going to drive to Dallas if the weather will improve.

7. When I'll get my paycheck, I'll pay my bills.

8. They cancel the picnic if it will rain tomorrow.

9. When the phone is going to ring, I'll answer it.

10. She'll be rich if she wins the lottery.

▶ Beyond the Classroom

Searching for Authentic Examples

Find examples of grammar in everyday life. Look for advertisements in an English-language newspaper or magazine, or on the Internet. Find five sentences with *if* clauses and bring them to class. What does each *if* clause express? Is it advice? a warning? a promise? a prediction? Discuss your findings with your classmates.

Writing

Imagine you are running for election as mayor of your town or city. Follow these steps to write a campaign flyer.

1. Work with a partner. Think about the topic. Brainstorm the changes that you will make as mayor.

2. Makes notes about what you want to say. Use these questions to help you.
   - What problems does your city have?
   - How will you solve these problems if the people elect you?
   - What will happen when you solve these problems?

3. Write a first draft. Use future time clauses and *if* clauses to make predictions, promises, and warnings.

4. Read your work carefully and circle grammar, spelling, and punctuation errors. Work with your partner to decide how to fix your errors and improve the content.

5. Rewrite your draft.
   - When I become mayor, I will work hard to improve our city.
   - If you elect me, I will not raise taxes.

Modals

Modals of Ability and Possibility

A A Real-Life Hero

A1 **Before You Read**

Discuss these questions.

What is a hero? Can an ordinary person be a hero? Do you know any heroes?

A2 **Read**

 Read this magazine article to find out why a man who played a hero in the movies is a real-life hero today.

feature story

A Real-Life Hero

Reeve as Superman

Everyone knows Superman. He's a comic book hero. He <u>can do</u> things that ordinary people can't do. And most people know Christopher Reeve. He's the 5 actor who played Superman in four movies. As Superman, Reeve <u>could fly</u>. He could see through walls. He had the strength of one hundred men, and his enemies could not defeat him. These 10 movies were very popular, and for most people Christopher Reeve was Superman— until May 26, 1995.

On that day Reeve was in a horse-jumping competition. His horse couldn't 15 jump over a hurdle, and Reeve fell. He injured his spinal cord very badly. Now he is paralyzed—he is not able to move any part of his body below his neck. He cannot write, walk, or even feed 20 himself. A machine helps him breathe. He is able to talk, but his voice is often difficult to understand.

What kind of life does Reeve have after this terrible accident? Does he

25 spend his time feeling sorry for himself?
No. In fact, he's still a very busy man. He
still acts in films and directs them. Most
importantly, he makes speeches and raises
money for the study of spinal cord
30 injuries. He has also started a research
center.

Reeve today

Reeve has brought hope to other
people who are paralyzed. He speaks to
people all over the country with similar
35 injuries. He tells them that they can still
have useful lives, and he explains his
idea of what makes a hero. According to
Reeve, a hero is an ordinary person who
can find the strength to continue even
40 with serious problems.

Christopher Reeve has made some
progress with special exercise. He has
recovered some feeling in his left leg and
parts of his left arm. Although doctors
45 think that he will always be paralyzed,
Christopher Reeve still has hope for the
future. Researchers may find a cure for
spinal cord injuries. Reeve believes that he
might even walk again. And who knows? For
50 this real-life hero, nothing is impossible.

competition: a contest or an athletic event
cure: something that makes a sick person healthy
defeat: to beat someone in a fight or battle
enemy: a person who hates or wants to hurt somebody

hurdle: a fence or wall that horses jump over in a race
spinal cord: a system of nerves in the back that
connects the brain to other parts of the body

A3 After You Read

Write *T* for true or *F* for false for each statement.

__F__ **1.** Christopher Reeve was not famous before his accident.

_____ **2.** Christopher Reeve is still a busy man.

_____ **3.** Christopher Reeve gives hope to people with spinal cord injuries.

_____ **4.** The doctors think Christopher Reeve will walk again.

_____ **5.** Christopher Reeve doesn't believe that ordinary people can be heroes.

_____ **6.** Christopher Reeve feels positive about the future.

B Modals of Ability: *Can* and *Could*; *Be Able To*

Examining Form

Look back at the article on page 156 and complete the tasks below. Then discuss your answers and read the Form charts to check them.

1. Look at the underlined examples of *can* + verb and *could* + verb. What form of the verb follows *can* and *could*?

2. Find the negative forms of *can* + verb and *could* + verb in the first paragraph. What is unusual about the negative form of *can* + verb? What are the contracted negative forms of *can* and *could*?

CAN FOR PRESENT AND FUTURE ABILITY

Affirmative Statements			
SUBJECT	MODAL	BASE FORM OF VERB	
I		**play**	the piano.
He	**can**		
They		**work**	tomorrow.

Negative Statements			
SUBJECT	MODAL + *NOT*	BASE FORM OF VERB	
I		**play**	the piano.
He	**cannot** **can't**		
They		**work**	tomorrow.

Yes/No Questions			
MODAL	SUBJECT	BASE FORM OF VERB	
	you	**play**	the piano?
Can	he		
	they	**work**	tomorrow?

Short Answers						
YES	SUBJECT	MODAL	NO	SUBJECT	MODAL + *NOT*	
	I			I		
Yes,	he	**can.**	**No,**	he	**can't.**	
	they			they		

Information Questions

WH- WORD	MODAL	SUBJECT	BASE FORM OF VERB	
What	can	you	**play?**	
How long		he	**work**	tomorrow?

WH- WORD (SUBJECT)	MODAL		BASE FORM OF VERB	
Who	can		**work**	tomorrow?
What			**fly?**	

- *Can* is a modal. Like all modals, it is followed by the base form of a verb and has the same form for all subjects.
- The negative form of *can* is *cannot*. Notice that *cannot* is written as one word.
- It is often difficult to hear the difference between *can* and *can't* because the final *t* in *can't* is not clearly pronounced. In sentences with *can* + verb, the vowel sound in *can* is very short and the stress is on the verb that follows *can:* I/kən/gȯ. In sentences with *can't* + verb, the stress is on *can't* and the *a* is pronounced like the *a* in *ant:* I/kæn/gȯ.

COULD FOR PAST ABILITY

Affirmative Statements

SUBJECT	MODAL	BASE FORM OF VERB	
I			
He	**could**	**read**	in kindergarten.
They			

Negative Statements

SUBJECT	MODAL + *NOT*	BASE FORM OF VERB	
I			
He	**could not** **couldn't**	**read**	in kindergarten.
They			

Yes/No Questions

MODAL	SUBJECT	BASE FORM OF VERB	
Could	you	**read**	in kindergarten?

Short Answers

YES	SUBJECT	MODAL	NO	SUBJECT	MODAL + *NOT*
Yes,	I	**could.**	**No,**	I	**couldn't.**

(Continued on page 160)

Information Questions

WH- WORD	MODAL	SUBJECT	BASE FORM OF VERB	
What	**could**	she	**read**	in kindergarten?

WH- WORD (SUBJECT)	MODAL		BASE FORM OF VERB	
Who	**could**		**read**	in kindergarten?

- *Could* is a modal. Like all modals, it is followed by the base form of a verb and has the same form for all subjects.

BE ABLE TO FOR PAST, PRESENT, AND FUTURE ABILITY

Affirmative Statements

SUBJECT	BE ABLE TO	BASE FORM OF VERB	
He	**was able to**	**work**	yesterday.
	is able to		today.
	will be able to		tomorrow.

Negative Statements

SUBJECT	BE + NOT + ABLE TO	BASE FORM OF VERB	
He	**was not able to**	**work**	yesterday.
	is not able to		today.
	will not be able to		tomorrow.

- *Be able to* is not a modal, but it has the same meaning as *can* and *could*. The verb *be* in *be able to* changes form and agrees with the subject.
- See Appendix 16 for contractions with *be* and *will*.

B1 **Listening for Form**

Listen to this paragraph. Write *can* or *can't*.

Michael is blind. He ___can't___ see. He _____ do amazing things, however. He
                           1   2
lives in Chicago, and he _____ walk around the city alone. Of course, he _____
                              3   4
read the street signs, so sometimes he asks for help. After he has been somewhere with a

friend, he _____ go there again by himself. Michael is good at sports, too. He's the best
                5
player on his bowling team, even though he _____ see the bowling pins.
                                                6

B2 **Building Sentences with *Can* and *Can't***

Build three logical sentences with *can* and three logical sentences with *can't*. Use a word from each column. Punctuate your sentences correctly.

People can climb trees.

people fish dogs	can can't	climb trees bark swim

B3 **Forming Statements and Questions with *Can* and *Could***

In your notebook, write a statement and a question for each set of words and phrases. Punctuate your sentences correctly.

1. Emily/party/can/our/come/to

   Emily can come to our party.
   Can Emily come to our party?

2. them/airport/could/we/the/take/to

3. his/languages/can/parents/speak/several

4. sister/your/can/Mandarin/speak

5. problem/us/can/she/this/with/help

B4 **Completing Conversations with *Be Able To***

Complete these conversations with the words in parentheses and the correct form of *be able to*. Use contractions where possible.

1. **A:** ___Were___ you ___able to finish___ (finish) the test yesterday?
            ¹   ²

   B: No, _____ (not), but I _____ (do) 45 out of
                ³   ⁴

   the 50 questions.

2. **A:** Did David help you clean the attic?

   B: No, he _____ (not/come) on Saturday. But I think he
                  ¹

   _____ (help) me this weekend.
      ²

3. **A:** _____ Susan _____ (practice) the piano at college last year?
        ¹   ²

   B: Well, not in the dorm, but she _____ (play) at the Student Center.
                        ³

4. **A:** _____ you _____ (call) me later?
        ¹   ²

   B: No. I'm busy tonight, but I _____ (see) you tomorrow.
                        ³

Past, Present, and Future Ability

Examining Meaning and Use

Read the sentences and answer the questions below. Then discuss your answers and read the Meaning and Use Notes to check them.

    a. Carl can type 40 words a minute.
    b. Last year Carl could type 20 words a minute.
    c. When Carl's typing class ends, he will be able to type 60 words a minute.

1. Which sentence talks about an ability that Carl has at the present time?

2. Which sentence talks about an ability Carl doesn't have yet?

3. Which sentence talks about an ability Carl had in the past?

Meaning and Use Notes

Present Ability with *Can*

1A   *Can* is used to talk about an ability in the present.

> The baby **can walk,** but she **can't talk** yet.
> Strong winds **can cause** a lot of damage.

1B   *Be able to* also describes an ability in the present, but *can* is more commonly used.

Less Common	*More Common*
He **is able to** speak French and Arabic.	He **can speak** French and Arabic.

Future Ability with *Be Able To* and *Can*

2A   Use *will be able to* to talk about a skill or other ability that you don't have yet, but will have in the future. Do not use *can* to describe an ability that you will have only in the future.

> After I complete this class, **I'll be able to type** 60 words a minute.
> *After I complete this class, I can type 60 words a minute. (INCORRECT)
> I **will be able to see** better after I get new glasses.
> *I can see better after I get new glasses. (INCORRECT)

2B Use *will be able to* or *can* to express ability that relates to decisions and arrangements for the future.

She $\left\{ \begin{array}{l} \textbf{'ll be able to} \\ \textbf{can} \end{array} \right\}$ **meet** you at the airport at 3:00.

I'm busy now, but I $\left\{ \begin{array}{l} \textbf{'ll be able to} \\ \textbf{can} \end{array} \right\}$ **help** you in ten minutes.

Past Ability with *Could* and *Be Able To*

3A Use *could* or *was/were able to* to talk about an ability that existed for a long period of time in the past.

Long Period of Time

When I was young I $\left\{ \begin{array}{l} \textbf{was able to} \\ \textbf{could} \end{array} \right\}$ **eat** dessert every night, and I didn't gain weight.

3B In affirmative statements with action verbs, do not use *could* to talk about an ability related to a single event. Use only *was/were able to*.

Single Event with Action Verb (Affirmative)
Yesterday I **was able to finish** my homework quickly.
*Yesterday I could finish my homework quickly. (INCORRECT)

3C In affirmative statements with certain stative verbs such as *see, hear, feel, taste, understand,* and *remember,* use *could* or *was/were able to* to talk about ability related to a single event in the past.

Single Event with Stative Verb (Affirmative)

Last night the sky was clear and we $\left\{ \begin{array}{l} \textbf{were able to} \\ \textbf{could} \end{array} \right\}$ **see** for miles.

3D In negative statements, use *couldn't* or *wasn't/weren't able to* for both ability during single events and ability over a long period of time.

Single Event (Negative)

Yesterday I $\left\{ \begin{array}{l} \textbf{wasn't able to} \\ \textbf{couldn't} \end{array} \right\}$ **finish** my homework quickly.

Long Period of Time

When I was younger, I $\left\{ \begin{array}{l} \textbf{wasn't able to} \\ \textbf{couldn't} \end{array} \right\}$ **finish** my homework quickly.

C1) Listening for Meaning and Use

🎧 Listen to each speaker. Choose the correct response.

1. **a.** OK, let's go today.
   ⓑ OK, we'll go tomorrow.

2. **a.** No, they can't. It's raining.
   b. Why not?

3. **a.** Were they very high?
   b. How disappointing!

4. **a.** Well, at least she tries.
   b. Of course she can. Her dad's a coach.

5. **a.** So what did they do?
   b. When did they learn?

6. **a.** Is she able to walk now?
   b. Will she be able to walk tomorrow?

C2) Talking About Future Abilities

Complete the sentences with *will/won't* + *be able to.* Use your own ideas.

1. Next year <u>I'll be able to drive.</u>

2. In 20 years people _____

3. In 50 years doctors _____

4. By 2020 scientists _____

5. In 10 years I _____

6. In 100 years humans _____

C3) Distinguishing Between Can and Be Able To

In your notebook, rewrite these sentences with *can* where possible.

1. The teacher will be able to help you with your homework this afternoon.
   The teacher can help you with your homework this afternoon.

2. Paul will be able to drive us to school tomorrow morning.

3. Larry will be able to get a job when he learns how to use a computer.

4. Will you be able to swim after you finish this swimming class?

5. The doctor will be able to see you at three o'clock this afternoon.

6. He will be able to walk again after the operation.

A. Work with a partner. Look at the topics below, and think about how people lived fifty years ago. Take turns making sentences with *could(n't)* and *was/were* (*not*) *able to.*

education	food	housing	relationships
energy	health	leisure time	transportation

A: *Fifty years ago many people weren't able to go to college.*
B: *Fifty years ago you could buy a house for ten thousand dollars.*

B. Share your ideas with your classmates.

C5 Comparing Long Periods of Time and Single Events ▶ Notes 3A–3D

A. In your notebook, rewrite these sentences with *could* or *couldn't* where possible. Do not change the meaning.

1. For many years, we were able to take long vacations.

   For many years, we could take long vacations.

2. They were able to get tickets for the play this morning.

3. Before he hurt his knee, he was able to run five miles a day.

4. Even as a young child, she was able to swim well.

5. We weren't able to get to the concert on time last night.

6. Were you able to see the fireworks from your window the other night?

7. Matt wasn't able to find his keys this morning.

8. I was able to park the car in front of the restaurant this morning.

B. Look back at the sentences in part A. Which sentences cannot be rewritten? Why?

Vocabulary Notes

Know How To

You can use *know how to* instead of *can* to talk about a skill (a particular ability that you develop through training or practice).

KNOW HOW TO

They **know how to** speak Portuguese.

She **doesn't know how** to drive a car.

CAN

They **can** speak Portuguese.

She **can't** drive a car.

We do not use *know how to* to talk about abilities that do not require training or practice. We use *can* instead.

CAN

Hurricanes **can** cause damage.
*Hurricanes know how to cause damage. (INCORRECT)

The doctor **can** see you now.
*The doctor knows how to see you now. (INCORRECT)

C6 Talking About Skills

A. Ask your classmates questions to find out who has the skills on the list. Ask four questions with *can* and four questions with *know how to*.

1. do the tango
   (or other dance)

   Can you do the tango? OR
   *Do you know how to do
   the tango?*

2. change a tire

3. use a computer

4. sew on a button

5. play the guitar
   (or other instrument)

6. play baseball

7. speak French

8. drive a motorcycle

B. Work in small groups. Talk about your classmates' abilities. Use *can* and *know how to*.

Carlos can do the tango, but Mei Ling can't. OR
*Carlos knows how to do the tango, but Mei Ling
doesn't.*

D Modals of Future Possibility

Examining Form

Read the sentences and complete the tasks below. Then discuss your answers and read the Form charts to check them.

    a. He might walk again.
    b. He has the strength of one hundred men.
    c. Researchers may find a cure.

1. Which sentences contain modals? Underline them. Which sentence contains a verb in the simple present?

2. Change all the sentences to negative statements. How are the negative statements with modals different from the negative statement in the simple present?

Affirmative Statements

SUBJECT	MODAL	BASE FORM OF VERB	
I	might		
You	may	leave	tomorrow.
He	could		
They	will		

Negative Statements

SUBJECT	MODAL + *NOT*	BASE FORM OF VERB	
I	might not		
You	may not	leave	tomorrow.
He	won't		
They			

Yes/No Questions

FUTURE FORM
Are you going to leave next weekend?
Will you leave next weekend?
Are you leaving next weekend?

Short Answers

AFFIRMATIVE	NEGATIVE
I may.	I may not.
I might.	I might not.
I could.	I may not. / I might not.

(Continued on page 168)

- *Could not (couldn't)* is not usually used to express future possibility.
- *May not* and *might not* are not contracted in American English.
- *Yes/No* questions about future possibility are not usually formed with *may, might,* or *could.* Instead, they are formed with *be going to, will,* or the present continuous as future. You can use *may, might,* or *could* in short answers.
- Use modal + *be* in short answers to questions with *be.*
  - **A:** Will you **be** home next weekend?
  - **B:** I **might be.**
- Information questions about future possibility are also usually asked with future forms. You can answer with *may, might,* or *could.*
  - **A:** When are you leaving?
  - **B:** I'm not sure. I **may leave** next weekend.
  - **A:** When is he going to call?
  - **B:** He **might call** today.

D1) Listening for Form

Listen to these conversations. Write the correct form of the modals you hear.

1. **A:** What will you do when you finish college?

   B: I ___might___ look for a job, or I _____ go to graduate school instead.

   ₁   ₂

2. **A:** The traffic is moving very slowly. We won't get to the theater on time.

   B: We _____. We still have plenty of time.

     ₁

3. **A:** When is the package arriving?

   B: It _____ be here tomorrow, or it _____ arrive until the next day.

     ₁   ₂

4. **A:** Will there be many people at the meeting?

   B: I don't know. There _____ be just a few of us.

     ₁

5. **A:** What do you think? Is it going to snow tonight?

   B: Well, according to the weather report, there _____ be a lot of snow, but

       ₁

   the storm _____ hit us at all.

     ₂

A. Form affirmative statements from these words and phrases. Punctuate your sentences correctly.

1. fail/the/I/might/test

   I might fail the test.

2. game/you/win/next/could/the/Saturday

   _____

3. might/Bob and Carol/married/get/year/next

   _____

4. rain/could/tomorrow/it

   _____

5. tonight/cook/Sara/dinner/will

   _____

6. on/we/go/may/Sunday/beach/the/to

   _____

7. will/Yuji/at six o'clock/come

   _____

8. have/Kim and Josh/a/party/might

   _____

9. Lynn/graduate/could/next semester

   _____

10. stay/may/home/Victor/next weekend

    _____

B. In your notebook, rewrite the sentences as negative statements. Which three sentences cannot be made negative? Why? Discuss your answers with a partner.

I might not fail the test.

Future Possibility

Examining Meaning and Use

Read the sentences and answer the questions below. Then discuss your answers and read the Meaning and Use Notes to check them.

a. Ana could leave tomorrow, or she could leave today.
b. Ana will leave tomorrow. She's ready to go.
c. Ana may leave tomorrow. She's ready to go, but it depends on the weather.
d. Maybe Ana will leave tomorrow. I'm not certain.
e. Ana might leave tomorrow. I'm not sure.

Which sentence is the most certain? Which sentences are less certain?

Meaning and Use Notes

> **Expressing Future Possibility with *Could*, *Might*, and *May***
>
> **1A** *Could*, *might (not)*, and *may (not)* express possibility about the future. *Could* and *might* sometimes express more uncertainty than *may*.
>
> I **could get** an A or a B in the course. It depends on my final paper.
> I **may take** history next semester. It seems like a good idea.
>
> ---
>
> **1B** You can talk about future possibility and future ability together with *might/may (not) + be able to.* You cannot use *might/may (not) + can.*
>
> It's already April, but I **might be able to go** skiing one more time.
>
> If I learn to speak Portuguese, I **may be able to get** a job in Brazil.
>
> *If I learn to speak Portuguese, I may can get a job in Brazil. (INCORRECT)
>
> ---
>
> **1C** Do not confuse *may be* and *maybe*. *May be* is the modal *may* and the verb *be*. *Maybe* is an adverb. It comes at the beginning of a sentence, and it is written as one word. *Maybe* can be used with *will* to express future possibility.
>
> May be *(Modal + Be)*   Maybe *(Adverb)*
> We **may be** away next week. = **Maybe** we'll be away next week.

1D Use *will* in *Yes/No* questions about future possibility. You can use *might* but it will sound overly formal. Do not use *may*.

Will	Might/May
Will he come home soon?	**Might** he come home soon? (OVERLY FORMAL)
	*May he come home soon? (INCORRECT)

Expressing Strong Certainty with *Will*

2 Use *will* when you are certain about something. If you are not certain, you can weaken *will* by adding the adverbs *probably, maybe,* and *perhaps.*

Certain	*Not Certain*
They'**ll move** in the summer.	They'**ll probably move** in the summer.
She'**ll find** a new job.	**Maybe she'll find** a new job.

E1 **Listening for Meaning and Use**   ▶ **Notes 1A, 1B, 2**

🎧 Listen to the conversation. Check (✓) the places that Mark and Dan are definitely going to see on their trip to Florida. Put a question mark (?) next to the places that they aren't sure about.

  ✓ **1.** Disney World   ____ **4.** Miami Beach

____ **2.** Epcot Center   ____ **5.** the Everglades

____ **3.** Cape Canaveral   ____ **6.** Key West

The Colony Hotel, Miami Beach

Complete this conversation by choosing the appropriate word or phrase in parentheses.

A: So what's your daughter Lisa going to do this summer?

B: She's not sure, but she (could /'ll) probably work for an architect. What's your son
1

going to do? (Will / May) he have the same job as last summer?
2

A: He isn't sure. He (might / 'll) work in a movie theater again. But there aren't
3

many jobs available, so he (couldn't / might not) find one.
4

B: They (can / might) be able to give him a job at my office. I'll speak to my boss.
5

(Maybe / May be) there will be an opening.
6

A: Oh, thank you! That (maybe / may be) a better way for him to spend the summer.
7

I (can / 'll) probably be able to convince him to apply.
8

Rewrite each sentence in your notebook. If the sentence uses *maybe,* rewrite it with *may be.* If it uses *may be,* rewrite it with *maybe.* Make all other necessary changes.

1. Lee's family may be in town next week.

   Maybe Lee's family will be in town next week.

2. Maybe the weather will be better on the weekend.

3. Maybe we'll be able to get tickets to the baseball game.

4. This may be an exciting game.

5. Maybe they won't be home this evening.

6. The final exam may not be very difficult.

7. He may be stuck in traffic.

8. Maybe they'll be able to help us clean the attic.

A. Use your imagination to complete these conversations. Use a modal of future possibility and a verb.

Conversation 1

A: What are your roommates going to do tonight?

B: I don't know. They <u>might go to the movies</u>, but they
₁

<u>may stay home and watch the game on TV</u>.
₂

Conversation 2

A: Can you come to Europe with us this summer?

B: I don't have much money, but I _____.
₁

Conversation 3

A: Tomorrow's Monday again! I don't want to go to school!

B: _____. Then we won't have to go
₁

to school.

Conversation 4

A: What are we having for dinner tonight?

B: We have a couple of choices. We _____, or we
₁

_____.
₂

Conversation 5

A: Where will you go on your next vacation?

B: I'm not sure. _____.
₂

B. With a partner, write two more short conversations about these situations. Use *could, might (not), may (not), maybe, will, won't,* or *be able to.*

A student asks a teacher about finishing a paper late.
A reporter asks an athlete about the next Olympics.

F Combining Form, Meaning, and Use

F1 Thinking About Meaning and Use

Choose the best answer to complete each conversation. Then discuss your answers in small groups.

1. **A:** At that time, she could speak Japanese like a native.

   B: _____

      a. Maybe she can teach me.

      (b.) How did she learn it?

2. **A:** He won't be able to leave the hospital for a long time.

   B: _____

      a. Who's going to take care of him at home?

      b. I'll try to visit him every day.

3. **A:** The whole house is clean.

   B: _____

      a. It's amazing that you were able to do it by yourself.

      b. Who could help you?

4. **A:** We couldn't find a babysitter, so we stayed home.

   B: _____

      a. Well, you made the right decision.

      b. I'm glad that you were able to.

5. **A:** We might go out to dinner tonight.

   B: _____

      a. OK. I was able to meet you there.

      b. Where do you think you'll go?

6. **A:** Do you know how to swim?

    B: _____

        a. Yes, but not very well.

        b. No, it's too cold today.

7. **A:** Were you able to go to the meeting last night?

    B: _____

        a. Yes, I could.

        b. Yes, I was.

8. **A:** What will you be able to do after this English class?

    B: _____

        a. I'll be able to speak English more fluently.

        b. I can speak English more fluently.

F2 Editing

Find the errors in this paragraph and correct them.

My friend Josh might take~~s~~ us
to the beach this weekend. The
beach isn't far from his house.
Josh can to walk there. He is a
great swimmer. He could swim
when he was three years old! My
roommate Nicole doesn't know
to swim, so I will probably teach

her this weekend. Nicole will able to swim by the end of the summer if she practices
every day. May be we'll go sailing this weekend, too. Last Saturday Josh and I was
able to go sailing because the weather was great. We could see dolphins near the
boat. They were beautiful. Unfortunately, we couldn't touch them. If we're lucky, we
can see some dolphins at the beach this weekend.

▶ Beyond the Classroom

Searching for Authentic Examples

Find examples of English grammar in everyday life. Look in an English-language newspaper or magazine, or on the Internet for articles dealing with a famous person's plans for the future. Find five examples of sentences containing modals of future possibility: *may, might,* or *will.* Can you find any examples of *maybe*? Bring your examples to class. How is each example used? Does it show possibility or certainty about a plan? Discuss your findings with your classmates.

Writing

Follow these steps below to write a paragraph about your future after college.

1. Think about the topic. Make notes about what you want to say. Use these questions to help you organize your ideas.

   • What things will you be able to do?

   • What things will you definitely do or not do?

   • What things will you possibly do or not do?

2. Write a first draft. Use modals of future ability and possibility where appropriate.

3. Read your work carefully and circle grammar, spelling, and punctuation errors. Work with a partner to decide how to fix your errors and improve the content.

4. Rewrite your draft.

   After I finish college, I'll probably be able to get a good job. I'll probably look for a job in a bank, but I may not look for a job right away. I could take some more classes at night, but first I might take some time to relax. Maybe I'll go on a vacation. . . .

Modals and Phrases of Request, Permission, Desire, and Preference

A How *Not* to Ask for a Raise

A1 Before You Read

Discuss these questions.

Have you ever asked for a raise (an increase in pay)? How did you ask? What did your boss say? What are some good ways to ask for a raise?

A2 Read

Read this book excerpt to find out about good and bad ways to ask for a raise.

How *Not* to Ask for a Raise

A Case Study

As the manager of her own company, Rachel Franz has been asked for raises by many employees. Sometimes she has agreed and sometimes she 5 hasn't. Franz's decision is often influenced by how an employee asks. Here is a typical request for a raise. Find the mistakes that the employee makes in this situation.

10   **Robert:** Ms. Franz, <u>could I speak</u> to you for a few minutes?

  Ms. Franz: Can we talk another time? It looks like we have a big problem with our computer system and . . .

  Robert: I would rather talk to you now, if possible. It will only take a few minutes.

  Ms. Franz: Well, OK, come in.

15   **Robert:** I don't know if you know this, but I'm getting married next month.

  Ms. Franz: No, I didn't know that, Robert. Congratulations!

  Robert: Thank you. Of course, getting married is quite expensive. Would you consider giving me a raise?

Ms. Franz: Well, Robert, your performance review is coming up in six months. I
20 would like to wait until your review.

Robert: But six months is a long time. Could we discuss a raise sooner?

Ms. Franz: We usually don't give raises between reviews, Robert. Now please excuse me. I have to find out about this computer problem. Can you please ask Kristen to come into my office when you leave?

Analysis

25 Robert made several errors. First of all, it is best to make an appointment with your boss in advance. Second, try to speak to your boss when things are going well, not badly. Listen when your boss says that it isn't a good time to talk, and arrange to speak to him or her later. Third, give your boss a good reason to give you a raise. Explain that you have more responsibilities at work now, or that you are working
30 longer hours. Show your boss how important you are to the company, not how badly you need the money. Last, do your homework. Robert didn't know that the company doesn't give raises between reviews. Robert didn't get a raise, and he has probably hurt his chances of getting one in the future!

Adapted from *Executive Female*

consider: to think about

do your homework: to prepare for something by finding out important information

influence: to have an effect on someone's behavior

performance review: a meeting in which a boss and an employee discuss the employee's work

responsibilities: things that you must do as part of your job

A3 **After You Read**

The writer says that Robert made several errors. Check (✓) the four errors that Robert made, according to the Analysis in the book excerpt.

✓ **1.** Robert didn't make an appointment with his boss in advance.

_____ **2.** Robert didn't speak politely to his boss.

_____ **3.** Robert chose a bad time to speak to his boss.

_____ **4.** Robert walked into his boss's office without her permission.

_____ **5.** Robert didn't have a good reason for his boss to give him a raise.

_____ **6.** Robert didn't know the company rules about raises before he spoke to his boss.

B Modals of Request; Modals of Permission; *Would Like, Would Prefer,* and *Would Rather*

Examining Form

Look back at the conversation in the book excerpt on page 178 and complete the tasks below. Then discuss your answers and read the Form charts to check them.

1. Find questions with the modals *can, could,* and *would.* (An example is underlined.) What is the subject of each question? What form of the verb follows the subject?

2. Find the expressions *would rather* and *would like.* Which one is followed by the base form of the verb? Which one is followed by an infinitive (*to* + verb)?

MODALS OF REQUEST

Yes/No Questions			
MODAL	SUBJECT	BASE FORM OF VERB	
Can		close	the window?
Could	you		
Will		give	me a raise?
Would			

Short Answers					
YES	SUBJECT	MODAL	NO	SUBJECT	MODAL + NOT
Yes,	I	can.	No,	I	can't.
		will.			won't.

- Modals of request are usually used in questions with *you.*
- We usually use *can* and *will* in affirmative short answers. *Could* and *would* are less common.
- We usually avoid using *won't* in negative short answers because it sounds very impolite and angry.

Affirmative Statements

SUBJECT	MODAL	BASE FORM OF VERB	
You	can / may	borrow	my car.

Negative Statements

SUBJECT	MODAL + *NOT*	BASE FORM OF VERB	
You	cannot / can't / may not	borrow	my car.

Yes/No Questions

MODAL	SUBJECT	BASE FORM OF VERB	
Can / Could / May	I / we	borrow	your car?

Short Answers

YES	SUBJECT	MODAL	NO	SUBJECT	MODAL + *NOT*
Yes,	you	can. / may.	No,	you	can't. / may not.

Information Questions

WH- WORD	MODAL	SUBJECT	BASE FORM OF VERB	
What	can	I	call	you?
When	could	we	make	a reservation?
Where	may	I	put	my coat?

- Modals of permission are most often used in questions with *I* and *we* and in statements with *you*.
- Use *can* and *may* in statements and short answers. Do not use *could*.
- Use *can*, *could*, and *may* in *Yes/No* questions.
- There is no contracted form of *may not*.

(Continued on page 182)

Affirmative Statements

SUBJECT	*WOULD RATHER*	BASE FORM OF VERB
I	would rather	leave.

SUBJECT	*WOULD PREFER/ WOULD LIKE*	INFINITIVE OR NOUN PHRASE
I	would prefer	to leave.
	would like	some tea.

Negative Statements

SUBJECT	*WOULD RATHER + NOT*	BASE FORM OF VERB
I	would rather not	leave.

SUBJECT	*WOULD PREFER + NOT*	INFINITIVE
I	would prefer not	to leave.

Yes/No Questions

WOULD	SUBJECT	*RATHER*	BASE FORM OF VERB
Would	you	rather	leave?

WOULD	SUBJECT	*PREFER/ LIKE*	INFINITIVE or NOUN PHRASE
Would	you	prefer	to leave?
		like	some tea?

Short Answers

YES,	SUBJECT	*WOULD*	*NO,*	SUBJECT	*WOULD + NOT*
Yes,	I	would.	No,	I	wouldn't.

YES,	SUBJECT	*WOULD*	*NO*	SUBJECT	*WOULD + NOT*
Yes,	I	would.	No,	I	wouldn't.

Information Questions

WH- WORD	*WOULD*	SUBJECT	RATHER	BASE FORM OF VERB
What	would	you	rather	eat?

WH- WORD	*WOULD*	SUBJECT	PREFER/ LIKE	INFINITIVE
What	would	you	prefer	to eat?
			like	

- *Would rather* is similar to a modal verb. It is followed by the base form of the verb.
- Unlike modals, *would like* and *would prefer* are followed by the infinitive (*to* + verb). They can also be followed by a noun phrase.
- *Would like* is not usually used in negative statements. Use *don't/doesn't want* instead.

    I don't want to leave.   **I don't want** tea.
- For contractions with *would,* combine the subject pronoun + *'d.*

B1   Listening for Form

🎧 **Listen to these conversations. Write the form of the modals you hear.**

1. **A:** Kevin, ____will____ you start dinner? I'm going shopping.
    ₁

   B: Hmm . . . _____ you get some chocolate ice cream?
    ₂

   A: I _____ buy more ice cream. You know we're both on a diet.
    ₃

2. **A:** _____ I speak with Mrs. Thompson, please?
    ₁

   B: No, I'm sorry. She's in a meeting. _____ you call back in an hour?
    ₂

3. **A:** _____ you _____ a cup of coffee?
    ₁   ₂

   B: No, thanks. I _____ a cup of tea.
    ₃

4. **A:** I _____ to go to the beach with my friends this weekend, but I don't
    ₁

   have any money. _____ I borrow $50?
    ₂

   B: No, you _____. You already owe me $100!
    ₃

B2   Building Questions with Modals

Build eight logical questions. Use a word or phrase from each column.

Can I come with you?

		give	to leave now
can		come	with you
could	I	prefer	me a ride
would	you	like	eat later
		rather	some coffee

Form • Modals and Phrases of Request, Permission, Desire, and Preference   **183**

B3 Completing Conversations

Complete these conversations using the words in parentheses. Use contractions where possible. Then practice the conversations with a partner.

1. **Guard:** Excuse me, sir. The sign says ___visitors may not take___ ₁ (not/take/may/visitors) pictures inside the museum.

   Visitor: Oh, I'm sorry. I didn't see it. _____ ₂ (leave/I/can/where) my camera?

2. **Salesclerk:** _____ ₁ (I/help/may) you?

   Customer: Yes. I'm looking for a birthday gift for my boyfriend.

   _____ ₂ (like/I/get/would/to) him something special.

3. **Visitor:** _____ ₁ (I/park/can) here?

   Guard: No, I'm sorry. _____ ₂ (can/visitors/park/not) in this section.

4. **Husband:** _____ ₁ (you/will/answer) the phone, please? My hands are wet.

   Wife: Sorry, _____ ₂ (I/not/can). I'm busy. They can leave a message on the answering machine.

5. **Father:** _____ ₁ (you/go/would/like/to) skiing with us this weekend?

   Daughter: No, thanks. _____ ₂ (rather/I/stay/would) home.

6. **Waitress:** _____ ₁ (order/like/you/would/to) now?

   Customer: Yes, I'll have the broiled chicken.

   Waitress: _____ ₂ (you/would/prefer) soup or salad as an appetizer?

B4 Working on Negative Sentences

Write the negative form of each sentence. Use contractions where possible. Remember to avoid the negative form of *would like*.

1. I would rather stay home tonight.

   I'd rather not stay home tonight.

2. We would prefer to exercise in the morning.

   _____

3. I would like to call you later.

   _____

4. They would rather live in the suburbs.

   _____

5. He would prefer to buy a new computer.

   _____

6. He would like to finish his work now.

   _____

B5 Writing Short Conversations

In your notebook, write short conversations with information questions and answers using these words and phrases. Punctuate your sentences correctly.

1. where/would rather/live/in Hong Kong/in New York City

   A: Where would you rather live, in Hong King or in New York City?
   B: I'd rather live in Hong Kong.

2. who/would prefer/meet/a famous athlete/a famous writer

3. where/would like/eat dinner tonight/at home/in a restaurant

4. what/would rather/do tonight/watch TV/go out

5. how/would rather/ travel/by car/by plane

6. what/would like/buy/a laptop computer/a digital camera

7. what/would rather/eat/cookies/cake

8. where/would prefer/live/in a big city/in a small town

C Modals of Request

Examining Meaning and Use

Read the sentences and answer the questions below. Then discuss your answers and read the Meaning and Use Notes to check them.

    a. Will you open the door?
    b. Would you open the door, please?
    c. Can you open the door, please?

Which request is the most polite? Which request is the least polite?

Meaning and Use Notes

Making Requests

1A Use *can, could, will,* and *would* to make requests. *Can* and *will* are less formal than *could* and *would.* We usually use *can* and *will* in informal conversations with friends and family. We use *could* and *would* to make polite requests in formal situations when we speak to strangers or to people in authority.

Less Formal	*More Formal*
To a Friend: **Can** you **tell** me the time?	*To a Stranger:* **Could** you **tell** me the time?
Mother to Child: **Will** you **be** quiet?	*To a Boss:* **Would** you **look** at my report?

1B Add *please* to a request to make it more polite.

Can you tell me the time, **please**?   Would you **please** look over my report?

Agreeing to and Refusing Requests

2A Use *will* and *can* to agree to requests. Do not use *would* or *could.* We generally use *can't* to refuse a request. *Won't* is used for strong refusals, and sounds impolite.

Agreeing to a Request	*Refusing a Request*
A: Will you help me for a minute?	A: **Can** you **help** me decorate for the party?
B: **Yes,** I **will.**	B: Sorry. I **can't** right now. (polite)
A: **Could** you **spell** your name for me?	A: Holly, will you clean up this room?
B: **Yes,** I **can.** It's C-L-A-R-K-E.	B: **No, I won't.** (impolite)

2B Instead of *can* or *will*, we often use expressions such as *OK, sure,* or *certainly* when agreeing to a request.

A: Will you help me for a minute?
B: **OK.**
A: Could you spell your name for me?
B: **Sure.** It's C-L-A-R-K-E.

2C We often say *I'm sorry* and give a reason in order to make our refusal more polite.

A: Can you help me decorate for the party?
B: **I'm sorry,** but I can't right now. **I have a doctor's appointment.**

C1 Listening for Meaning and Use ▶ Notes 1A, 1B

A. 🎧 Listen to each conversation. Is the request you hear informal or formal? Check (✓) the correct column.

	INFORMAL	FORMAL
1.	✓	
2.		
3.		
4.		
5.		
6.		

B. 🎧 Listen to the conversations again. Who are the speakers? Look at the choices, and write the correct letter for each conversation. Then discuss your answers with your classmates.

1. __b__   **a.** wife and husband

2. _____   **b.** mother and daughter

3. _____   **c.** two strangers

4. _____   **d.** two friends

5. _____   **e.** student and teacher

6. _____   **f.** employee and boss

A. Choose the best response to complete each telephone conversation.

1. **Student:** Could you connect me with Professor Hill's office?

   Secretary: _____

         a. No, I won't. He's busy.

         b. I'm sorry. He's not in right now. Would you like to leave a message?

2. **Secretary:** Good morning, History Department.

   Student: I'd like to register for History 201. Is it still open?

   Secretary: _____

         a. Yes. Give me your name.

         b. Yes, it is. Could you give me your name, please?

3. **Jenny's friend:** Will you please tell Jenny that I called?

   Jenny's sister: _____

         a. No, I won't. I'm going out.

         b. I won't be here when she gets home, but I'll leave her a note.

4. **Mark's friend:** Hi. Is Mark there?

   Mark's brother: _____

         a. Sure. Can you hold on a minute?

         b. Certainly. Would you hold, please?

5. **Client:** Would you please ask Ms. Banes to call me this afternoon?

   Secretary: _____

         a. I'm sorry, but she's out of the office until next week.

         b. Sorry, I can't.

6. **Student:** Could you send me some information about scholarships?

   Secretary: _____

         a. Certainly.

         b. No, I can't. That's impossible right now.

B. Discuss your answers with a partner. Why did you choose each response? Why was the other response inappropriate?

C. Now practice the conversations with your partner.

C3 Making Formal and Informal Requests

► Notes 1A, 1B

A. Work with a partner. Complete the requests with *can, will, could,* or *would.* (More than one answer is possible for each situation.)

1. **Neighbor A:** ____Can____ you take in our mail while we're away?

   Neighbor B: I'm sorry, but I can't. I'll be away then, too.

2. **Young Woman:** Excuse me, officer. _____ you please help me?

   Police Officer: Of course. What's the problem?

3. **Parent:** _____ you help me for a minute?

   Child: OK.

4. **Customer:** _____ you put that in a box, please?

   Salesclerk: I'm sorry, ma'am. I don't have any boxes.

5. **Employee:** When you get a chance, _____ you please show me how to use this new computer program?

   Manager: Certainly. How about right now?

B. Work with a different partner. Compare your answers. Be prepared to explain the modals you choose.

C4 Agreeing to and Refusing Requests

► Notes 1–2

Work with a partner. Read each situation. Then take turns making and responding to requests. Use *can, will, could,* or *would* in your requests. Use expressions such as *OK, sure, certainly,* and *I'm sorry* in your responses, and give reasons for refusals.

1. You are at a supermarket. You want the cashier to give you change for a dollar.

   A: Could you give me change for a dollar, please?
   B: Certainly.
      OR
   I'm sorry. The manager doesn't allow us to make change.

2. You are moving to a new apartment. You want your friend to help you move.

3. You would like your friend to lend you $50 until next week.

4. You are on vacation. You want the hotel desk clerk to give you a larger room.

5. You missed class yesterday, and you want your classmate to lend you her notes.

6. You would like your mechanic to repair your car by the end of the week.

D   Modals of Permission

Examining Meaning and Use

Read the sentences and answer the questions below. Then discuss your answers and read the Meaning and Use Notes to check them.

1a. Can I look at your book?   **2a.** May I borrow your book?
1b. Can you speak Russian?   **2b.** Can I borrow your book?

1. Look at 1a and 1b. Which question asks for permission to do something? Which question asks about ability?

2. Look at 2a and 2b. Which question is more formal?

Meaning and Use Notes

> **Asking for Permission**

> **1A** Use *can, could,* and *may* to ask for permission. *Can* and *could* are less formal than *may*. We usually use *may* in formal situations when we speak to strangers or to people in authority. You can use *please* to make your request more polite.
>
> *Less Formal*
> *Child to Parent:* **Can I go** outside and play now?
> *Friend to Friend:* **Could I borrow** your pen for a minute?
>
> *More Formal*
> *Business Call:* A: **May I speak** to Ms. Jones, **please**?
>   B: Certainly. **May I ask** who's calling?

> **1B** Because *may* is more formal, it is often used in announcements and signs or other printed materials.
>
> *Announcement:* Flight 26 has arrived. Passengers **may proceed** to Gate 2B for boarding.
>
> *Sign:* Visitors **may not park** in numbered spaces.

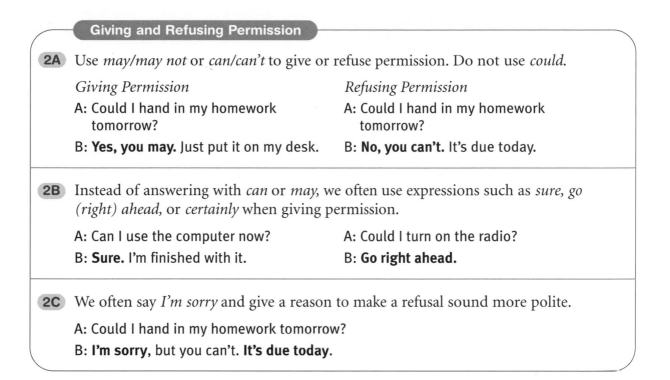

Giving and Refusing Permission

2A Use *may/may not* or *can/can't* to give or refuse permission. Do not use *could*.

Giving Permission	Refusing Permission
A: Could I hand in my homework tomorrow?	A: Could I hand in my homework tomorrow?
B: **Yes, you may.** Just put it on my desk.	B: **No, you can't.** It's due today.

2B Instead of answering with *can* or *may*, we often use expressions such as *sure, go (right) ahead,* or *certainly* when giving permission.

A: Can I use the computer now?	A: Could I turn on the radio?
B: **Sure.** I'm finished with it.	B: **Go right ahead.**

2C We often say *I'm sorry* and give a reason to make a refusal sound more polite.

A: Could I hand in my homework tomorrow?

B: **I'm sorry,** but you can't. **It's due today.**

D1) Listening for Meaning and Use ► Notes 1A, 1B

Listen to these conversations. In each, the first speaker is asking for permission. Who is the second speaker? Look at the choices and write the correct letter for each conversation.

1. __d__   **a.** a boss

2. _____   **b.** a stranger

3. _____   **c.** a mother

4. _____   **d.** a friend

5. _____   **e.** a police officer

6. _____   **f.** a salesclerk

7. _____   **g.** a brother

8. _____   **h.** a teacher

Look at the pictures. Make sentences to ask permission. Use informal and formal modals as appropriate.

1.

3.

5.

May I look at your map?

2.

4.

6.

Work with a partner. Take turns asking for and giving or refusing permission in these situations. Use *can, may,* or *could* in your questions. Use expressions such as *sure, go (right) ahead, certainly,* and *I'm sorry* in your responses.

1. You need to use your classmate's pencil.

   A: *Can I use your pencil for a minute?*
   B: *Sure. Here you are.*

2. You want to rent an apartment. The landlord shows it to you at night. You want to see it again in the daytime.

3. You want to borrow your friend's car this afternoon.

4. You are hungry, and your roommate has some leftover pizza in the refrigerator.

5. You are buying gas. You want to pay by check.

Would Like, Would Prefer, and Would Rather

Examining Meaning and Use

Read the sentences and complete the tasks below. Then discuss your answers and read the Meaning and Use Notes to check them.

1a. I want the check now. **2a.** Do you like ice cream?
1b. I'd like the check, please. **2b.** Would you like ice cream?

1. Compare 1a and 1b. Which sounds more polite?

2. Compare 2a and 2b. Which is an offer? Which asks about likes or dislikes?

Meaning and Use Notes

Stating Desires and Making Requests with *Would Like*

1A *Would like* has the same meaning as *want*. It is often used to talk about desires.

Stating a Desire with Would Like
I'd like to go to China next year. (= I **want** to go to China next year.)

1B *Would like* is also used to make requests. In making requests, *would like* is more polite than *want*. Add *please* to make the request even more polite.

Making a Request with Would Like
I'd like the check, please.   *I want the check. (not polite)

Making Offers with *Would Like*

2 Use *would like* in a question to make a polite offer.

A: **Would** you **like** some coffee?
B: Yes, please. With milk and sugar.

⚠ Be careful not to confuse *would like* and *like*.

Would Like (*to Make an Offer*)
A: **Would** you **like** some coffee?
B: Yes, please. With milk and sugar.

Like (*to Ask About Likes and Dislikes*)
A: Do you **like** coffee?
B: Yes, I do. I drink it every morning.

(Continued on page 194)

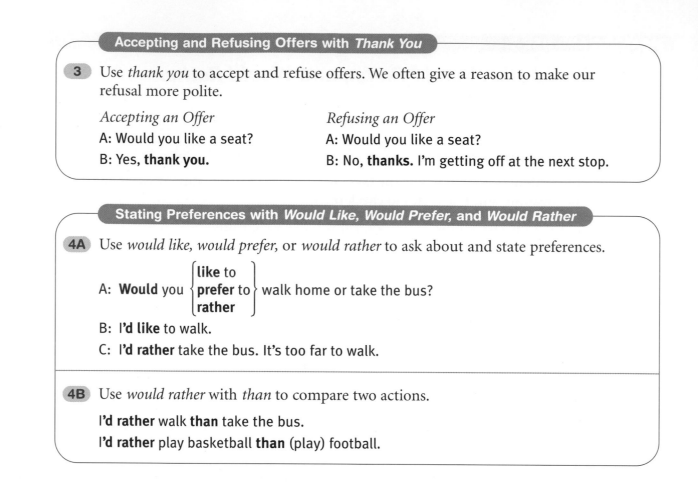

Accepting and Refusing Offers with *Thank You*

3 Use *thank you* to accept and refuse offers. We often give a reason to make our refusal more polite.

Accepting an Offer
A: Would you like a seat?
B: Yes, **thank you.**

Refusing an Offer
A: Would you like a seat?
B: No, **thanks.** I'm getting off at the next stop.

Stating Preferences with *Would Like, Would Prefer,* and *Would Rather*

4A Use *would like, would prefer,* or *would rather* to ask about and state preferences.

A: **Would** you
$$\begin{cases} \textbf{like} \text{ to} \\ \textbf{prefer} \text{ to} \\ \textbf{rather} \end{cases}$$
walk home or take the bus?

B: **I'd like** to walk.
C: **I'd rather** take the bus. It's too far to walk.

4B Use *would rather* with *than* to compare two actions.

I'd rather walk **than** take the bus.
I'd rather play basketball **than** (play) football.

E1 **Listening for Meaning and Use** ▶ Notes 1, 2, 4A, 4B

 Listen to each statement. Is the speaker making a request, making an offer, or stating a preference? Check (✓) the correct column.

	REQUEST	OFFER	PREFERENCE
1.	✓		
2.			
3.			
4.			
5.			
6.			
7.			
8.			

Work with a partner. Look at the pictures and take turns making offers, asking about preferences, and responding appropriately. Use *would like, would prefer,* or *would rather.*

1.

4.

A: *Would you like some help?*
B: *Yes, thank you.* OR
   No, thanks. I can carry them myself.

2.

5.

3.

6.

E3 **Asking About and Stating Preferences** ▶ Notes 4A, 4B

Work with a partner. Read each situation. Take turns asking and answering
questions with *would prefer, would rather,* and *would like.*

1. You and your friend are making plans for the evening. You could see a movie, or
   you could go to a concert.

   A: Would you rather see a movie or go to a concert?
   B: I'd rather see a movie.
   OR
   A: Would you prefer to see a movie or go to a concert?
   B: I'd prefer to go to a concert.

2. You and your roommate are trying to decide what to eat for dinner: chicken or
   fish.

3. You need to finish a project by tomorrow. Your boss asks if you want to stay late
   today or come in early tomorrow.

4. You are making arrangements to travel from Paris to Rome. The travel agent asks
   you if you want to fly or go by train.

5. You want your roommate to help with the housework. You give him a choice: do
   the dishes or vacuum.

E4 **Discussing Preferences** ▶ Notes 4A–4C

Work with a small group. Look at these winter vacation ideas and choose where
you would like to go. Then discuss your preferences by explaining what you would
like to do. Use *would prefer, would rather,* and *would like.*

1. Mountain resort   watch ski competitions, go downhill skiing, go cross-country skiing,
                      hike, watch birds, visit nearby towns

2. Caribbean cruise   swim, play volleyball, play tennis, sunbathe, go scuba diving, visit
                      islands, eat fancy buffet dinners

3. Trip to Europe   shop, visit art museums, try foreign foods, speak foreign languages,
                      visit cities, see famous buildings, take photographs

   *I'd prefer to go on a Caribbean cruise because I'd rather be in the tropics than in the
   mountains. Once I get there, I'd rather play tennis than volleyball. I'd also like to go
   scuba diving, but I prefer not to eat fancy buffet dinners. I'm on a diet!*

F Combining Form, Meaning, and Use

F1 Thinking About Meaning and Use

Choose the best answer to complete each conversation. Then discuss your answers in small groups.

1. **A:** Could you help me?

   B: I'm sorry. _____
   a. I didn't have the time.
   b. I'm busy right now. *(circled)*

2. **A:** Could I borrow your car later?

   B: No, I'm sorry, but _____.
   a. you can't
   b. you couldn't

3. **A:** Would you help me choose a present for my wife?

   B: _____
   a. Yes, I may
   b. Certainly.

4. **A:** Do you like to dance?

   B: _____
   a. Not really.
   b. Yes. I'd love to.

5. **A:** Could you give me a ride to work?

   B: Sure, _____.
   a. no problem
   b. no way

6. **A:** Would you rather go to the party or stay home?

   B: _____
   a. Yes, I would.
   b. I'd rather stay home tonight.

F2 Editing

Some of these sentences have errors. Find the errors and correct them.

1. I would rather ∧ an apple.   *(have inserted above)*

2. You could not borrow my van next week.

3. May we leave now?

4. You mayn't leave until the exam is over.

5. Where you prefer to go this weekend?

6. I'd rather not to go now.

7. She'd like learn to drive.

8. What would you rather do tonight?

▶ Beyond the Classroom

Searching for Authentic Examples

Find examples of English grammar in everyday life. Watch an English-language television program or movie. Listen for examples of people making requests, asking for permission, expressing their desires, or stating their preferences. Write down three examples and bring them to class. Which examples are more formal and polite? Which are less formal and less polite? Discuss your findings with your classmates.

Speaking

Follow these steps to present a role-play to your class.

1. In pairs, write a dialogue for one of the situations below. Use modals of request, permission, desire, and preference where appropriate.

   • an employee asking for a raise

   • a shy man asking a woman out for a first date

   • a teenager asking parents for permission to have a party

2. Act out the dialogue for your classmates.

>   Lee: *Uh, excuse me, Mrs. Smith, could I ask you something?*
> Mrs. Smith: *Yes, Lee. What would you like to discuss?*

Modals and Phrasal Modals of Advice, Necessity, and Prohibition

A The Rules

 Before You Read

Discuss these questions.

Do you think it is important to get married? Why or why not? How do men and women meet and marry in your culture?

 Read

Read the on-line book review about dating on the following page. Would you buy the book?

A3 **After You Read**

Write *T* for true or *F* for false for each statement.

_T_ **1.** *The Rules* is written for women.

_____ **2.** According to *The Rules*, a woman should call a man on the phone.

_____ **3.** According to *The Rules*, a man should buy a woman a romantic gift for her birthday.

_____ **4.** According to the writer of the book review, women should play games to make men fall in love with them.

_____ **5.** The writer of the book review agrees with the advice in *The Rules*.

BUNDLES OF BOOKS

⌂ **Home**   🔍 **Search**   @ **Contact**   # Book Review

Are these two playing by *The Rules*?

The Rules
Ellen Fein and Sherrie Schneider

An unexpected best-seller, this is a self-help book for women who want to find their ideal man. The basic idea of *The Rules* is that women must play

5 hard to get. For example, *The Rules* states that a woman must not call a man on the phone, ask him to dance, or begin a conversation. She <u>must refuse</u> a date for Saturday if the invitation

10 comes after Wednesday. Further, the authors say that a woman should stop dating a man if he doesn't buy her a romantic gift for special occasions such as Valentine's Day or her birthday.

Ellen Fein and Sherrie Schneider, the authors, say that all women who want to
15 get married have to follow these rules. However, I believe that women should not follow the advice in this book—women who do will end up alone or married to the wrong man.

In my opinion, any woman who follows this advice had better buy a copy of the book for her boyfriend. If she doesn't, how will he know the rules? Women don't
20 have to play games to make men fall in love with them. I believe that a man and a woman ought to know each other very well before they get married. How can two people get to know each other when one of them is following a set of artificial rules?

Reviewed by Janice Harper

---

artificial: not natural

get to know: to spend time with someone and learn about him or her

play games: to behave dishonestly in order to get what you want

play hard to get: to try to attract someone by pretending that you aren't interested in him or her

Valentine's Day: a day (February 14) when people send cards to the people they love

Grammar in Discourse • Modals and Phrasal Modals of Advice, Necessity, and Prohibition   201

B # Modals and Phrasal Modals of Advice, Necessity, and Prohibition

Examining Form

Look back at the review on page 201 and complete the tasks below. Then discuss your answers and read the Form charts to check them.

1. An example of the modal *must* is underlined. Find another example. What form of the verb follows *must*?

2. Find an example of the modal *should*. What form of the verb follows it?

3. Find an example of each of these phrasal modals: *have to, ought to,* and *had better*. What form of the verb follows each of them?

4. Find the negative forms of *must, should,* and *have to*. How is the negative form of *have to* different from the negative forms of *should* and *must*?

MODALS OF ADVICE, NECESSITY, AND PROHIBITION

Affirmative Statements

SUBJECT	MODAL	BASE FORM OF VERB	
You He They	could might should must	buy	a gift.

Negative Statements

SUBJECT	MODAL + *NOT*	BASE FORM OF VERB	
You He They	should not shouldn't must not	buy	a gift.

Yes/No Questions

MODAL	SUBJECT	BASE FORM OF VERB	
Should	I	buy	a gift?

Short Answers

YES	SUBJECT	MODAL		NO	SUBJECT	MODAL + *NOT*
Yes,	you	should.		No,	you	shouldn't.

Information Questions

WH- WORD	MODAL	SUBJECT	VERB	
Where	should	we	go	for dinner?

- *Could, might, should, and must* are used to give advice. *Should* and *must* are also used to express necessity. *Must not* is used to express prohibition.
- Like all modals, *could, might, should,* and *must* are followed by the base form of the verb and have the same form for all subjects.
- The contracted form *mustn't* is not usually used in American English.
- Do not use *couldn't* in negative statements of advice.
- *Could, might,* and *must* are not usually used in questions of advice.
- We usually use *have to* (see below) instead of *must* in questions of necessity.

PHRASAL MODALS OF ADVICE AND NECESSITY

Affirmative Statements

SUBJECT	PHRASAL MODAL	BASE FORM OF VERB	
I	**have to** **have got to**		
She	**has to** **has got to**	**call**	him.
They	**have to** **have got to**		

CONTRACTIONS			
I've	**got to**	**call**	him.
She's			

Negative Statements

SUBJECT	*DO/DOES* + *NOT*	PHRASAL MODAL	BASE FORM OF VERB	
I	**do not** **don't**			
She	**does not** **doesn't**	**have to**	**call**	him.
They	**do not** **don't**			

CONTRACTIONS				
I	**don't**	**have to**	**call**	him.
She	**doesn't**			

Affirmative Statements

SUBJECT	PHRASAL MODAL	BASE FORM OF VERB	
I			
She	**ought to** **had better**	**call**	him.
They			

CONTRACTIONS			
I'd better	**call**	him.

Negative Statements

SUBJECT	PHRASAL MODAL + *NOT*	BASE FORM OF VERB	
I			
She	**had better not**	**call**	him.
They			

CONTRACTIONS			
I'd better not	**call**	him.

(Continued on page 204)

Yes/No Questions				
DO/DOES	SUBJECT	PHRASAL MODAL	BASE FORM OF VERB	
Do	I			
Does	she	**have to**	**call**	him?
Do	they			

Short Answers						
YES	SUBJECT	*DO/DOES*	*NO*	SUBJECT	*DO/DOES + NOT*
	you	**do.**		you	**don't.**
Yes,	she	**does.**	**No,**	she	**doesn't.**
	they	**do.**		they	**don't.**

Information Questions				
WH- WORD	*DO/DOES*	SUBJECT	PHRASAL MODAL	BASE FORM OF VERB
Who	**do**	I		
What			**have to**	**pay?**
When	**does**	she		
Why				

- *Have to, have got to, ought to,* and *had better* are used to give advice. *Have to* and *have got to* are also used to express necessity.
- Unlike other phrasal modals, *have to* and *have got to* have different forms for the third-person singular.
- *Had better* looks like a past form, but isn't. It is used to talk about the present and the future.

    You'd better call him now.   **We'd better** leave tomorrow.

- In spoken English, we usually use contracted forms of *had better* and *have got to*. The contracted form of *had* for all persons is *'d. Have to* does not have a contracted form.

    You'd better call him.   **You've got to** call him   ***You've to call him.** (INCORRECT)

- We do not usually use *have got to* or *ought to* in negative statements or in questions.
- We do not usually use *had better* in questions.

Listen to these sentences. Circle the modal forms you hear.

1. **a.** should
   b. shouldn't *(circled)*

2. **a.** has to
   b. doesn't have to

3. **a.** We'd better
   b. We'd better not

4. **a.** must
   b. must not

5. **a.** have to
   b. don't have to

6. **a.** should
   b. shouldn't

7. **a.** You've got to
   b. You have to

8. **a.** have got to
   b. have to

A. Rewrite these statements as *Yes/No* questions.

1. He should buy a new car. _Should he buy a new car?_

2. We have to eat at 12. _____

3. They should bring a gift. _____

4. She has to go to class today. _____

5. You have to get a new passport. _____

6. He should see a doctor. _____

B. Write an information question about each underlined word or phrase.

1. <u>Susan</u> should give us the money. _Who should give us the money?_

2. He has to write <u>a paper for his history class</u>. _____

3. You have to stay in the hospital <u>for two days</u>. _____

4. We should go to the gym <u>on Monday</u>. _____

5. They have to take this form <u>to the Registration Office</u>. _____

6. You should talk to the professor <u>after the class</u>. _____

B3 Writing Contracted Forms

Rewrite these sentences with contractions where possible. If you cannot use a contraction in a sentence, write *No contraction possible.*

1. You had better tell her the truth. <u>You'd better tell her the truth.</u>

2. You have to look for a better job. _____

3. She ought to see a doctor. _____

4. He has got to study more. _____

5. You should not wear jeans to work. _____

6. She has to spend more time with the kids. _____

7. You had better not argue with him. _____

8. You have got to take a trip to the Caribbean! _____

9. He should not waste any more time. _____

10. You do not have to call. _____

B4 Writing Negative Statements

Rewrite these affirmative statements as negative statements. Use contractions where possible.

1. You should ask him to dance. <u>You shouldn't ask him to dance.</u>

2. Jake has to do his homework now. _____

3. Visitors must park here. _____

4. You had better tell your roommate the news. _____

5. Employees have to attend the sales meeting. _____

6. They should buy their son a car this year. _____

7. You must get on that train. _____

8. You should ask for a raise. _____

9. He had better wait until tomorrow. _____

10. You have to be home early. _____

Informally Speaking

Reduced Forms of *Ought To, Has To, Have To,* and *Have Got To*

🎧 Look at the cartoon and listen to the conversation. How are the underlined forms in the cartoon different from what you hear?

In informal conversation, *ought to* is often pronounced as /ˈɔt̬ə/, *has to* as /ˈhæstə/, *have to* as /ˈhæftə/, and *have got to* as /hævˈgɑt̬ə/ or /ˈgɑt̬ə/.

STANDARD FORM	WHAT YOU MIGHT HEAR
I **ought to** go.	"I /ˈɔt̬ə/ go."
She **has to** do the work.	"She /ˈhæstə/ do the work."
We **have to** see him now.	"We /ˈhæftə/ see him now."
You**'ve got to** finish today.	"You've /ˈgɑt̬ə/ finish today." OR "You /ˈgɑt̬ə/ finish today."

B5 Understanding Informal Speech

🎧 Matt and Linda are getting married today. Listen to their conversations. Write the standard form of the words you hear.

Conversation 1: At Matt's house

Matt: It's 9:00. We ____ought to____ leave now.
⠀⠀⠀⠀⠀⠀⠀⠀⠀⠀⠀⠀⠀⠀⠀⠀⠀1

Friend: The wedding is at 10:00. We don't _____ leave until 9:30.
⠀⠀⠀⠀⠀⠀⠀⠀⠀⠀⠀⠀⠀⠀⠀⠀⠀⠀⠀⠀⠀⠀⠀⠀⠀⠀⠀⠀2

Matt: But we _____ be there before the guests arrive.
⠀⠀⠀⠀⠀⠀⠀⠀⠀⠀⠀3

Conversation 2: Later, at the church

Linda: Where's Matt? He _____ come soon! We're getting
⠀⠀⠀⠀⠀⠀⠀⠀⠀⠀⠀⠀⠀⠀⠀⠀⠀⠀⠀⠀1

married in 15 minutes!

Sister: Maybe I _____ call him at home.
⠀⠀⠀⠀⠀⠀⠀⠀⠀⠀⠀⠀⠀2

Father: Don't worry. He'll be here. We _____ stay calm and wait.
⠀⠀⠀⠀⠀⠀⠀⠀⠀⠀⠀⠀⠀⠀⠀⠀⠀⠀⠀⠀⠀⠀⠀⠀⠀3

C Modals and Phrasal Modals of Advice

Examining Meaning and Use

Read these sentences and answer the questions below. Then discuss your answers and read the Meaning and Use Notes to check them.

    a. You ought to take that job.
    b. You could take that job now, or you could wait awhile.
    c. You had better take that job soon, or someone else will.
    d. You have to take that job. You need a job!
    e. You should take that job.

1. Which two sentences offer advice and have the same meaning?

2. Which sentence expresses the strongest advice?

3. Which sentence makes two suggestions?

4. Which sentence expresses a warning?

Meaning and Use Notes

> ### Weak and Strong Advice
>
> **1** Use *could, might, should (not), ought to, had better (not), have to, have got to,* and *must* to give advice, suggestions, and warnings.
>
> *It's Mary's birthday tomorrow.*
>
> *Weak*
> - could, might — You **could buy** her flowers.
> - should (not), ought to — You **should ask** her what she wants.
> - had better (not) — You**'d better buy** something before it's too late.
> - have to, have got to, must — You **have to buy** her that new book.
>
> *Strong*

2 Both *could* and *might* are used to make casual suggestions, especially when there is more than one choice.

> If you want to get to know him, you **might** invite him for coffee after class, or you **could** call him.
> You **could** meet for lunch or dinner.

Advice with *Should* and *Ought To*

3A Use *should (not)* and *ought to* to give advice. *Should (not)* is more common than *ought to.*

> You **should get** married in June, when the weather is warm.
> You **ought to look** for a new job.

3B You can also use *should (not)* and *ought to* in general statements to express a personal opinion about something.

> People **shouldn't** drive when they're tired.
> The President **ought to** do more for the environment.

3C Use words such as *I think, maybe,* and *perhaps* to soften your advice or opinion.

> <u>I think</u> the President **ought to do** more for the environment.
> <u>Maybe</u> you **should get** married in June.

Warnings with *Had Better*

4 *Had better (not)* is stronger than *should (not)* or *ought to.* It is used to give advice with a warning about possible bad consequences. As with *should (not)* or *ought to,* you can use expressions such as *I think, maybe,* and *perhaps* to soften the meaning.

> You**'d better study** for the test. If you don't, you'll fail.
> You**'d better not make** so many personal phone calls at work, or you'll lose your job.
> <u>I think</u> you**'d better see** the doctor, or your cold will get worse.

(Continued on page 210)

Strong Advice with *Have To, Have Got To,* and *Must*

5A *Have to, have got to,* and *must* are used to give strong advice. They often suggest that the situation is serious or urgent.

Your cough sounds terrible. You $\begin{Bmatrix} \textbf{have to} \\ \textbf{'ve got to} \\ \textbf{must} \end{Bmatrix}$ **see** a doctor immediately.

5B Another type of strong advice with *have to, have got to,* and *must* is more casual. It shows that the speaker has a strong opinion about something, even though the situation is not serious.

You $\begin{Bmatrix} \textbf{have to} \\ \textbf{'ve got to} \\ \textbf{must} \end{Bmatrix}$ **try** that new restaurant. I ate there yesterday and the food is great!

C1 **Listening for Meaning and Use** ► Notes 1–5

Listen to two people give advice. Who gives stronger advice: Speaker A or Speaker B? Check (✓) the correct column.

	SPEAKER A	SPEAKER B
1.		✓
2.		
3.		
4.		
5.		
6.		
7.		
8.		

Write two suggestions for each question or statement. Use *could* in one suggestion and *might* in the other.

1. Friend: My grades in French are really bad. What should I do?

    You: <u>You could study harder.</u>

             <u>You might get a tutor to help you.</u>

2. Friend: I need to earn some extra money this summer. How can I find a job?

    You: _____

        _____

3. Sister: Let's go somewhere special for Mom's birthday. Where could we go?

    You: _____

        _____

4. Friend: I'm so bored. There's nothing to do around here.

    You: _____

        _____

C3 **Giving Your Opinion** ▶ Notes 3A–3C

A. Work with a partner. Take turns asking and answering questions using these words and phrases. Use *should* in your questions. Use *should* or *ought to* in your answers. You can soften your advice with *I think, maybe,* or *perhaps.*

  1. men/give women romantic birthday gifts

    A: Should men give women romantic birthday gifts?
    B: Yes, they should. I think men ought to give women romantic gifts all year.

  2. women with small children/work

  3. men/do housework

  4. women/invite men to go out

  5. married woman/keep her family name/take her husband's last name

B. Work on your own. Make up two more opinion questions with *should.* Then ask your classmates their opinions.

A. Work with a partner. Give two pieces of advice to the person(s) in each situation. Use *you should* in one and *you ought to* in the other. You can soften your advice with *maybe, perhaps,* or *I think*.

   1. Sasha has an old car. The car is making a strange noise.

   You ought to buy a new car. Maybe you should fix your car.

   2. Today is Monday. Emily has to work today, but she woke up with a sore throat.

   _____

   3. Dan isn't doing very well in his math class.

   _____

   4. Mr. and Mrs. Chen love their apartment, but it's a little expensive.

   _____

B. The situations have become worse. Give two pieces of strong advice for each situation. Use *you have to, you've got to,* or *you must*.

   1. Now Sasha's car has broken down.

   You must not fix this car. You've got to buy a new car.

   2. It's Monday night. Emily has a high fever. She feels very sick.

   _____

   3. Now Dan is failing math. If he fails, he won't graduate.

   _____

   4. The Chens' landlord has increased the rent and they can't afford it.

   _____

C. Work by yourself. Write down three situations of your own. Then ask your partner to give advice.

Look at the pictures and write a warning for each one. Use *had better* or *had better not*.

1. _He had better stop the car._

4. _____

2. _____

5. _____

3. _____   6. _____

D Modals of Necessity and Prohibition

Examining Meaning and Use

Read the sentences and answer the questions below. Then discuss your answers and read the Meaning and Use Notes to check them.

1a. Students must show an ID to enter the building.
1b. You have to show an ID to enter the building.

2a. Students must not bring food into the library.
2b. You shouldn't bring food into the library.

1. Which sentence in each pair is formal, and sounds like a rule or a law?

2. Which sentence in each pair sounds more conversational?

Meaning and Use Notes

> **Necessity**
>
> **1A** *Should, ought to, have to, have got to,* and *must* express necessity. *Must* expresses the strongest necessity and is used in formal or more serious situations. We often use *should, ought to, have to,* and *have got to* in conversation to avoid sounding too formal.
>
> Students **should study** their notes before the exam.
> I **have to hurry.** I'm going to be late!
> We**'ve got to send** out the invitations today. The party is next week.
> You **must take** the final exam if you want to pass the course.
>
> ---
>
> **1B** Use *must* to express rules, laws, and requirements, especially in written documents.
>
> Bicyclists **must obey** all traffic lights in the city.
> All couples **must apply** for a marriage license in person.
>
> ---
>
> **1C** *Should, have to,* and *have got to* are often used instead of *must* to talk about rules and laws in less formal English.
>
> The manual says that bicyclists **should obey** all traffic lights in the city.
> I found out that we **have to apply** for a marriage license in person.

Lack of Necessity vs. Prohibition

2 *Don't/doesn't have to* and *must not* have very different meanings. *Don't/doesn't have to* means that something is not necessary—there is a choice of whether to do it or not. *Must not* means that something is prohibited (not allowed). There is no choice involved.

Don't/Doesn't Have To *(Not Necessary)*	Must Not *(Prohibited)*
Your children **don't have to take** these vitamins. If they eat a healthy diet, they'll be fine.	Your children **must not take** these vitamins. They are for adults only.

D1 **Listening for Meaning and Use** ▶ Notes 1A, 1B, 2

🎧 Listen to these conversations between an employee at the Department of Motor Vehicles and people who call with questions. What does the employee say about each of the topics in the chart? Check (✓) the correct column.

		NECESSARY	NOT NECESSARY	PROHIBITED
1.	take an eye test	✓		
2.	take the eye test at the Department of Motor Vehicles			
3.	need a California license to drive in California			
4.	pay with a credit card			
5.	go to driving school			
6.	drive alone without a learner's permit			

A. Read these public signs. Then explain the signs by completing the statements with *must, don't have to,* or *must not.*

1. SWIMMING POOL FOR APARTMENT RESIDENTS ONLY

   This means that you _____have to_____ be a resident of the apartment

   building to swim in the pool.

2. NO PETS ALLOWED

   This means that you _____ bring your pet into the building.

3. CHILDREN UNDER 12 FREE

   This means that children under 12 years old _____ pay

   to go in.

4. NO APPOINTMENT NECESSARY

   This means that you _____ make an appointment.

5. NO EXIT

   This means that you _____ go out this door.

6. ID REQUIRED

   This means that you _____ show identification.

7. HOSPITAL ZONE — NO HORNS

   This means that you _____ blow your car horn in this area.

8. SHIRT AND SHOES, PLEASE

   This means that you _____ wear a shirt to go into this place,

   but you _____ wear a tie.

B. Work with a partner. Discuss the signs in part A. Where do you think you
might you find each one?

D3 Writing About Rules and Laws

► Notes 1B, 1C, 2

A. Look at each sign and write a sentence to explain its meaning. Use *must* and *must not*.

1. <u>You must not smoke</u>   3. _____   5. _____

<u>here.</u>   _____   _____

2. _____   4. _____   6. _____

_____   _____   _____

B. Work with a partner. What other signs have you seen? Write down the words or draw the images and show them to your classmates. Explain each sign using *have to, have got to,* or *must not.*

You have to turn right.

D4 Stating Necessity, Lack of Necessity, and Prohibition

► Notes 1A, 2

Work with a partner. Think about your English class. Write sentences about what is necessary, what is not necessary, and what is not allowed. Use *have got to, have to, don't have to, must,* and *must not.*

1. <u>We have to speak English in class.</u> _____

2. _____

3. _____

4. _____

5. _____

E Combining Form, Meaning, and Use

E1 Thinking About Meaning and Use

Choose the best answer to complete each conversation. Then discuss your answers in small groups.

1. **A:** Emergency Room. How can I help you?

   B: My daughter fell down the stairs and she's unconscious! Should I bring her in?

   A: _____ wait for an ambulance.

     a. You'd better

     b. You could

2. **A:** Do you like my new dress?

   B: _____.

     a. Not really. You shouldn't wear that color.

     b. Yes, you don't have to wear that color.

3. **A:** I'd like to pick up my car. Is it ready?

   B: Yes, but you _____ come right away. We're closing in a few minutes.

     a. might

     b. should

4. **A:** I don't have my glasses. What does that sign say?

   B: It says, "Visitors _____ check in at the front desk."

     a. must

     b. ought to

5. **A:** Can we put posters on the wall in our dorm room?

   B: Yes, but you _____ make holes in the walls. It's against the rules.

     a. don't have to

     b. shouldn't

6. A: My boss will fire me if I come late again.

   B: _____
   - **a.** Then you'd better be on time from now on.
   - **b.** Then maybe you must not be late.

7. A: What do you want for dinner?

   B: I don't care. _____
   - **a.** You should make hot dogs.
   - **b.** We could have spaghetti.

8. A: Look at all those people at the exit. We'll never get out.

   B: We _____ use that exit. There's another one in the back.
   - **a.** don't have to
   - **b.** must not

E2 Editing

Find the errors in this paragraph and correct them.

There are many wedding traditions in the United States. One of them is that the bride ought ^to^ wear "something old, something new, something borrowed, something blue, and a sixpence in her shoe." The old, new, borrowed, and blue parts are easy enough. However, a sixpence is an old English coin. It is impossible to find these days, so most people feel that the bride doesn't has to use a sixpence—any coin will do. Another tradition is that the groom must not to see the bride before the wedding. People think that it is bad luck. In addition, many people think that first-time brides ought wear white and second-time brides could not. However, second and third marriages are so common these days that many brides feel they must not follow this rule. One final tradition is that when people get married, they've to save a piece of their wedding cake for good luck.

▶ Beyond the Classroom

Searching for Authentic Examples

Find examples of English grammar in everyday life. Look in an advice column in a newspaper or magazine or on the Internet for examples of sentences with modals of advice. Bring at least four examples to class. Why is each modal used? Discuss your findings with your classmates.

Writing

Imagine you are the director of a small company. Follow the steps below to write a memo explaining the office rules to new employees.

1. Think about all the things a new employee needs to know. Make notes about what you want to say. Use these categories to help you.

   - office hours
   - lateness
   - appropriate clothing
   - lunch breaks
   - vacation policy
   - sick leave
   - personal phone calls
   - Internet use

2. Write a first draft. Use modals and phrasal modals of advice, necessity, and prohibition.

3. Read your work and circle grammar, spelling, and punctuation errors. Work with a partner to help you decide how to fix your errors and improve the content.

4. Rewrite your draft.

   To: All New Employees
   From: Bob Chang

   Welcome to Architectural Design Solutions. Please read this memo carefully. Before you start work here, you have to . . .

Tag Questions and Other Additions

PART

5

Tag Questions

Women's Language and Men's Language

Discuss these questions.

Do you have more female friends or male friends? Are your conversations with female friends different from your conversations with male friends? How?

Read this magazine article to find out about the different ways in which men and women talk to their friends.

Women's Language and Men's Language

FOR MANY YEARS RESEARCHERS HAVE studied how men and women use language. They have been trying to find out if there are differences related to
5 gender. Deborah Tannen, a professor at Georgetown University, is the author of several books on this subject. According to Tannen, men and women relate to their friends very differently and this difference
10 shows in their use of language.

Read these two conversations between friends. Can you guess which conversation is between two men and which one is between two women?

Conversation 1

15 **A:** Hi. It's a great day for tennis, isn't it?

B: Yeah. I can't wait to get on the tennis court and forget about work. I'm so tired of my job.

A: I know what you mean. I'm really tired
20 of my job, too.

B: You aren't going to quit, are you?

A: Well, actually, I've been offered another job. The pay is a lot better.

B: That's great! Let's go play some tennis.

Conversation 2

25 **A:** Hi there. How are you doing?

B: Not great. I had a bad day at work.

A: Have a seat and tell me about it. We can play tennis later.

B: Thanks. Well, you see, I keep making
30 mistakes. Today I lost some very important papers, and my boss got angry with me. I'm so tired of this job. I try so hard, but it's never good enough.

A: How is the job search going? You're
35 still looking for another job, aren't you?

B: Yeah. In fact, I have an interview next week with that company I told you about.

A: That's great! So tell me about last night. You didn't go to that awful
40 restaurant again, did you?

Did you guess that Conversation 1 was between two men and Conversation 2 was between two women? The conversations show very different communication styles.

45 According to Tannen, the differences in the ways that men and women relate to friends begin in childhood. Little girls usually spend a lot of time talking and sharing their feelings. A girl's best friend

50 is the person who knows all her secrets. Talk is the "glue" that holds the female friendship together. However, this is not true for boys. A boy's best friend is a person that he does everything with.

55 Although a boy will defend his friend in a fight, he often doesn't know his best friend's secrets or private feelings. Tannen says that women often tell their friends the intimate details of their lives, but men

60 rarely do this. Male friendships focus on activities; female friendships focus on talk.

Female friendships focus on talk.

Male friendships focus on activities.

defend: fight to protect someone or something
gender: being male or female

intimate: private, personal
relate: to interact or have a relationship with

A3 After You Read

Write *T* for true or *F* for false for each statement.

__F__ **1.** Women's friendships are the same as men's friendships.

_____ **2.** Differences in the way men and women relate to friends begin in childhood.

_____ **3.** Women don't usually tell each other how they feel.

_____ **4.** Men tell their friends everything about their lives.

_____ **5.** For men, doing things together is more important than talking.

B Tag Questions

Examining Form

Look back at the magazine article on page 224 and complete the tasks below. Then discuss your answers and read the Form charts to check them.

1. An example of a tag question is underlined. Find three more.

2. Look at the statement that comes before each tag question. What kind of tag question follows an affirmative statement? What kind of tag question follows a negative statement?

TAG QUESTIONS WITH *BE, HAVE,* OR MODAL

AFFIRMATIVE STATEMENT	NEGATIVE TAG	
STATEMENT WITH *BE, HAVE,* OR MODAL	*BE, HAVE,* or MODAL + *NOT*	SUBJECT
I'm right,	aren't	I?
He was tired,	wasn't	he?
It was raining,	wasn't	it?
We have finished,	haven't	we?
They should come,	shouldn't	they?

SHORT ANSWERS	
AFFIRMATIVE	NEGATIVE
Yes, you are.	No, you aren't.
Yes, he was.	No, he wasn't.
Yes, it was.	No, it wasn't.
Yes, you have.	No, you haven't.
Yes, they should.	No, they shouldn't.

NEGATIVE STATEMENT	AFFIRMATIVE TAG	
STATEMENT WITH *BE, HAVE,* OR MODAL	*BE, HAVE,* or MODAL	SUBJECT
I'm not right,	am	I?
He wasn't tired,	was	he?
It wasn't raining,	was	it?
We haven't finished,	have	we?
They shouldn't come,	should	they?

SHORT ANSWERS	
AFFIRMATIVE	NEGATIVE
Yes, you are.	No, you aren't.
Yes, he was.	No, he wasn't.
Yes, it was.	No, it wasn't.
Yes, you have.	No, you haven't.
Yes, they should.	No, they shouldn't.

Overview

- A tag question (or tag) is an addition to a sentence. It is a short *Yes/No* question that is added to the end of a statement. It is separated from the statement by a comma.
- Use a negative tag after an affirmative statement. A negative tag is usually contracted.
- Use an affirmative tag after a negative statement. An affirmative tag is never contracted.

Tag Questions with *Be, Have,* and Modals

- After statements where *be* is a main verb, use the correct form of *be* in the tag.

  He **was** tired, **wasn't** he?   He **wasn't** tired, **was** he?

  They**'re** here, **aren't** they?   They **aren't** here, **are** they?

- Note that affirmative statements with *I am* are followed by the negative tag *aren't I?*

  I'm right, **aren't I?**

- After statements with verb tenses formed with *be, have,* or a modal + a main verb, use the correct form of *be, have,* or the modal in the tag. Do not repeat the main verb.

  It **was** raining, **wasn't** it?   It **wasn't** raining, **was** it?

  We **have** finished, **haven't** we?   We **haven't** finished, **have** we?

  They **should** come, **shouldn't** they?   They **shouldn't** come, **should** they?

- We form answers to tag questions in the same way that we form answers to *Yes/No* questions.

  A: You're not tired, are you?   A: We haven't finished, have we?

  B: **Yes, I am.** OR **No, I'm not.**   B: **Yes, you have.** OR **No, you haven't.**

TAG QUESTIONS WITH *DO*

AFFIRMATIVE STATEMENT	NEGATIVE TAG	
SIMPLE PRESENT or SIMPLE PAST STATEMENT	*DO + NOT*	SUBJECT
I **play** badly,	**don't**	I?
It **costs** a lot,	**doesn't**	it?
You **live** nearby,	**don't**	you?
They **sang** well,	**didn't**	they?

SHORT ANSWERS	
AFFIRMATIVE	NEGATIVE
Yes, you **do.**	**No,** you **don't.**
Yes, it **does.**	**No,** it **doesn't.**
Yes, we **do.**	**No,** we **don't.**
Yes, they **did.**	**No,** they **didn't.**

(Continued on page 228)

NEGATIVE STATEMENT		AFFIRMATIVE TAG
SIMPLE PRESENT or SIMPLE PAST STATEMENT	**DO**	**SUBJECT**
I **don't play** badly,	**do**	I?
It **doesn't cost** a lot,	**does**	it?
They **didn't sing** well,	**did**	they?

SHORT ANSWERS	
AFFIRMATIVE	**NEGATIVE**
Yes, you **do.**	**No,** you **don't.**
Yes, it **does.**	**No,** it **doesn't.**
Yes, they **did.**	**No,** they **didn't.**

- After simple present and simple past statements with all verbs except *be*, use the correct form of *do* in the tag.

  You **live** nearby, **don't** you?   It **doesn't cost** a lot, **does** it?

  They **sang** well, **didn't** they?   They **didn't** sing well, **did** they?

- Answer tag questions with *do* in the same way you answer *Yes/No* questions with *do*.

  A: It costs a lot, doesn't it?   A: They didn't sing well, did they?

  B: **Yes, it does.** OR **No, it doesn't.**   B: **Yes, they did.** OR **No, they didn't.**

SUBJECT PRONOUNS IN TAG QUESTIONS

STATEMENT	TAG
He seems shy,	doesn't **he?**
John seems shy,	doesn't **he?**
This is fun,	isn't **it?**
That's true,	isn't **it?**
These are Ana's,	aren't **they?**
Those are mine,	aren't **they?**
There's more hot water,	isn't **there?**

- When a personal pronoun is used in the statement, it is always repeated in the tag.
- When a noun is used in the statement, use the appropriate pronoun in the tag.

  <u>Gina</u> is nice, **isn't she?**   <u>His car</u> is really old, **isn't it?**

- When *this* or *that* is used in the statement, substitute *it* in the tag.
- When *these* or *those* is used in the statement, substitute *they* in the tag.
- When *there* is used in the statement, repeat *there* in the tag.

🎧 Listen to each conversation. Choose the tag question you hear.

1. **a.** aren't you?   3. **a.** does he?   5. **a.** are there?
   b. are you?   **b.** doesn't he?   **b.** is there?

2. **a.** did you?   4. **a.** can you?   6. **a.** am I?
   b. didn't you?   **b.** can't you?   **b.** aren't I?

Complete these conversations with tags. Then practice them with a partner.

1. **A:** There's no one home, _is there_?

   B: No, there's not.

2. **A:** I'm going to drive downtown.

   B: You couldn't give me a ride,

   _____?

3. **A:** He didn't tell you the answers,

   _____?

   B: No, he didn't.

4. **A:** Ben, I want to discuss your test.

   B: I did okay, _____?

5. **A:** The traffic was terrible. I'm not

   late, _____?

   B: No, you're not.

6. **A:** Rita came in late last night,

   _____?

   B: I'm not sure. Ask Beth.

A. Work with a partner. Add a tag to each statement.

1. You aren't hungry, _are you_?

2. You're studying English, _____?

3. You like this class, _____?

4. You've flown, _____?

5. You have a dog, _____?

6. You don't live alone, _____?

B. Take turns asking and answering the questions in part A.

A: You aren't hungry, are you?
B: No, I'm not. OR *Yes, I am.*

Reduced Statements with Tag Questions

🎧 Look at the cartoon and listen to the conversation. How are the underlined forms in the cartoon different from what you hear?

He's not very good, is he?

No, he's absolutely awful.

In informal conversation, we often leave out subject pronouns and forms of *be* in statements with tag questions.

STANDARD FORM	WHAT YOU MIGHT HEAR
It's hot in here, isn't it?	"Hot in here, isn't it?"
She's not a good speaker, is she?	"Not a good speaker, is she?"
You're leaving at six, aren't you?	"Leaving at six, aren't you?"

B4 Understanding Informal Speech

🎧 Listen to these reduced statements with tag questions. What subject pronoun + form of *be* does the speaker leave out at the beginning of each statement? Choose the correct answer.

1. **a.** It's
   b. They're ⟵ (circled)

2. **a.** She's
   b. She was

3. **a.** They're
   b. It's

4. **a.** They aren't
   b. They're

5. **a.** You're
   b. You aren't

6. **a.** It's
   b. It has been

Tag Questions

Examining Meaning and Use

Read the sentences and answer the questions below. Then discuss your answers and read the Meaning and Use Notes to check them.

1a. Is dinner at six?

1b. Dinner is at six, isn't it?

2a. It's a nice day, isn't it?

2b. You couldn't give me that pen, could you?

1. Look at 1a and 1b. Which sentence shows that the speaker has a previous idea about the time of dinner? Which sentence shows that the speaker has no previous idea about the time of dinner?

2. Look at 2a and 2b. In which sentence is the speaker making a request? In which sentence is the speaker expecting agreement?

Meaning and Use Notes

Tag Questions vs. *Yes/No* Questions

1 Tag questions are different from *Yes/No* questions. Use a tag question when you have a previous (earlier) idea or opinion about something and want to confirm it. Use a *Yes/No* question when you have no previous idea or opinion. Tag questions are more common in spoken English than in written English.

Tag Question	*Yes/No Question*
You**'re** a student, **aren't** you?	Are you a student?
(I think you're a student.)	(I have no idea.)

Intonation Patterns and Certainty

2A Use tag questions with falling intonation if you are very certain of your previous idea or opinion. Use tag questions with rising intonation if you are less certain.

Falling Intonation

He makes a lot of money, **doesn't he?**
  (I'm sure he makes a lot of money.)

Rising Intonation

He makes a lot of money, **doesn't he?**
  (I think he makes a lot of money, but I'm not sure.)

(Continued on page 232)

2B We often use tag questions with rising intonation to express doubt or surprise. We also use them to make polite requests with modals, especially when we're not sure that the listener will agree to our request.

Expressing Doubt or Surprise
That box won't fit in the trunk, **will it?**

Making a Polite Request
You couldn't lend me five dollars, **could you?**

2C We often use tag questions with falling intonation to confirm information we are already sure of, or to ask for agreement.

Confirming Information
We've met before, **haven't we?**

Asking for Agreement
We haven't had rain for a long time, **have we?**

Negative Words in Affirmative Statements

3 An affirmative statement that uses a negative adverb of frequency (such as *rarely, hardly, seldom,* and *never*) or a word with *no* (such as *nobody, nowhere,* and *nothing*) has a negative meaning. It requires an affirmative tag.

You <u>never</u> go to class, **do** you?
There's <u>nobody</u> here, **is** there?

C1 **Listening for Meaning and Use** ▶ Notes 1–3

A. Listen to these statements with tag questions. Draw arrows to show falling or rising intonation.

1. We spent too much money, didn't we?

2. That's a very expensive restaurant, isn't it?

3. You didn't walk here, did you?

4. He has Ms. Walker for history, doesn't he?

5. You couldn't watch my children for an hour, could you?

6. You've never met the Smiths, have you?

B. 🎧 Listen again. Is the speaker certain or uncertain? Check (✓) the correct column.

	CERTAIN	UNCERTAIN
1.	✓	
2.		
3.		
4.		
5.		
6.		

C2 **Practicing the Intonation of Tag Questions** ▶ Note 2A

A. Read each conversation. Think about the meaning and decide if the tag question expresses certainty or uncertainty. Draw an arrow over each tag question to show falling (certain) or rising (uncertain) intonation.

1. **A:** Sam got an A in calculus.

   B: He's really smart, isn't he?

2. **A:** I'm sorry, but Mark left.

   B: He's coming back, isn't he?

3. **A:** I've got some bad news. Your car needs a new engine.

   B: Oh, no! It's going to be really expensive, isn't it?

4. **A:** Look how cloudy it is outside!

   B: It's going to rain, isn't it?

5. **A:** Thanks for inviting us to dinner.

   B: You're welcome. You eat meat, don't you?

6. **A:** Can you believe it? My boss asked me to take work home over the holiday.

   B: You didn't agree, did you?

B. Work with a partner. Practice the conversations in part A. Use the correct intonation.

C3 Expressing Doubt

► Note 2B

Work with a partner. Take turns expressing doubt about these incorrect facts. Use negative statements with affirmative tags and rising intonation. Reply with the correct fact, using the information in parentheses.

1. Columbus sailed to America in 1489. (1492)

   A: Columbus didn't sail to America in 1489, did he?
   B: No, he didn't. He sailed to America in 1492.

2. Africa is the largest continent. (Asia)

3. Saturn is the farthest planet from the sun. (Pluto)

4. Toronto is the capital of Canada. (Ottawa)

5. There are 31 days in November. (30)

6. They use pesos in Japan. (yen)

7. Albert Einstein invented the telegraph. (Samuel Morse)

8. A yard is equal to 24 inches. (36)

C4 Making Polite Requests

► Note 2B

Read each situation. Then make a polite request. Use a negative statement with an affirmative tag and rising intonation.

1. You are a waiter. You can't work tomorrow, and you hope your friend can take your place. You ask your friend.

   You couldn't take my place tomorrow, could you?

2. You have a doctor's appointment, and you need a ride to the clinic. You ask your roommate.

3. You need someone to take care of your son after school today. You ask your neighbor.

4. You need help tonight with your paper for English class. You ask your sister.

5. You're going on vacation. You need someone to feed your cats next week. You ask your neighbor.

6. You want to go away for the weekend, but you don't have a car. Maybe your father can lend you his car. You ask him.

Vocabulary Notes

Other Ways of Answering Tag Questions

Using short answers is not the only way to respond to tag questions. We can also use other expressions to show agreement or disagreement. In negative responses, we often correct the speaker's statement.

A: The movie starts at six, doesn't it?

B: That's right. OR No, it starts at seven.

A: You don't like your new roommate, do you?

B: Not really. OR Actually, I think she's great!

C5 Using and Answering Tag Questions

A. Work with a partner. Use the questions as a guide to help you confirm what you know about each other. Take turns using and answering tag questions. Use appropriate intonation in your tag questions and a variety of expressions and short answers in your responses.

1. How does your partner get to school?

    A: *You drive to school, don't you?*
    B: *That's right.* OR *No, I don't. Actually, I usually walk.*

2. Where does you partner live?

3. Where is your partner from?

4. How long has your partner studied English?

5. What other languages does your partner speak?

6. Does your partner work?

7. Does your partner like classical music?

8. Does your partner have brothers and sisters?

9. Does your partner play tennis?

10. Does your partner like to swim?

B. Think of two more pieces of information to confirm with your partner. Then ask your partner to confirm the information using statements with tag questions.

A: *Pizza is your favorite food, isn't it?*
B: *Not really. Actually, I prefer Mexican food.*

Beyond the Sentence

Beginning Conversations Using Statements with Tag Questions

Using statements with tag questions is a good way to begin a conversation with someone that you do not know. We often do this by using a statement with a tag question to comment on a shared experience. Using a statement with a tag question is an effective way to begin a conversation because the listener is expected to respond.

At a Train Station

> A: These trains never come on time, do they?
> B: No, they don't. And I'm always late for work.

In a Cafeteria

> A: The cafeteria is very crowded today, isn't it?
> B: Yes, it is. This line is really long.

C6 Beginning Conversations

A. Work with a partner. How would you begin a conversation in each situation?

1. You're leaving the classroom after the first day of class. The teacher has told you that you have to read 50 pages for the next class.

   She gives a lot of homework, doesn't she?

2. You're standing at a bus stop on a beautiful spring day, waiting for a bus.

   _____

3. You're in a very long line at the supermarket. The cashier is very slow.

   _____

4. You're at a party. There is a live band playing music. The band is very good.

   _____

5. You're on an airplane eating dinner. The food isn't very good.

   _____

6. You're at a conference. There are a lot of people there.

   _____

B. Now think of two more situations. Write them down and ask your partner to think of a statement with a tag question to begin each conversation.

D Combining Form, Meaning, and Use

D1 Thinking About Meaning and Use

Choose the best answer to complete each conversation. Then discuss your answers in small groups.

1. **A:** Someone stole my bike.

   B: _____
      a. You didn't call the police, did you?
      b. You called the police, didn't you?

2. **A:** _____

   B: It sure is. Dan's parties are always fun.
      a. It's a great party, isn't it?
      b. It isn't a very good party, is it?

3. **A:** You always study hard, don't you?

   B: _____
      a. Yes, I did.
      b. No, not always.

4. **A:** You couldn't lend me your car, could you?

   B: _____
      a. Of course I couldn't.
      b. Sure. When do you need it?

5. **A:** It's a beautiful day, isn't it?

   B: _____
      a. Yes. We're having great weather.
      b. I'm not sure.

6. **A:** We didn't pay the phone bill, did we?

   B: _____
      a. Oh, no! You're right, we didn't.
      b. Why not?

Some of these sentences have errors. Find the errors and correct them.

1. Tom has been here before, ~~is~~ he? *(hasn't)*

2. I shouldn't tell the teacher, could I?

3. There are many French speakers in Canada, aren't they?

4. I'm not going to see you again, are I?

5. He never visits his parents on Saturday, doesn't he?

6. Frank didn't get married, did Frank?

7. Barbara isn't traveling alone, will she?

8. Your sneakers don't fit, don't they?

▶ Beyond the Classroom

Searching for Authentic Examples

Find examples of English grammar in everyday life. Watch an English-language movie or television show, or listen to a radio interview. Listen for examples of statements with tag questions. Write them down and bring them to class. Try to explain why each example was used.

Speaking

Work with a partner. Create a conversation for the situation below. Use at least three different statements with tag questions. Act out your conversation for another pair of students.

Two people meet at a party. They think they have met before but aren't sure where. They ask questions about places where they think they have seen each other.

A: Haven't I met you before? You used to work at the library, didn't you?
B: No, I never worked at the library. . . . I know! You were at Cindy's wedding last year, weren't you?
A: That's right. Now I remember. You were the best man, weren't you?

Additions with Conjunctions

A Equal Rights for Apes?

Discuss these questions.

Do you believe that animals can feel happy or sad? Do you believe that they can think? Why or why not?

 Read this letter to a newspaper editor to find out the writer's views on the rights of apes.

LETTER TO THE EDITOR

"Equal Rights for Apes?"

I read your recent article "Equal Rights for Apes?" in Friday's paper. I'm upset, and I'm sure others are too. Humans and animals share many similarities and
5 deserve the same respect. Humans shouldn't live in fear of their lives, and animals shouldn't either. Your article contains several inaccuracies that I would like to correct.

10   One of the main reasons that people believe that animals and humans are different is that humans have language, but animals don't. However, scientific studies have shown that apes can learn to
15 use language. A gorilla named Koko learned to communicate with sign language, and so did a chimpanzee named

Koko

Washoe. In fact, on an intelligence test Koko scored 91.7 (a slightly below-
20 average score for a human being).

People also say that humans can appreciate beauty, but animals can't. I don't agree, and neither do many scientists. Apes appreciate beauty in 25 ways that seem very "human." Scientists, for example, have seen chimpanzees in the wild sit and watch sunsets.

Some people say that humans are different from animals because we have 30 feelings, but they don't. This is not true. A gorilla at a Chicago zoo showed that she had feelings when a three-year-old boy fell into the ape exhibit. Binti, an eight-year-old female gorilla, saved his life. She 35 picked him up and held him in her arms for a few moments to calm him down, and then she carried him to safety.

Clearly, apes are not so different from human beings. If they don't deserve the 40 right to be free and live in peace, maybe humans don't either.

Charles Walker
Holly Grove, IL

Apes have feelings too.

---

apes: animals such as gorillas and chimpanzees

exhibit: the place where animals live in a zoo

inaccuracies: mistakes or errors

rights: things that you are morally or legally allowed to do or have

sign language: a way to communicate by using your hands instead of your voice

the wild: a natural environment; nature

A3 **After You Read**

Read these statements. Check (✓) the ones you think the writer would agree with.

__✓__ **1.** Apes and humans are not very different.

_____ **2.** Apes can't use language to communicate with others.

_____ **3.** Some apes are as intelligent as some humans.

_____ **4.** Some apes like to look at sunsets.

_____ **5.** Apes don't have feelings.

_____ **6.** Animals deserve the right to live in peace.

B *And . . . Too, And . . . Either,* and *But*

Examining Form

Read the sentences and complete the tasks below. Then discuss your answers and read the Form charts to check them.

    a. Derek is busy, but Eve isn't.   (= Derek is busy. Eve isn't busy.)
    b. Derek is busy, and Eve is too.   (= Derek is busy. Eve is busy.)
    c. Derek isn't busy, and Eve isn't either.   (= Derek isn't busy. Eve isn't busy.)
    d. Eve isn't busy, but Derek is.   (= Eve isn't busy. Derek is busy.)

1. Which sentence is a combination of two affirmative sentences? What two words connect the second clause to the first clause?

2. Which sentence is a combination of two negative sentences? What two words connect the second clause to the first clause?

3. Which sentences are a combination of an affirmative sentence and a negative sentence (in either order)? What word connects the second clause to the first clause in both sentences?

4. Look back at the underlined examples in the article on page 240. Circle the connecting words. Do they connect two affirmative clauses, two negative clauses, or an affirmative and a negative clause?

And . . . Too					
AFFIRMATIVE		*AND*	AFFIRMATIVE		
SUBJECT	**VERB PHRASE**	*AND*	**SUBJECT**	**BE, HAVE, MODAL, or DO**	**TOO**
Bob	**is** angry,		Amy	**is**	
He	**was** running,		they	**were**	
We	**have** eaten,	and	he	**has**	too.
I	**could** go,		you	**could**	
You	**like** sports,		he	**does**	
We	**sang** well,		they	**did**	

And . . . Either

| | NEGATIVE | | | NEGATIVE | | |
SUBJECT	VERB PHRASE + *NOT*	*AND*	SUBJECT	*BE, HAVE*, MODAL, or *DO* + *NOT*	*EITHER*
Bob	**isn't** angry,		Amy	**isn't**	
He	**wasn't** running,		they	**weren't**	
We	**haven't** eaten,	**and**	he	**hasn't**	**either.**
I	**couldn't** go,		you	**couldn't**	
You	**don't like** sports,		he	**doesn't**	
We	**didn't sing** well,		they	**didn't**	

But

SUBJECT	VERB PHRASE	*BUT*	SUBJECT	*BE, HAVE*, MODAL, or *DO* + *NOT*
Bob	**is** angry,		Amy	**isn't.**
He	**was** running,	**but**	they	**weren't.**
We	**have** eaten,		he	**hasn't.**

SUBJECT	VERB PHRASE + *NOT*	*BUT*	SUBJECT	*BE, HAVE*, MODAL, or *DO*
I	**couldn't** go,		you	**could.**
You	**don't like** sports,	**but**	he	**does.**
We	**didn't sing** well,		they	**did.**

- Use the conjunctions *and . . . too*, *and . . . either*, and *but* to combine two sentences with similar verb phrases but different subjects. In the combined sentence, the second clause (the addition) is a shortened form of the second sentence.

    Bob is angry. Amy is angry. → Bob is angry, **and** Amy is **too.**

- Use *and . . . too* to combine two affirmative sentences. Use *and . . . either* to combine two negative sentences. Use *but* to combine an affirmative and a negative sentence (in either order).

- To combine two sentences where *be* is the main verb, use a form of *be* in the addition and omit the rest of the verb phrase.

- To combine two sentences with verb tenses formed with *be, have,* or a modal, use a form of *be* or *have* or the modal in the addition and omit the rest of the verb phrase.

- To combine two sentences in the simple present or the simple past, use the correct form of *do* in the addition and omit the rest of the verb phrase.

Listen to each sentence. Does the speaker use *and . . . too, and . . . either,* or *but*? Check (✓) the form you hear.

	AND . . . TOO	*AND . . . EITHER*	*BUT*
1.			✓
2.			
3.			
4.			
5.			
6.			
7.			
8.			
9.			
10.			

B2 **Understanding Additions**

Look at the underlined addition in each sentence. Which words are missing? Omit the conjunction and rewrite the addition as a complete sentence.

1. She had fun at the party, <u>but he didn't</u>.

   <u>He didn't have fun at the party.</u>

2. Koji is hungry, <u>and I am too</u>.

   _____

3. I watch a lot of television, <u>but he doesn't</u>.

   _____

4. The students needed to leave early, <u>and the teachers did too</u>.

   _____

5. Our telephone wasn't working, and <u>theirs wasn't either</u>.

   _____

6. We couldn't speak French, <u>and they couldn't either</u>.

_____

7. Pedro enjoys jazz, <u>but Holly doesn't</u>.

_____

8. I liked the concert, <u>and she did too</u>.

_____

9. My aunt has visited Iowa, <u>but my uncle hasn't</u>.

_____

10. Kim isn't going to work this summer, <u>and Josh isn't either</u>.

_____

 Working on Form

Complete each sentence with the correct form of *be, have,* a modal, or *do.*

1. I didn't do the homework last night, and Alex ___*didn't*___ either.

2. Our neighbors have a swimming pool, and we _____ too.

3. Rita lives in an apartment, but Ben _____. He owns a house.

4. Miguel is worried about the test, and Sara _____ too.

5. My friend couldn't go to the party last night, and I _____ either.

6. Steve wasn't at home when I called, but his wife _____. I left her a message.

7. My roommate has been to Thailand, but I _____. I'd like to go one day.

8. I wasn't listening to the teacher, and my partner _____ either. What did she say?

9. I got to work late, and Rick _____ too.

10. Larry will come tonight, but Eva _____.

11. You shouldn't drink so much coffee, and I _____ either.

12. Lee and Chang have learned Chinese, but their sister _____.

Combine each pair of sentences. Use *and . . . too, and . . . either,* or *but.*

1. Koji fell asleep during the movie. Yuji didn't fall asleep during the movie.

   <u> Koji fell asleep during the movie, but Yuji didn't. </u>

2. I don't like getting up early. Jane doesn't like getting up early.

   _____

3. Dan has a car. Rita has a car.

   _____

4. She was feeling sick. He wasn't feeling sick.

   _____

5. I didn't play sports in high school. Carlos didn't play sports in high school.

   _____

6. He's going to the conference. She's not going to the conference.

   _____

7. Ana doesn't eat meat. I don't eat meat.

   _____

8. Soo-jin has studied chemistry. Won-joon has studied chemistry.

   _____

B5) Completing Sentences

Work in small groups. Complete these statements about yourself and the other members of your group. Use additions with *and . . . too, and . . . either,* or *but.*

1. I have a <u> sister </u>, and <u> Reiko does too </u>.

2. I'm wearing _____, and _____.

3. I never eat _____, and _____.

4. Five years ago I was _____, but _____.

5. I'm going to _____ this weekend, and _____.

6. I haven't _____ yet, and _____.

C Additions with *And So* and *And Neither*

Examining Form

Read the sentences and complete the tasks below. Then discuss your answers and read the Form charts to check them.

1a. Humans are intelligent, and so are apes.
1b. Humans are intelligent, and apes are too.

2a. Humans aren't always happy, and neither are apes.
2b. Humans aren't always happy, and apes aren't either.

1. Compare 1a and 1b. Underline the subject and circle the verb in each addition. How is the word order different in these additions?

2. Compare 2a and 2b. Underline the subject and circle the verb in each addition. How is the word order different?

3. Does *and so* connect two affirmative or two negative sentences? Does *and neither* connect two affirmative or two negative sentences?

	And So			
AFFIRMATIVE			AFFIRMATIVE	
SUBJECT	**VERB PHRASE**	*AND SO*	*BE, HAVE,* **MODAL**, or *DO*	**SUBJECT**
Bob	**is** angry,		**is**	Amy.
He	**was** running,		**were**	they.
We	**have** eaten,	and so	**has**	he.
I	**could** go,		**could**	you.
You	**like** sports,		**does**	he.
We	**sang** well,		**did**	they.

(Continued on page 248)

And Neither					
— NEGATIVE —			— NEGATIVE —		
SUBJECT	**VERB PHRASE + NOT**	**AND NEITHER**	**BE, HAVE, MODAL, or DO**	**SUBJECT**	
Bob	**isn't** angry,		**is**	Amy.	
He	**wasn't** running,		**were**	they.	
We	**haven't** eaten,		**has**	he.	
I	**couldn't** go,	**and neither**	**could**	you.	
You	**don't** like sports,		**does**	he.	
We	**didn't** sing well,		**did**	they.	

- The conjunctions *and so* and *and neither* are used to combine two sentences with similar verb phrases but different subjects. They form additions with *be, have,* a modal, or *do,* but the additions have a different word order than additions with *and . . . too* and *and . . . either.*
- Use *and so* to combine two affirmative sentences. Notice the word order after *and so. Be, have,* a modal, or *do* comes before the subject.
- Use *and neither* to combine two negative sentences. Since *neither* has a negative meaning, the verb form that follows it is affirmative. Notice the word order after *neither. Be, have,* a modal, or *do* comes before the subject.

⚠ Do not use *not* in additions with *neither. Neither* expresses the negative meaning.

C1 **Listening for Form**

🎧 Listen to these sentences. Write the additions with *and so* or *and neither.*

1. Los Angeles is a big city, _and so is Chicago._

2. He didn't need a hotel room, _____

3. February doesn't have 31 days, _____

4. Teresa should go home, _____

5. Carol can't ski, _____

6. They've left, _____

C2 Combining Sentences

Combine each pair of sentences. Use *and so* and *and neither*.

1. I'm going away to college next year. My friend Paul is going away to college next year.

   I'm going away to college next year, and so is my friend Paul.

2. Science isn't an easy subject for me. Math isn't an easy subject for me.

   _____

3. Children will enjoy that movie. Adults will enjoy that movie.

   _____

4. My sisters don't live at home anymore. My brother doesn't live at home anymore.

   _____

5. The stores here close early. The restaurants here close early.

   _____

6. We didn't know the answer. The teacher didn't know the answer.

   _____

C3 Completing Sentences

A. Work with a partner and complete these sentences. For sentences 1–4, use *and so* or *and neither* in the addition. For sentences 5–8, use an appropriate first clause.

1. I don't have a pet, _and neither does my neighbor_____.

2. Spaghetti is an Italian food, _____.

3. People deserve to be happy, _____.

4. Coffee isn't good for you, _____.

5. _____, and so does my best friend.

6. _____, and neither did my parents.

7. _____, and neither have I.

8. _____, and so should I.

B. In your notebook, write the first clause of two more sentences. Then exchange notebooks with your partner and complete each other's sentences.

D Expressing Similarities and Differences

Examining Meaning and Use

Read the sentences and answer the questions below. Then discuss your answers
and read the Meaning and Use Notes to check them.

  a. Carl lives in Florida, and Lee does too.
  b. Carl doesn't live in Florida, and Lee doesn't either.
  c. Carl lives in Florida, and so does Lee.
  d. Carl doesn't live in Florida and neither does Lee.

Which sentences have the same meaning? Does each sentence express a similarity between
the two subjects or a difference?

Meaning and Use Notes

Expressing Similarities

1A Use additions with *and . . . too, and . . . either, and so,* and *and neither* to show that
the information about the subject of the addition is the same as the information
about the subject of the first clause.

> We live in Seattle, **and** they do **too**.   I don't like pizza, **and** she doesn't **either**.
> Lisa has a pet, **and so** does Susan.   He didn't get sick, **and neither** did she.

1B *And . . . too* and *and so* have the same meaning. *And . . . either* and *and neither*
have the same meaning.

> I have a car, **and she does too.** = I have a car, **and so does she.**
> He didn't come, **and she didn't either.** = He didn't come, **and neither did she.**

1C *Too, so, not either,* and *neither* can be used in conversation to form a response that
shows agreement with the speaker. (Such responses are also called rejoinders.)
And is usually omitted. Use *too* or *so* to agree with an affirmative statement. Use
not either or *neither* to agree with a negative statement.

> *Agreeing with an Affirmative Statement*   *Agreeing with a Negative Statement*
> A: I thought the test was really hard.   A: I couldn't do the math homework.
> B: **I did too. / So did I.**   B: **I couldn't either. / Neither could I.**

Expressing Differences

> **2** Use additions with *but* to show that the information about the subject of the addition is different from the information about the subject of the first clause.
>
> I can ice skate, **but** she can't.
>
> Their class has a computer, **but** our class doesn't.

D1 Listening for Meaning and Use

▶ Notes 1A, 1B, 2

 Listen to each sentence. Do the two clauses contain the same information about the subjects or different information? Check (✓) the correct column.

	SAME INFORMATION	DIFFERENT INFORMATION
1.		✓
2.		
3.		
4.		
5.		
6.		

D2 Expressing Similarities and Differences

▶ Note 1C

A. Complete these statements about yourself.

1. I don't like *cooking*_____.

2. I really like _____.

3. I often _____ with my friends.

4. I don't usually _____ on the weekend.

5. When I was a child, I used to _____.

6. When I was a child, I never _____.

B. Work with a partner. Take turns making the statements in part A and giving short responses to express your similarities and differences.

A: I don't like cooking.
B: Really? I do. OR *Neither do I.*

Informally Speaking

Pronouns in Short Responses

🎧 Look at the cartoon and listen to the conversation. How are the underlined forms in the cartoon different from what you hear?

> I want to try bungee jumping.

> I do too!

> I'm not sure about this.

> Neither am I!

In informal speech, we often use object pronouns *(me, him, her, us, them)* instead of subject pronouns *(I, he, she, we, they)* in responses with *too*. Informal responses with *either* and *neither* can only begin with *me*.

STANDARD FORM	WHAT YOU MIGHT HEAR
I am too. / I do too.	"Me too."
She is too. / She does too.	"Her too."
He is too. / He does too.	"Him too."
We are too. / We do too.	"Us too."
They are too. / They do too.	"Them too."
I'm not either. / I don't either.	"Me either."
Neither am I. / Neither do I.	"Me neither."

D3 Understanding Informal Speech

🎧 Listen and choose the standard form of the responses you hear.

1. **(a.)** I didn't either.
   b. I did too.

2. **a.** We are too.
   b. We do too.

3. **a.** So do I.
   b. Neither do I.

4. **a.** We are too.
   b. So do we.

5. **a.** They are too.
   b. They aren't either.

6. **a.** Neither can I.
   b. So can I.

7. **a.** She did too.
   b. She didn't either.

8. **a.** I am too.
   b. Neither am I.

9. **a.** She does too.
   b. She is too.

A. Work with a partner. Take turns choosing categories. Your partner will read a statement to you. Add to the statement, using the noun in parentheses. Use additions with *and . . . too, and so, and . . . either, and neither,* or *but.*

A: *Geography.*
B: *Egypt has a canal.*
A: *Egypt has a canal, and Panama does too.*
   OR
   Egypt has a canal, and so does Panama.

Geography

1. Egypt has a canal. (Panama)

2. Turkey isn't in Europe. (France)

3. Guam is an island. (Puerto Rico)

4. Austria isn't near the sea. (Switzerland)

Food

1. Prunes are dried fruit. (raisins)

2. Strawberries are red. (bananas)

3. Fish isn't fattening. (ice cream)

4. Potatoes don't have seeds. (carrots)

Animals

1. Chickens don't swim. (turkeys)

2. Dogs can't communicate with sign language. (apes)

3. Snails have shells. (turtles)

4. Elephants live in Africa. (lions)

B. Work alone. Write two more statements for each category. Then work with your partner. Take turns reading your statements and making additions using *and . . . too, and so, and . . . either, and neither,* or *but.*

A: *Canada has glaciers.*
B: *Canada has glaciers, and so does Iceland.*

Work in small groups. Look at the college scholarship applications. Imagine that your group will give a scholarship to one of the two students. Make sentences comparing and contrasting the students. Use additions with *and . . . too, and so, and . . . either, and neither,* or *but.* Then make your decision.

Jenny Chang has good grades, and Pedro Gonzalez does too.
Jenny Chang did volunteer work, but Pedro Gonzalez didn't.

College Scholarship Application Form	*College Scholarship Application Form*

Name: Jenny Chang

Major: Don't know yet

High School Grades (Average):		
English: A	Math: B	Spanish: A
History: A	Science: B	

SCHOOL ACTIVITIES

Was student a member of clubs?
  Yes; Spanish Club, sophomore, junior, and senior years

Did student participate in sports?
  No

Did student participate in student government?
  Yes; president of senior class

Did student work on school newspaper?
  No

Did student receive awards?
  Yes; Most Outstanding English Student

ACTIVITIES OUTSIDE SCHOOL

Did student do volunteer work?
  Yes; volunteer language tutor (Spanish, Cantonese) at community center

Did student work?
  Yes; worked in a camp for children during the summer (3 years)

Name: Pedro Gonzalez

Major: Biology, interested in medical research

High School Grades (Average):		
English: A	Math: A	German: B
History: B	Science: A	

SCHOOL ACTIVITIES

Was student a member of clubs?
  Yes; Science Club, junior and senior years

Did student participate in sports?
  No

Did student participate in student government?
  No

Did student work on school newspaper?
  No

Did student receive awards?
  Yes; first prize in school science fair senior year

ACTIVITIES OUTSIDE SCHOOL

Did student do volunteer work?
  No

Did student work?
  Yes; worked at a science laboratory (1 year)

Beyond the Sentence

Combining Ideas

When you compare people or things, it is important to combine your ideas by using additions with *and . . . too, and . . . either, and so, and neither,* and *but*. If you do not combine ideas, your writing will be very repetitive. Compare these two paragraphs. Notice how combining ideas makes the second paragraph sound less repetitive.

Repetitive

> My best friend and I have many similarities. I have a sister. Carol has a sister. I like vanilla ice cream. Carol likes vanilla ice cream. I'm not good at math. Carol isn't good at math. There is one big difference. Carol lives in the United States. I don't live in the United States. I live in Costa Rica.

Not Repetitive

> My best friend and I have many similarities. I have a sister, **and so does** Carol. I like vanilla ice cream, **and** Carol does, **too**. I'm not good at math, **and neither** is Carol. There is one big difference. Carol lives in the United States, **but** I don't. I live in Costa Rica.

D6 Avoiding Repetition

Read this paragraph. Underline the parts that are repetitive. Then rewrite the paragraph combining sentences where possible.

The United States and the United Kingdom have many similarities and differences. One of the similarities is language. <u>People in the United States speak English. People in the United Kingdom speak English.</u> Some people say that Americans don't speak very clearly. Some people say that the British speak very clearly. American and British food is also similar in some ways. Americans like to eat meat and potatoes. The British like to eat meat and potatoes. The two countries also have similar holidays. Christmas is a very important holiday in both countries. Most Americans don't work on Christmas. Most British people don't work on Christmas. One big difference is the political system. The United Kingdom has a queen. The United States doesn't have a king or a queen. In the United States voters elect a president. In the United Kingdom voters don't elect a president. They elect a prime minister.

E Combining Form, Meaning, and Use

E1 Thinking About Meaning and Use

Choose the best answer to complete each conversation. Then discuss your answers in small groups.

1. **A:** You have to take the test, but I don't.

   B: _____

   (a.) That's not fair.

   b. Good. Let's study together.

2. **A:** She's never late.

   B: _____

   a. So am I.

   b. Neither am I.

3. **A:** I'm going to get a new computer next month.

   B: _____

   a. So am I.

   b. Neither am I.

4. **A:** We have to leave before noon.

   B: _____

   a. I do too.

   b. I don't either.

5. **A:** She'll be able to speak English very well next year.

   B: _____ I practice all the time.

   a. Me neither.

   b. So will I.

6. **A:** They seldom get to class on time.

   B: Well, _____
   - **a.** you don't either.
   - **b.** you do too.

7. **A:** I haven't seen him in years.

   B: _____ I wonder what he's doing these days.
   - **a.** I have too.
   - **b.** I haven't either.

8. **A:** I usually go to bed before twelve.

   B: _____
   - **a.** Me too.
   - **b.** Me neither.

E2 **Editing**

Some of these sentences have errors. Find the errors and correct them.

1. I want to go to Hawaii, and so ~~he does.~~ _does he_

2. They don't have enough money, but we do too.

3. The books cost a lot of money, and the paper was too.

4. She hasn't finished cleaning her room, and I have either.

5. Susan is angry, but I'm not.

6. We are going to go by plane, and so they are.

7. He is doing well in class, but she is.

8. The coffee was hot, and so was the tea.

9. He never gets a raise, and I do too.

10. Megan doesn't wear makeup, and neither doesn't Donna.

▶ Beyond the Classroom

Searching for Authentic Examples

Find examples of English grammar in everyday life. Listen to a conversation between two or three people in an English-language film or on a television program. Listen for examples of statements followed by short responses such as *I do too, Me too, Me either,* and *Neither do I.* Write down each statement and response. Bring your examples to class and discuss them with your classmates.

Writing

Follow these steps to write a letter to the editor about the writer's views in the letter on page 240.

1. Think about the topic. Divide a piece of paper into two columns. In one column, make notes about the writer's opinions. In the second column, make notes about your opinions.

2. Write a first draft. Use *and . . . too, and so, and . . . either, and neither,* and *but* to compare and contrast your ideas with the writer's ideas.

3. Read your work carefully and circle grammar, spelling, and punctuation errors. Work with a partner to help you decide how to fix your errors and improve the content.

    Dear Editor,

    I am responding to Charles Walker's letter in yesterday's newspaper. Mr. Walker thinks animals should have the right to live in peace, and so do I. We agree about this. However, Mr. Walker doesn't think apes are very different from humans, but I do. . . .

Nouns, Quantity Expressions, and Articles

Nouns and Quantity Expressions

A Mood Foods

A1 Before You Read

Discuss these questions.

What is your favorite food? Why do you like it? How do you feel after you eat it? Are there any foods that make you feel sleepy? Are there any foods that give you energy or help you stay awake?

A2 Read

Read the magazine article on the following page to find out how certain foods can affect the way you feel.

A3 After You Read

Answer these questions according to the information in the magazine article. Use the choices below.

cayenne pepper	cheese	eggs	honey
chamomile tea	coffee	gingko biloba	mint

1. Which two give you long-lasting energy? ___*cheese, eggs*___

2. Which two calm your nerves? _____

3. Which one helps you stay awake but doesn't make you nervous? _____

4. Which one helps you wake up, but also makes you nervous? _____

5. Which one may help you concentrate? _____

6. Which one helps the body absorb calcium? _____

MOOD FOODS

We all know that the food we eat can affect the way we look physically. But did you know that food can also have an impact on the way you feel?

The Situation	The Food	The Result
1. You have little energy in the morning.	Don't eat pancakes or toast. Have some cheese or an egg instead.	Eggs and cheese have a great deal of protein, which builds muscles and gives you long-lasting energy to start your day. Pancakes are high in carbohydrates, which can give you a lot of energy, but only for a short time.
2. You are preparing for an important meeting or for a final exam. You have to stay up late.	Don't have a cup of coffee. Mix one teaspoon of cayenne pepper with a quart of tomato juice. Then drink it.	The caffeine in coffee will keep you awake, but it will also make you nervous. Cayenne pepper gives you energy, but won't make you nervous. The tomato juice just covers up its hot taste.
3. You have looked at a report for three hours, and you can't concentrate anymore.	Take some ginkgo biloba, eat a few prunes, or drink a cup of ginger tea.	Many nutrition experts say that prunes, gingko biloba, and ginger may improve memory and concentration.
4. It's exam time, and you're really nervous.	Drink chamomile or peppermint tea. If you don't like tea, have a few pieces of mint candy.	Both chamomile and mint calm your nerves. (Some people also say that mint helps your digestion.)
5. You can't sleep, and your interview is only hours away.	Drink a cup of warm milk mixed with one teaspoon of honey.	Milk contains calcium and tryptophan, both of which have a calming effect. Honey may help the body absorb calcium.

Adapted from *Seventeen* magazine

---

absorb: to take something in (e.g., a sponge absorbs water)

concentrate: to focus your thoughts on something

digestion: the body's ability to break down food

gingko biloba: an herbal preparation that comes from the leaves of the gingko tree

impact: effect, influence

nutrition: food science

Nouns and Quantity Expressions

Examining Form

Read the sentences and complete the tasks below. Then discuss your answers and read the Form charts to check them.

> **1a.** There is <u>milk</u> in this drink.
> **1b.** There is a lot of <u>milk</u> in this drink.
>
> **2a.** There is one <u>calorie</u> in this drink.
> **2b.** There are a lot of <u>calories</u> in this drink.

1. Look at the underlined nouns. Which are count nouns? Which is a noncount noun?

2. Look back at the magazine article on page 263. Find the nouns below and write the quantity expressions that are used with them. (Some appear more than once.)

_____ energy   _____ prunes   _____ protein   _____ people

--- COUNT AND NONCOUNT NOUNS ---

Count Nouns			
A, AN, THE, NUMBER, or Ø	**COUNT NOUN**	**VERB**	
An The One	**egg**	has	70 calories.
The Four	**eggs**	have	280 calories.
Ø	**Eggs**	have	a lot of protein.

Noncount Nouns			
THE or Ø	**NONCOUNT NOUN**	**VERB**	
The	**juice**	is	in the refrigerator.
Ø	**Juice**		sweet.

Count Nouns

- Count nouns can be counted. They have both singular and plural forms.

  one **egg**   four **eggs**

- *A, an, the,* a number *(one, two, . . .),* or Ø (no article) can come before count nouns.

- The plural of a count noun is usually formed by adding *-s* or *-es* to the singular form. See Appendix 1 for the spelling of nouns ending in *-s* or *-es.*

- Some count nouns have irregular plural forms. See Appendix 8 for a list of common irregular plural nouns.

Noncount Nouns

- Noncount nouns cannot be counted. They do not have plural forms.

- *The* or Ø (no article) can come before noncount nouns. *A, an,* or a number cannot come before them.

GENERAL QUANTITY EXPRESSIONS

Plural Count Nouns

	QUANTITY EXPRESSION	COUNT NOUN	
There are	**many several a few few**	**apples**	in the bag.
There aren't	**many**	**eggs**	in the basket.

Noncount Nouns

	QUANTITY EXPRESSION	NONCOUNT NOUN	
We have	**a great deal of a little little**	**food.**	
We don't have	**much**	**milk.**	

Plural Count Nouns or Noncount Nouns

	QUANTITY EXPRESSION	COUNT NOUN	
There are	**a lot of some no**	**apples**	on the tree.
There aren't	**any**	**grapes**	in the bowl.

	QUANTITY EXPRESSION	NONCOUNT NOUN	
There is	**a lot of some no**	**food**	in the bag.
There isn't	**any**	**milk**	in the cup.

Questions with *How Many* and *How Much*

HOW MANY	COUNT NOUN	
How many	**sandwiches**	should I buy?

HOW MUCH	NONCOUNT NOUN	
How much	**sugar**	do you want?

(Continued on page 266)

General Quantity Expressions with Count Nouns

- Use *many*, *several*, *a few*, and *few* before count nouns.

General Quantity Expressions with Noncount Nouns

- Use *a great deal of*, *much*, *a little*, and *little* only before noncount nouns.
- *Much* is not usually used in affirmative statements. Use *a lot of* instead.
    This recipe has **a lot of sugar** in it.
    * This recipe has much sugar in it. (INCORRECT)

General Quantity Expressions with Count or Noncount Nouns

- *A lot of*, *lots of*, *plenty of*, *some*, *any*, and *no* can be used before both plural count nouns and noncount nouns.
- Use *any* before plural count nouns or noncount nouns in negative statements and questions.

Questions with *How Many* and *How Much*

- Use *how many* with plural count nouns to ask about quantity.
- Use *how much* with noncount nouns to ask about quantity.

SPECIFIC QUANTITY EXPRESSIONS

Plural Count Nouns or Noncount Nouns			
	QUANTITY EXPRESSION	COUNT NOUN	
There is	**a carton of**	eggs	in the refrigerator.
There are	**two cartons of**		

	QUANTITY EXPRESSION	NONCOUNT NOUN	
There is	**a cup of**	sugar	in the recipe.
There are	**three teaspoons of**		

- Many specific quantity expressions end in *of*. They can go before plural count nouns and noncount nouns.

A. Listen to each sentence. Are the nouns you hear count or noncount? Check (✓) the correct column.

	COUNT	NONCOUNT
1.		✓
2.		
3.		
4.		
5.		
6.		
7.		
8.		

B. Complete these conversations with the quantity expressions you hear.

Conversation 1

A: Do you have any news about those jobs you applied for?

B: Yes. I've had ___several___ interviews. I'm sure I'll get an offer, but I need
        1

_____ information about the companies before I decide.
    2

Conversation 2

A: Were there _____ people in the park?
                      1
B: There were _____ children! I forgot that summer vacation started last week.
                     2

Conversation 3

A: Would you like _____ milk with your sandwich?
                        1
B: No, thanks. I'd rather have _____ coffee.
                                    2

Conversation 4

A: _____ food should I buy?
         1
B: There are _____ people coming. You should buy _____ food.
                   2   3

Choose the correct general quantity expression to complete each sentence.

1. Desserts usually have _____ sugar.

   a. lots of   **b.** many

2. _____ salt often makes food taste better.

   a. A few   **b.** A little

3. Does ice cream have _____ calories?

   a. many   **b.** much

4. On hot days you should drink _____ water.

   a. plenty of   **b.** many

5. One reason junk food isn't good for you is that it has _____ vitamins.

   a. little   **b.** few

6. John ate _____ pancakes for breakfast.

   a. a great deal of   **b.** a lot of

B3 **Asking Questions with *How Many . . . ?* and *How Much . . . ?***

Work with a partner. Use *How many* and *How much* to ask questions about the list of ingredients in this recipe for chocolate cake.

How many cups of sugar are in the recipe? OR *How much sugar is in the recipe?*

Chocolate Cake

Ingredients

1½ cups of sugar
5 eggs
1½ teaspoons of vanilla extract
1 teaspoon of almond extract
2 cups of sour cream
1½ teaspoons of baking powder
¼ teaspoon of salt
4 tablespoons of powdered cocoa
2 cups of chocolate chips
¾ cup of milk
1 stick (8 tablespoons) of butter
¾ cup of flour

Informally Speaking

Reducing *Of* in Informal Speech

🎧 Look at the cartoon and listen to the conversation. How are the underlined forms in the cartoon different from what you hear?

Well, Liz, we have <u>a lot of</u> gas and <u>plenty of</u> time.

Good thing we also have <u>a lot of</u> friends.

The word *of* in quantity expressions is often reduced in informal speech.

STANDARD FORM	WHAT YOU MIGHT HEAR
You need **plenty of** time.	"You need /ˈplɛniə/ time."
There are **a lot of** cars here.	"There are /əˈlɑt̬ə/ cars here."
He has **lots of** money.	"He has /ˈlɑtsə/ money."

B4 Understanding Informal Speech

🎧 Listen and write the standard form of the words you hear.

1. _____Lots of_____ people enjoy playing golf.

2. _____ my friends are coming over tonight.

3. If you're going to Las Vegas, take _____ money.

4. This dishwasher uses a great _____ hot water.

5. Are you hungry? There's _____ food left over from the party.

6. There are _____ lakes in Minnesota.

7. He took _____ classes last year.

8. We won't be late. We have _____ time.

Form • Nouns and Quantity Expressions   269

General Quantity Expressions

Examining Meaning and Use

Read the sentences and complete the tasks below. Then discuss your answers and read the Meaning and Use Notes to check them.

1a. Ben has many friends.
1b. Eva has few friends.
1c. Josh has lots of friends.
1d. Tony has a lot of friends.

2a. There's little time left. I don't think we can get there by 8:30.
2b. There's a little time left. We can get there by 8:30 easily.

1. Look at 1a–1d. Underline the quantity expressions. Who has a large number of friends? Who has a small number of friends?

2. Look at 2a and 2b. Underline the quantity expressions. In which sentence is there not enough time?

Meaning and Use Notes

> ### Expressing Large and Small Amounts
>
> **1** General quantity expressions are used to refer to larger and smaller amounts. They don't refer to exact amounts. *Many, much, a lot of, lots of, plenty of,* and *a great deal of* all have the same meaning, but *lots of* and *plenty of* are more informal and are more commonly used in spoken English.
>
> | | | |
> |---|---|---|
> | *Larger Amount* ↑ | • many, much, a lot of, lots of, plenty of, a great deal of | There are **many** calories in potato chips.
Milk has **lots of** calcium. |
> | | • some/several | There is **some** juice in the refrigerator. |
> | | • a few/a little | There are **a few** people here. |
> | *Smaller Amount* ↓ | • few/little | We have **little** money, so we rarely go on vacation. |

Many vs. Much

2A Use *many* in affirmative and negative statements and questions. Use *much* in negative statements and questions.

Many	Much
I have **many** friends.	—
I do**n't** have **many** friends.	We do**n't** get **much** rain here.
Do you have **many** friends?	Do you get **much** rain here?

2B *Much* is not usually used alone in affirmative statements. Use *a lot of* instead.

We get **a lot of** rain here.

A Few/A Little vs. Few/Little

3A Use *a few/a little* or *few/little* to talk about smaller amounts. However, notice the difference in meaning:

Few *vs.* A Few

We have **few** sandwiches left. We'll have to make more.
(We have a small number of sandwiches, but not enough.)

We have **a few** sandwiches left. Would you like one?
(We have a small number of sandwiches, but it's enough.)

Little *vs.* A Little

I can't pay my rent this month. I have **little** money in the bank.
(I have a small amount of money, and it isn't enough.)

I can pay my rent this month. I have **a little** money in the bank.
(I have a small amount of money, but it's enough.)

3B *Not . . . many* and *not . . . much* are more common in speech than *few* and *little*.

We do**n't** have **many** sandwiches left. We'll have to make more.

I can't pay my rent this month. I do**n't** have **much** money in the bank.

Expressing None

4 Use *no* or *not any* to express *none*. *No* is used in affirmative statements, but it has a negative meaning. *Not any* is used to form a negative statement. *Not* usually contracts with the verb.

{ There is **no** sugar / There is**n't any** sugar } in this dessert.   { There are **no** eggs / There are**n't any** eggs } in this recipe.

(Continued on page 272)

5A You can use *so* and *too* before *many* and *much* to emphasize a larger amount. *Too* usually has a negative meaning.

Plural Count Nouns with Many

There are **so many** choices on this menu. Isn't it wonderful?

There are **too many** choices on this menu. I can't decide what to eat.

Noncount Nouns with Much

She's made **so much** money this year. She's very happy about it.

She's made **too much** money this year. She'll have to pay a lot in taxes.

5B Use *only* before *a few* or *a little* to emphasize an even smaller amount. Use *quite* with *a few* (but not with *a little*) to emphasize a larger amount.

Plural Count Nouns with A Few

Only a few houses are available. (There are a small number of houses.)

Quite a few houses are available. (There are a large number of houses.)

Noncount Nouns with A Little

A: Would you like some milk in your coffee?

B: **Only a little**, please.

C1 **Listening for Meaning and Use** ▶ Notes 1–5

 Listen to this conversation. Listen carefully for the nouns in the chart. Is the speaker talking about a large quantity of each noun, a small quantity, or none at all? Check (✓) the correct column.

		LARGE QUANTITY	SMALL QUANTITY	NONE
1.	work	✓		
2.	milk			
3.	cars			
4.	homework			
5.	food			
6.	books			
7.	caffeine			
8.	tests			
9.	money			
10.	friends			

Choose the best answer to complete each conversation.

1. A: I have a little money.

   B: _____
   a. So do I. Let's go out to dinner.
   b. Then we'd better not go out to dinner. Let's have spaghetti at home.

2. A: Can you help me with my homework?

   B: Sorry. I _____ time right now.
   a. have much
   b. don't have much

3. A: The kids do a lot of housework these days.

   B: _____
   a. That's great! They're finally old enough to help you.
   b. That's not good. You should ask them to help you more.

4. A: So far we have no information.

   B: _____
   a. I don't, either.
   b. I do, too.

5. A: There are too many people here.

   B: _____
   a. I agree. Why don't we leave?
   b. I know. It's wonderful, isn't it?

6. A: Can we still get tickets to the concert?

   B: I'm not sure. There are _____ a few tickets left.
   a. only
   b. quite

C3 Talking About Small Quantities

► Note 3

Work with a partner. Consider the meaning of each sentence and complete it with *a few, few, a little,* or *little.*

1. The students thought the exam was very difficult. They complained that

   _____few_____ people got high grades.

2. Amy has to visit a friend in the hospital. She can probably go on Monday

   because she has _____ time in the afternoon.

3. Not everyone was able to sit down because there were _____

   chairs.

4. Pedro is trying to teach Gina to play guitar. Gina doesn't practice, so she's

   making _____ progress. She needs to practice a lot more.

5. Luckily, the school library has _____ books on the history of

   India, so I'll be able to finish my history project tonight.

6. Koji's new computer isn't working correctly. He calls the store and says, "I'm

   having _____ trouble with my new computer."

C4 Using Quantity Expressions

► Notes 1–3, 5

Rick's office had a party. One hundred people attended the party. Rick ordered the food, but he made some mistakes. Make sentences about the amounts of food that Rick ordered. Use quantity expressions in affirmative and negative sentences.

150 hot dogs, 30 hot dogs buns   1 apple pie, 10 chocolate cakes

50 hamburgers, 100 hamburger buns   1 gallon of lemonade, 3 bottles of soda

5 bags of potato chips   10 gallons of coffee, 1 gallon of iced tea

2 bowls of salad   50 cups, 100 plates, 25 napkins

He bought plenty of hot dogs, but he didn't buy many hot dog buns.

A. Work with a partner. Look at the charts. Take turns asking and answering questions about the two cereals. Use quantity expressions.

A: Does Healthy Grains have much fiber?
B: Yes, it has plenty of fiber. What about Chocolate Puffies?
*   How much fiber does it have?*
A: It has only a little.

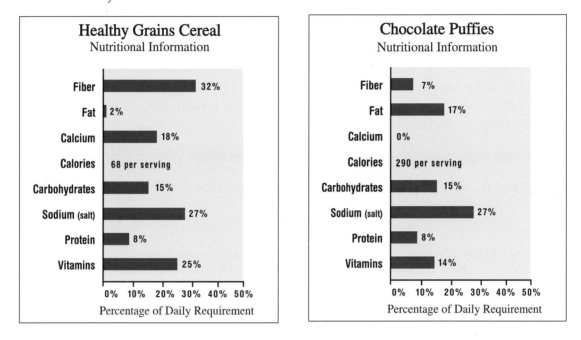

B. Look at the nutritional information on the package of a food that you eat often. Write four sentences about the nutritional value of this food.

Spaghetti has a lot of carbohydrates. It has very little fat and . . .

Specific Quantity Expressions

Examining Meaning and Use

Read these instructions for making pancakes and answer the questions below.
Then discuss your answers and read the Meaning and Use Notes to check them.

Mix a lot of flour with a little baking powder. Beat some eggs with some milk.
Mix the eggs and milk with the flour and baking soda. Put a lot of blueberries in the
mix. Add a little vanilla. Melt some butter in a frying pan. Pour in some of the
batter. After a while, turn the pancake over. When it is brown, remove it from the
pan and serve immediately.

1. Can you make pancakes by following these instructions? Why or why not?

2. Can you think of any specific quantity expressions that should be in the
   instructions above?

Meaning and Use Notes

Expressing Specific Amounts

1A General quantity expressions indicate only whether quantities are large or small.
Specific quantity expressions give exact amounts.

General Quantity Expression	*Specific Quantity Expression*
I ate **too much** pizza.	I ate **six slices of** pizza.
He bought **a lot of** potato chips.	He bought **ten bags of** potato chips.

1B Specific quantity expressions can be used with plural count nouns or noncount
nouns.

Plural Count Nouns	*Noncount Nouns*
a box of matches	**a box of** cereal
a cup of raisins	**a cup of** sugar

1C Specific quantity expressions make noncount nouns countable.

one bowl of milk	**six ounces of** beef
two cans of soup	**four gallons of** gas

1D The expression *a piece of* can be used with a number of noncount nouns to express a specific amount.

a piece of
{
cake
bread
furniture
clothing
advice
news
}

1E There are many different types of specific quantity expressions. Some include:

Containers
a carton of eggs/milk
a jar of mayonnaise
a bag of potato chips
a can of soda/tuna fish
a box of cereal/candy

Portions
a slice of bread
a piece of candy/cake
a bowl of soup
a glass of milk
a cup of coffee

Groups
a bunch of bananas
a dozen eggs
a herd of cattle
a flock of birds
a school of fish

Measurements
a quart/gallon of juice
an inch/foot/yard of cloth
a cup/teaspoon/tablespoon of salt
an ounce/pound of butter

Shapes
a grain of rice/sand
a pile/stack of leaves
a drop of water
a stick of butter

D1 **Listening for Meaning and Use** ► Notes 1A–1E

🎧 Listen to this description. Listen carefully for each food in the chart. Does the speaker mention a specific or general amount? Check (✓) the correct column.

		SPECIFIC	GENERAL
1.	tomatoes	✓	
2.	ground beef		
3.	salt		
4.	onions		
5.	cream		
6.	spaghetti		
7.	water		
8.	bread		

Work with a partner. Each item has one specific quantity expression that is incorrect. Cross it out.

1. a piece of cloth

   ~~a pound of cloth~~

   a yard of cloth

2. a drop of milk

   a pound of milk

   a quart of milk

3. a piece of bread

   a slice of bread

   a tablespoon of bread

4. a grain of rice

   a bunch of rice

   a cup of rice

5. an ounce of fish

   a pound of fish

   a gallon of fish

6. a slice of cereal

   a cup of cereal

   a box of cereal

7. a bag of peanut butter

   a jar of peanut butter

   a teaspoon of peanut butter

8. a can of food

   a bowl of food

   a yard of food

9. a bunch of bananas

   a pound of bananas

   a quart of bananas

10. a drop of papers

    a pile of papers

    a box of papers

Work with a partner. Look at the shopping list and take turns asking and telling your partner about how much of each item you're going to buy. Use specific quantity words and expressions.

A: How much juice are you going to buy?
B: I think I'll get three quarts of juice.

juice
milk
peanut butter
bananas
eggs
cookies
candy
pizza

Combining Form, Meaning, and Use

E1 Thinking About Meaning and Use

Choose the best answer to complete each conversation. Then discuss your answers in small groups.

1. **A:** We have plenty of food.

   B: _____
   - **a.** OK. I'll get some more.
   - **(b.)** OK. I won't bring any.

2. **A:** I have little free time.

   B: _____
   - **a.** Oh. Then you can't help me.
   - **b.** Good. Then you can help me.

3. **A:** My car gives me little trouble.

   B: _____
   - **a.** Why don't you get it fixed?
   - **b.** You're lucky.

4. **A:** Is a gallon enough for ten people?

   B: _____
   - **a.** No. Buy more meat.
   - **b.** No. Buy more soda.

5. **A:** We don't have any milk.

   B: _____
   - **a.** Good. I need a cup for this recipe.
   - **b.** I'll go buy some.

6. **A:** It snowed here last night.

   B: _____
   - **a.** How many inches did you get?
   - **b.** How many quarts did you get?

E2 Editing

Some of these sentences have errors. Find the errors and correct them.

1. There is several fruit in the basket.
   are several pieces of fruit

2. We bought many food.

3. There isn't much salt in the soup.

4. There isn't much traffic at night.

5. I have little money, so I guess we can go out to dinner tonight.

6. I bought a grain of eggs.

7. How many does a pound of beef cost?

8. We had foot of snow last night.

9. Could I have a piece of cake?

10. She'll graduate soon. She only has a little more courses to take.

▶ Beyond the Classroom

Searching for Authentic Examples

Find examples of English grammar in everyday life. Look for an article on healthy foods in an English-language magazine or newspaper, or on the Internet. Find five specific and five general quantity expressions with nouns. Write them down and bring them to class. What other quantity expressions could be used with these nouns? Discuss your answers with your classmates.

Writing

You write a food column for a magazine called *Health Nut*. You have just received this letter.

> Dear Health Nut,
>
> I am a teenager. My favorite foods are pizza and hamburgers. I also like potato chips, candy, and soda. My parents say that these foods are not good for me, but I feel fine. What do you think? Are these foods good or bad? What should I eat?
>
> Yours truly,
>
> Junk Food Jan

Follow the steps below to write a reply to the letter.

1. Think about the topic. Make notes about what you want to say.

2. Write a first draft. Use count and noncount nouns with quantity expressions where possible.

3. Read your work carefully and circle grammar, spelling, and punctuation errors. Work with a partner to help you decide how to fix your errors and improve the content.

4. Rewrite your draft.

   Dear Junk Food Jan,
       Your parents are right. It is not good to eat too much of these kinds of food. . . .

Indefinite and Definite Articles

A Meat-Eating Plants

 Before You Read

Discuss these questions with your classmates.

Do you know about any unusual plants? What makes them unusual? Have you ever heard of a meat-eating plant? What kind of meat do you think it eats?

 Read

Read the book excerpt on the following page to find out how meat-eating plants attract insects and other small animals.

A3 **After You Read**

Write *T* for true or *F* for false for each statement.

__T__ **1.** Venus flytraps are one kind of carnivorous plant.

_____ **2.** Flies can easily escape from a Venus flytrap.

_____ **3.** Carnivorous plants have moving parts.

_____ **4.** There are about 450 kinds of carnivorous plants.

_____ **5.** Carnivorous plants eat large animals.

_____ **6.** Some carnivorous plants smell sweet.

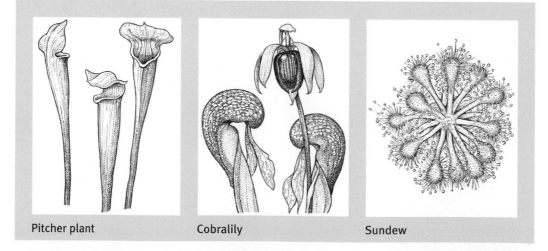

Pitcher plant   Cobralily   Sundew

Meat-Eating Plants

A black fly hovers in the air over a strange-looking plant. Attracted by a sweet smell, the fly lands on one of the plant's flat, red leaves. The 5 fly begins to crawl across the leaf. Suddenly, the leaf moves! Before the fly can get away, the leaf closes around it. Two rows of teeth close together. Escape is impossible. The fly tries to get 10 out, but the trap closes more tightly. Soon the fly is dead. In a few days there is nothing left but the hard parts of its body.

The plant that ate this fly is called a 15 Venus flytrap. It is one of about 450 species, or kinds, of carnivorous plants. A plant that is carnivorous actually eats meat. It traps and eats insects, and in some cases, small animals such as frogs 20 and mice.

How do these unusual plants work? They must attract animals. Unlike a frog or a bird, a carnivorous plant cannot reach out and grab an insect. It must 25 wait until an insect comes to it. Some carnivorous plants give off a sweet smell that attracts insects such as flies, bees, and ants. Other carnivorous plants have bright colors and patterns. And one 30 species has leaves covered with sparkling droplets that attract insects with bright color and light, as well as with a sweet smell.

Venus flytrap

Adapted from *Carnivorous Plants*

crawl: to move slowly with the body close to the ground, like a baby

droplet: a very small drop of liquid

grab: to take hold of something quickly

hover: to stay in the air without moving forward

insect: a small animal such as an ant, fly, or bee

sparkling: shiny and bright from light, like water in sunshine

B Indefinite and Definite Articles

Examining Form

Look back at the book excerpt on page 283 and complete the tasks below. Then discuss your answers and read the Form charts to check them.

1. Complete each sentence from the reading with an article (*a, an,* or *the*).

   a. _____ black <u>fly</u> hovers in _____ <u>air</u> over _____ strange-looking <u>plant.</u>

   b. Suddenly, _____ <u>leaf</u> moves.

   c. In a few days there is nothing left but _____ hard <u>parts</u> of its body.

2. Look at the underlined nouns in the sentences above. Are they count nouns or noncount nouns? In these examples, which article(s) are used with singular count nouns? Which are used with plural count nouns? Which are used with noncount nouns?

Indefinite Article	
A/AN	**SINGULAR COUNT NOUN**
a	flower uniform
an	insect hour

Definite Article	
THE	**SINGULAR COUNT NOUN**
the	flower uniform insect hour

Ø or SOME	**PLURAL COUNT NOUN**
Ø **some**	flowers uniforms insects hours

THE	**PLURAL COUNT NOUN**
the	flowers uniforms insects hours

Ø or SOME	**NONCOUNT NOUN**
Ø **some**	water information money

THE	**NONCOUNT NOUN**
the	water information money

Indefinite Article

- The indefinite article is *a* or *an*. It can be used before a singular count noun (*a book*) or an adjective + a singular count noun (*an interesting book*).
- Use *a* before words that begin with a consonant sound (*a flower, a uniform*). Use *an* before words that begin with a vowel sound (*an insect, an hour*).
- Do not use *a* or *an* before plural count nouns or noncount nouns. We show this with the symbol Ø, which means "no article."
- *Some* often acts like an indefinite article before plural count nouns and noncount nouns.

Definite Article

- The definite article is *the*. It can be used before singular count nouns, plural count nouns, and noncount nouns.
- The definite article can be used before a noun (*the flower*) or an adjective + noun (*the beautiful flower*).
- When *the* comes before a noun that begins with a consonant sound, it is often pronounced /ðə/. When *the* comes before a noun that begins with a vowel sound, it is often pronounced /ði/.

/ðə/	/ði/
the plant	the insect

B1 Listening for Form

 Listen to these sentences. Listen carefully for the nouns in the chart. Which article do you hear before each noun? Check (✓) the correct column.

		A	*AN*	*THE*	Ø (NO ARTICLE)
1.	scientist	✓			
2.	botany				
3.	plants				
4.	hour				
5.	books				
6.	fork				
7.	apple				
8.	children				
9.	pen				
10.	flowers				

Working on the Indefinite Article

Some of these sentences have errors. Find the errors and correct them.

1. I'd like ~~an~~ ^a hot drink.

2. Can you give me a example?

3. I waited an whole hour for you. Where were you?

4. If you're going to London, don't forget a umbrella.

5. We saw a huge old elephant at the zoo.

6. You've met the Senator? What a honor!

7. She's thinking about buying an used car.

8. He isn't a honest man.

9. Can I use a one dollar bill in the soda machine?

10. Cornell is an university in New York state.

B3 **Working on Singular and Plural Forms**

Look at the underlined count nouns in these sentences. Rewrite the sentences in the plural. Change singular nouns to plural nouns, and plural nouns to singular nouns. Change the form of the verb where necessary.

1. A new <u>store</u> is opening here soon. <u>New stores are opening here soon.</u>

2. Celia is taking a <u>class</u> now. _____

3. The <u>sandwich</u> is good. _____

4. We saw some interesting <u>movies</u>. _____

5. We've been here for <u>hours</u>. _____

6. The new <u>people</u> at work are nice. _____

7. Mr. Smith has a <u>cow</u> and some <u>horses</u>. _____

8. The <u>girls</u> need <u>uniforms</u> for school. _____

9. There was an <u>insect</u> in the bathroom. _____

10. Some <u>men</u> were talking to my father. _____

Indefinite and Definite Articles

Examining Meaning and Use

Read the sentences and complete the task below. Then discuss your answers and read the Meaning and Use Notes to check them.

1a. Let's go shopping. I need <u>a lamp</u> for my bedroom.
1b. We'll need to use a flashlight. <u>The lamp</u> in the bedroom is broken.

2a. Excuse me, sir. I'm looking for <u>a bank</u>. Do you know where one is?
2b. Excuse me, sir. Where is <u>the bank</u> in this mall?

Compare the meaning of the underlined articles and nouns in each pair of sentences. In which sentences do the speakers have a specific object or place in mind? In which sentences do the speakers have only a general idea of the object or place they mention?

Meaning and Use Notes

The Indefinite Article for Introducing a Noun

1A Use *a* or *an* to introduce a singular count noun. *There is* or *there are* often begins a sentence or clause that introduces a noun with an indefinite article.

> Woman: Did you see **a little boy** walk by here five minutes ago?
> Police Officer: I'm not sure. What does he look like?
> Woman: He has brown hair, and <u>there's</u> **a big soccer ball** on his sweatshirt.

1B Use *some* or Ø (no article) to introduce plural count nouns or noncount nouns.

> I need **some batteries** for my camera.
> I called for **some information**.
> I need **Ø batteries** for my camera.
> I called for **Ø information**.

1C When a speaker uses an indefinite article, the noun is not a specific thing in the mind of the listener. In the speaker's mind, however, sometimes the noun is specific and sometimes it is not.

> Bob: I bought **a new car.** (Bob has a specific car in mind, but the listener doesn't.)
> Bob: I need **a new car.** (Neither Bob nor the listener have a specific car in mind.)

(Continued on page 288)

The Definite Article for Identifying a Noun

Use *the* to refer to a noun that both you and a listener can identify. This is possible when you and the listener share information about the noun.

2A Use the definite article after a noun has already been introduced with an indefinite article.

Introduced (with Indefinite Article)
I bought Koji <u>a sweater</u> and <u>a watch</u> for his birthday.

Mentioned Again (with Definite Article)
The sweater doesn't fit and **the watch** doesn't work!

2B Use the definite article for objects that you can see or hear.

Nouns You Can See or Hear
Could you pass **the butter**, please?
That must be a big fire. I can hear **the sirens** from here!

2C Use the definite article when you and a listener share general knowledge about something in your environment.

Noun of General Knowledge
A: Oh, no! **The copy machine** is broken again!
B: I can't believe it!
   (Both workers use a particular copy machine,
   so they know which one is broken.)

2D Use the definite article when other information in the sentence identifies the noun.

Noun Identified in Sentence
Turn off **the light** <u>near the door</u>.
   (The phrase *near the door* tells which light.)
Please hand me **the book** <u>about England</u>.
   (The phrase *about England* tells which book.)

2E Use the definite article with certain nouns (*store, doctor, hospital, movies, bank, park, TV, telephone*) that are familiar to you and a listener in everyday life.

Familiar Noun

A: I'm going to **the doctor** this morning. Can I borrow your car?

B: Sure.

A: Hello. I'm here to see Ms. Stephens.

B: I'm sorry, she's on **the telephone.** Would you like to sit down and wait?

2F Use the definite article for a noun that is unique (the only one of its type).

Unique Noun

The earth revolves around **the sun.**

Tokyo is **the capital** of Japan.

C1 **Listening for Meaning and Use**

▶ Notes 1A, 2A, 2C, 2E

Listen to these sentences. Listen carefully for the nouns in the chart. Is each speaker introducing a noun or referring to a noun that the listener can identify? Check (✓) the correct column.

		INTRODUCING A NOUN	REFERRING TO A NOUN THAT THE LISTENER CAN IDENTIFY
1.	present	✓	
2.	children		
3.	car		
4.	teacher		
5.	restaurant		
6.	man		
7.	bank		
8.	article		
9.	car keys		
10.	meeting		

C2 Choosing the Correct Article

► Notes 1, 2A, 2D

Choose the articles that best complete this description.

The Venus flytrap is (**(a)**/ some) famous carnivorous plant that grows
1
in North and South Carolina. (The / Ø) entire plant is about a foot tall.
2
In spring it has (the / Ø) small white flowers. But the most interesting
3
parts of (a / the) plant are its leaves.
4

(The / Ø) leaves grow in (a / some) circle around the bottom
5   6
of (Ø / the) plant. Each leaf opens into two halves. On (the / Ø) surface
7   8
of the leaves there are (some / the) short hairs. They are called (Ø / some)
9   10
trigger hairs. If (an / the) insect lands on one of (Ø / the) leaves and
11   12
touches (a / the) trigger hairs in a certain way, (the / some) two halves
13   14
close tightly around (an / the) insect.
15

To find more information about (Ø / the) carnivorous plants, look
16
in (Ø / the) plant guides, (an / Ø) encyclopedia, or on the Internet.
17   18

C3 Using Definite and Indefinite Articles

► Notes 1–2

Complete each sentence with *the, a, an,* or Ø.

1. **A:** Excuse me. Where's Room 203?

   B: Room 203 is ___the___ room at the end of the hall, next to the stairs.

2. Two women are eating lunch. There's a bottle of water on the table. One

   says, "Please pass me _____ water, Julie."

3. **A:** How do you get to school?

   B: I walk, but it takes too long. I think I'll buy _____ bike next semester.

4. Look at _____ sky! It's beautiful, isn't it?

5. My friend made a cake and a pie. I tasted _____ pie, and it was delicious!

6. Two roommates are cleaning their apartment. One says, "Could you help

   me move _____ couch? I need to sweep under there."

7. Oh, no! There's _____ fly in my salad.

8. This evening I'm going to visit my aunt. She's in _____ hospital.

9. **A:** May I borrow your camera?

   B: Yes, but you need to buy _____ film for it.

10. Two co-workers are standing near a printer. One of them says,

    "I think _____ printer is out of paper."

C4 **Guessing About Contexts** ► Notes 1–2

Work with a partner. Discuss the two sentences in each situation. How does the speaker's use of the indefinite or definite article change the meaning? Make guesses about the context of each sentence.

1. Two young women are talking. One says:
   a. "I hope I get the job."
   b. "I hope I get a job."

   A: In the first sentence the definite article means that the job is specific for both her and her friend. Maybe the young woman has applied for a specific job that her friend knows about.

   B: In the second sentence the indefinite article means that she doesn't have a specific job in mind. It sounds like she's not working and will take just about any job.

2. A married couple is talking. The man says:
   a. "I bought the book on Tahiti."
   b. "I bought a book on Tahiti."

3. Two young men are talking. One says:
   a. "I got the letter today."
   b. "I got a letter today."

4. A middle-aged woman is talking to her son. She says:
   a. "Did you buy a suit?"
   b. "Did you buy the suit?"

Vocabulary Notes

Phrases such as *In School* and *In the School*

After the preposition *in,* some nouns change meaning depending on whether they are used with an article or not. Some examples are *school, college, prison, court, church, bed,* and *class.* Use these nouns without an article to refer to what people usually do in them. Use these nouns with an article to refer to the physical place or object.

Ø ARTICLE	WITH AN ARTICLE
Are your children **in school**? (Are they students?)	Are your children **in the school**? (Are they in the school building?)
Davis is **in prison**. (He's a prisoner.)	Davis is **in the prison**. (He's not a prisoner, but he's in the building.)
Professor Lee is **in class**. (He's teaching.)	There aren't enough chairs **in the class**. (in the class = in the room)

C5 Using Nouns that Change Meaning

Work with a partner. Complete each sentence with *the* or Ø (no article).

1. He's still in _____Ø_____ school, but he's graduating next year.

2. On the tour, a guide showed us some beautiful stained glass windows in _____ church.

3. Professor Johnson teaches two courses. He's in _____ class all morning, and he has office hours in the afternoon.

4. There is a job opening for a social worker in _____ prison. They're looking for someone with a lot of experience.

5. Right now, there's no gym in _____ college, so I can't exercise here.

6. As an attorney, she spends a lot of her time in _____ court.

7. When I was in _____ college, I lived at home.

8. I know three people in my history course. Rita, Holly, and Omar are in _____ class.

D **Nouns in General Statements**

Examining Meaning and Use

Read the sentences and complete the tasks below. Then discuss your answers and read the Meaning and Use Notes to check them.

1a. <u>Students</u> often don't get enough sleep.
1b. How much sleep do <u>the students</u> in your class get?

2a. <u>Plants</u> usually need light and water.
2b. <u>The plants</u> in my garden don't need much water.

Compare the meaning of the underlined nouns in each pair of sentences.

1. In which sentences do they refer to a group of people or plants in general?

2. In which sentences do the underlined nouns refer to specific people or plants?

Meaning and Use Notes

> ### Making General Statements
>
> **1A** Sometimes a noun is used to make a general statement about a whole class or group. These nouns do not identify a specific person, place, or thing. They represent all members of that class or group.
>
> **Ants** are insects.
> **Chocolate** is made from cacao seeds.
>
> ---
>
> **1B** When making general statements about a whole class or group, we use *a/an* with singular count nouns, and Ø with plural count nouns and noncount nouns.
>
> *Singular Count Noun*
> **A cheetah** can run very fast.
>
> *Plural Count Noun*
> **Cheetahs** can run very fast.
>
> *Noncount Noun*
> **Oxygen** is necessary for our survival.

(Continued on page 294)

1C You may also see or hear *the* before singular count nouns in more formal discussions about plants, animals, and machines. Musical instruments usually occur with *the* in general statements.

The giant panda is an endangered animal.
It is difficult to play **the violin**.

1D General statements are often used to classify and define nouns.

A diary is a daily record of a person's life.
A carnivorous plant is a plant that eats meat.

1E General statements are also often used to express opinions.

Sharks are beautiful creatures.

D1 **Listening for Meaning and Use** ▶ Notes 1A–1C

Listen to each sentence. Listen carefully for the nouns in the chart. What does each one represent: a specific person, place, or thing, or a whole class or group? Check (✓) the correct column.

		SPECIFIC PERSON, PLACE, OR THING	WHOLE CLASS OR GROUP
1.	a. teachers		✓
	b. tests		✓
2.	a. kids		
	b. dogs		
3.	a. girl		
	b. information		
4.	a. dolphin		
	b. animal		
5.	a. radio station		
	b. advertisements		
6.	a. doctor		
	b. hospital		

A. Look at the pictures. Match each group noun below to the appropriate specific noun.

ape   fish   plant   dog   insect   flower

1. cactus - _plant_   **3.** poodle - _____   **5.** chimp - _____

2. butterfly - _____   **4.** rose - _____   **6.** shark - _____

B. Work with a partner. Take turns asking for and giving definitions of the specific nouns in part A.

A: What's a cactus?
B: A cactus is a plant.

Work with a partner. Discuss your opinion about the topics below.

cats   football   politicians   television
doctors   housework   rock music   the guitar

A: Television wasn't a good invention.
B: I agree. People don't read enough books these days. TV has made us lazy.

A. Complete the statements with *a, an,* or ∅. Be sure to capitalize the first word of each sentence where necessary.

1. __∅__ ~~rainforests~~ *Rainforests* are very warm, wet, dense forests. They cover about 6% of the earth's land surface.

2. _____ parrot is a well-known rainforest bird.

3. _____ teak and mahogany are two kinds of exotic wood that come from rainforest trees.

4. _____ jaguars are large beautiful rainforest cats. They are in danger of becoming extinct.

5. _____ rhinoceros beetle is a beetle that has a curved horn on its head. It is one of the more exotic-looking rainforest insects.

B. Complete these sentences with *a, an, the,* or ∅. Be sure to capitalize the first word of each sentence where necessary.

1. __∅__ ~~wolves~~ *Wolves* usually live in groups.

2. _____ chair is a piece of furniture that you can sit on.

3. _____ flute is my favorite instrument.

4. _____ rice is a popular food in Asia.

5. _____ trumpet is very hard to play.

6. _____ palm trees are common in places with a tropical climate.

7. _____ calcium is important for strong bones.

8. _____ mango is a tropical fruit.

Combining Form, Meaning, and Use

E1 Thinking About Meaning and Use

Read the conversations and the statements that follow. Write *True, False,* or *It's not clear* next to each statement.

Conversation 1

A: Have you met the new teacher?
B: No, I haven't.

1. B knows that there is going to be a new teacher. _____True_____

2. B knows the new teacher. _____

Conversation 2

A: Betty works in a department store.
B: Really? Does she like it?

1. A knows the name of the department store. _____

2. B knows the name of the department store. _____

Conversation 3

A: Did you buy a computer?
B: Yes. They're delivering it tomorrow.

1. A knows what kind of computer B bought. _____

2. B knows what kind of computer he or she bought. _____

Conversation 4

A: Please open the window. It's hot in here.
B: I can't. It's broken.

1. A and B are talking on the telephone. _____

2. There is only one window in the room. _____

Find the errors in this paragraph and correct them.

The leaves of Venus flytraps are ~~the~~ clever traps. Each leaf has the "trigger" hairs. When these hairs move, a trap closes. When leaf is open, the trap is set, ready for a insect to come. Plant attracts insects with the sweet smell. When an insect crawls across the leaf, it moves the trigger hairs. This is a signal for a trap to close. But the trap must receive two signals before it closes. It will close only if one hair moves twice or if two hairs move. This way, the plant makes sure that it has caught the live creature and not the piece of grass or a leaf.

Beyond the Classroom

Searching for Authentic Examples

Find examples of English grammar in everyday life. Look at an English-language recipe in a cookbook, magazine, or on the Internet. Find five examples of definite and indefinite articles and bring them to class. Are the articles you found used to introduce a noun, to refer to a noun that the listener can identify, or to make a general statement? Discuss your findings with your classmates.

Speaking

Follow these steps to make a group presentation of a story.

1. Work in small groups. Choose a story that you all know. It can be a true story, a fairy tale, a story from a movie or book, or a story that you make up. Make sure that the story isn't too long. You should be able to tell it in about five minutes.

2. Make notes about your story. Then assign each person a different part.

3. Practice telling your part of the story from your notes. Think about how you will use indefinite and definite articles.

4. Present the story to your class.

   Once upon a time there was a beautiful young girl. The girl lived in a small village. She had a very mean stepmother. . . .

Adjectives
and Adverbs

Adjectives

Unusual Gifts for Unusual People

A1 Before You Read

Discuss these questions.

Do you ever buy things from mail-order catalogs? Do you ever buy things from on-line catalogs? If so, what do you buy? Do you prefer to shop at a store? Why or why not?

A2 Read

Read the catalog entries on the following page. Would you buy any of these items?

A3 After You Read

Choose the answer that best completes each sentence.

1. The crossword puzzle has _____.
   a. 91,000 clues   **b.** 100 squares   **c.** 28,000 words

2. The potholders are _____.
   a. washable   **b.** removable   **c.** round

3. The thermometer has _____ balls.
   a. wooden   **b.** glass   **c.** leather

4. Each ball in the thermometer has a _____ tag.
   a. silver   **b.** black   **c.** gold

5. The backpacker guitar is _____.
   a. easy to carry   **b.** heavy   **c.** soft

Unusual Gifts for Unusual People

The World's Largest Crossword Puzzle

This challenging crossword puzzle can take months to finish. It has 91,000 squares and contains fascinating clues for over
5 28,000 words. A 100-page clue book provides additional help. The puzzle is printed on strong paper so that you can hang it on any wall. *Comes with storage box.*
Item #66813............$29.95

Backpacker Guitar

10 This extremely light, compact guitar weighs less than three pounds. It is so lightweight and portable that it has gone on trips on the Space Shuttle, to the summit of Mount Everest, and to both the North and South Poles. It has a
15 wooden body and neck, and metal tuners, and it comes with a soft, padded carrying case.
Item #66545 ....$224.95

Galileo Liquid Thermometer

20 Galileo was the first to make this unusual liquid thermometer. The clear glass tube holds a number of handmade glass balls that
25 float in a special liquid. Each colored ball responds to temperature changes by rising or falling. The lowest ball gives you the correct temperature.
30 The temperatures are easy to read because each ball has a gold tag with large numbers.
Item #48210............$49.95

Washable Leather Potholders

35 These strong, long-lasting potholders are excellent for protecting your hands from heat. The potholders are made from two soft, attractive leather pieces. They're washable, too.
Item #60934............$19.95

Adapted from the *Hammacher Schlemmer* catalog

---

challenging: difficult, but exciting and interesting

clue: a piece of information that helps you solve a crossword puzzle

compact: small and convenient

potholder: a thick piece of material used to handle hot pots, pans, or dishes

summit: the top of a mountain

temperature: measure of how hot or cold something is

B # Adjectives

Examining Form

Complete the tasks below. Then discuss your answers and read the Form charts to check them.

1. Underline the adjective and circle the noun in each phrase below. Does the adjective come before or after the noun?

fascinating clues   strong paper   gold tag

2. Look back at the catalog entries on page 303. Find three more examples of adjective + noun phrases.

3. Find the adjective in the sentence below. Does it follow an action verb or a stative verb? What does it describe?

The potholders are washable.

PLACEMENT OF ADJECTIVES

Before Nouns				
	ARTICLE	ADJECTIVE	NOUN	
I saw	an	**entertaining**	play	last night.
	The	**angry**	man	shouted at me.
He explained	the	**main**	point.	
We went to	the	**same**	school.	

After Certain Nouns		
	NOUN	ADJECTIVE
He is six	feet	**tall.**
I'm fifty	years	**old.**
It's	nothing	**important.**
Did you meet	anyone	**famous?**

After Stative Verbs		
	STATIVE VERB	ADJECTIVE
The play	was	**entertaining.**
The man	looked	**angry.**
The sky	became	**cloudy.**
The child	seemed	**afraid.**

Before Nouns

- Adjectives modify (or describe) nouns.
- Adjectives usually come after an article and before a noun. Be sure to use the form of *a* or *an* that agrees with the beginning sound of the adjective (*a unique experience*, *an entertaining play*, *an honest man*).

After Certain Nouns

- Adjectives come after nouns in most expressions of measurement such as height and age.
- Adjectives also come after pronouns such as *nothing, anyone,* and *someone.*

After Stative Verbs

- Adjectives can occur alone (without a noun) following stative verbs such as *be, become, feel, seem, look,* and *appear.*
- Some adjectives cannot come before a noun. These include *glad, pleased,* and certain adjectives beginning with the letter *a,* such as *awake, asleep, afraid, alone,* and *alike.*

  The dog is **asleep** on the couch.   * The asleep dog is on the couch. (INCORRECT)

- Some adjectives can only come before a noun. (These include *main, chief, principal, same, only, future, former,* and *previous.*)

  Hamlet is the **main** character.   * The character of Hamlet is main. (INCORRECT)

- Use *and* to separate two adjectives that follow a verb. If more than two adjectives follow the verb, separate them with commas and the word *and.*

  The official is **lazy and dishonest**.   We were **wet, tired, and hungry**.

FORMATION OF ADJECTIVES

	ARTICLE	ADJECTIVE	NOUN
The police saw	a	**speeding**	car.
The child held	the	**excited**	puppy.
The house had	a	**broken**	window.

	ARTICLE	ADJECTIVE	NOUN
She wears		**fashionable**	clothes.
Bears are		**furry**	animals.
My father is	a	**successful**	doctor.

- Many adjectives are formed by adding *-ing* to verbs.

  speed → speed**ing** (a **speeding** car)   bore → bor**ing** (a **boring** book)

- Many adjectives have the same form as past participles.

  excite → excit**ed** (an **excited** puppy)   break → **broken** (a **broken** window)

- Many adjectives are formed by adding endings such as *-able, -ish, -ic, -y, -ful,* and *-less* to nouns.

  fashion → fashion**able** (a **fashionable** tie)   success → success**ful** (a **successful** play)

- Many nouns function as adjectives when they are used to modify other nouns.

  window seat   **music** box

Listening for Form

🎧 Listen to each conversation. Listen carefully for the adjectives in the chart. Which noun does each describe? Check (✓) the correct column.

Conversation 1

		MOVIE	STARS	MAN
1.	entertaining	✓		
2.	same			
3.	famous			
4.	boring			
5.	asleep			

Conversation 2

		KIDS	RIDES	ADULTS
1.	excited			
2.	frightening			
3.	fine			
4.	tired			
5.	hungry			

Identifying Adjectives

Circle the adjectives in each sentence. Then draw arrows to the nouns described.

1. Matt loves that comfortable old leather chair.

2. My new dress is fancy, so I can't wear it to an informal party.

3. The tall dark man was the main character in the play.

4. When she returned my favorite silk dress, it had a huge coffee stain on it.

5. The salesman told us the rusty old car was a real bargain.

6. The theater tickets were cheap, but our balcony seats were awful.

7. The lost little boy has blond hair and blue eyes.

8. The tired old dog was asleep under the shady tree.

A. Work with a partner. Look at these adjectives. Do you see a noun form in each one? Circle it. Then underline the ending that makes each noun an adjective.

1. (child)less   4. friendless   7. heroic   10. hairy

2. childish   5. homeless   8. successful   11. curly

3. helpful   6. dirty   9. angelic   12. useless

B. Study the meaning of the adjective endings below. Then rewrite these sentences in a way that explains the meaning of the underlined words. Discuss your answers with your partner.

     -ish = like a

     -ic   = like a

     -y   = full of; having the quality of; having a lot of

     -ful = full of; having the quality of; having a lot of

     -less = without, do/does not have

1. Our neighbors are <u>childless</u>, but they have a lot of pets.
   Our neighbors don't have children, but they have a lot of pets.

2. His behavior is <u>childish</u>.

3. This computer manual is <u>helpful</u>.

4. He was <u>friendless</u> when he arrived in this city.

5. In this city there are many <u>homeless</u> people.

6. The kitchen floor is <u>dirty</u>.

7. Everyone thought the policeman was <u>heroic</u>.

8. My parents are lawyers, and they are both <u>successful</u>.

9. The little girl has an <u>angelic</u> smile.

10. He always wears shirts with long sleeves because he has <u>hairy</u> arms.

11. She has beautiful <u>curly</u> hair.

12. That guidebook is <u>useless</u>. It's over twenty years old.

Form sentences from these words. Punctuate your sentences correctly. Compare your sentences with a partner's.

1. and/job/challenging/her/is/rewarding

   Her job is challenging and rewarding. OR _Her job is rewarding and_

   challenging.

2. somewhere/go/want/exotic/we/expensive/to/and

   _____

3. car/bought/old/they/an

   _____

4. see/I/interesting/didn't/anything

   _____

5. feet/was/wide/room/ten/the

   _____

6. beach/sandy/the/looked/beautiful

   _____

7. do/never/I/right/anything

   _____

8. Amy/house/to/a/brick/moved

   _____

9. brother/asleep/my/is

   _____

10. a/dinner/that/delicious/was

   _____

Describing with Adjectives

Examining Meaning and Use

Read the sentences and complete the tasks below. Then discuss your ideas and read the Meaning and Use Notes to check them.

   a. Italian leather shoes are on sale today.
   b. He was wearing a large blue riding helmet.
   c. He bought an expensive European racing bike.
   d. I can't find my favorite cotton sweatshirt.

Underline the adjectives in the sentences above. Then think about the meaning of the adjectives and place them in the categories below.

quality/opinion: _____   origin: _____

size: _____   material: _____

color: _____   kind/purpose: _____

Meaning and Use Notes

Order of Adjectives

1A Adjectives can describe many different features of a noun.

Quality/Opinion: comfortable, colorful	*Color:* blue, gray
Size: large, small	*Origin:* Chinese, Russian
Age: old, antique, young	*Material:* wooden, cotton
Shape: round, square	*Kind/Purpose:* riding, rocking

1B If two or more adjectives come before a noun, they usually follow this order: quality/opinion, size, age, shape, color, origin, material, and kind/purpose.

Quality/ Opinion	Size	Age	Shape	Color	Origin	Material	Kind/ Purpose
beautiful	tall	old	round	blue	Greek	cotton	racing
expensive	small	new	square	green	Italian	wooden	rocking

That's an **Italian racing** bike.   They have a **beautiful new rocking** chair.
He wore a **blue cotton** shirt.   He sat at an **expensive wooden** desk.

(Continued on page 310)

1C We do not usually use more than three adjectives before a noun. It is more common to use two or three adjectives and then add other descriptive phrases to the end of the sentence.

I bought **expensive black leather** boots <u>from Italy</u>.

Adjectives Ending in *-ing* and *-ed*

2 Adjectives ending in *-ing* and *-ed* refer to emotions or feelings. The *-ing* adjective describes a noun that causes an emotion or feeling. The *-ed* adjective describes a noun (usually a person) that feels or experiences an emotion or feeling.

Adjective ending in -ing	*Adjective ending in -ed*
It's an **exciting** match.	The **excited** fans cheered wildly.
(= The match causes excitement.)	(= The fans felt excitement.)
We heard a **frightening** scream.	The **frightened** child cried all night.
(= The scream caused fear.)	(= The child felt fear.)

C1) **Listening for Meaning and Use** ▶ Note 2

Listen to each sentence. Does the adjective you hear describe a noun that causes an emotion, or does it describe a noun that feels an emotion? Check (✓) the correct column.

	CAUSES AN EMOTION	FEELS AN EMOTION
1.	✓	
2.		
3.		
4.		
5.		
6.		
7.		
8.		
9.		
10.		

A. Put the adjectives below in the correct columns of the chart. (The completed chart will have four blank boxes.)

lovely	French	leather	metal	fashionable
medical	tan	round	enormous	soft
brown	glass	long	plastic	small
toy	middle-aged	handmade	triangular	circular
Greek	unusual	yellow	purple	modern
honest	huge	beautiful	Japanese	hardworking
wooden	Indian	elegant	short	white
evening	suede	antique	tiny	wool
old	rectangular	decorative	square	cylindrical
European	racing	new	elderly	purple
silk	large	wedding	computer	oval
pink	young	miniature	gray	pear-shaped

QUALITY/ OPINION	SIZE	AGE	SHAPE	COLOR	ORIGIN	MATERIAL	KIND/ PURPOSE
lovely							medical

B. Work with a partner. Use the adjectives in the chart in part A or others of your own to describe the things below. Use at least three adjectives from different categories in each description.

1. your favorite piece of clothing

   I have a yellow silk dress from India. It's very elegant.

2. a piece of furniture

3. a person you know very well

4. a book or movie that you enjoyed

5. a car you would like to own

6. a favorite childhood toy

Read these conversations and choose the correct adjective.

Conversation 1

A: Did you see the program *Life of a Bug* on TV last night? It was

(fascinating / fascinated).
1

B: I started to watch it, but I turned it off. I felt (disgusting / disgusted)
2

by all those insects.

A: Do you think insects are (disgusting / disgusted)? To me they are really
3

(interesting / interested) creatures.
4

Conversation 2

A: That's an (exciting / excited) idea.
1

B: I'm glad you like it. Unfortunately, my boss didn't seem (exciting / excited)
2

when I told her about it. I felt really (disappointing / disappointed).
3

Conversation 3

A: I've never heard such a (boring / bored) speaker.
1

B: I know. I felt (boring / bored), too. It was (surprising / surprised), though,
2   3

because she's quite famous.

C4 **Describing People, Places, and Things**   ▶ Notes 1A–1C, 2

Work with a partner. Talk about these people, places, and things.

| your best friend | your boss/teacher | your job |
| your bedroom | your hometown | your neighbors |

A: What's your best friend like? or *Describe your best friend.*
B: He's short, and his hair is thick and curly. He has a big moustache and green eyes.

Look at these pictures from a catalog, and write a description of each item. Use the adjectives from the list in exercise C2 or others of your own. Use at least three adjectives from different categories in each description.

1. <u>This soft wool sweater will keep you warm all winter. . . .</u>

3. _____

5. _____

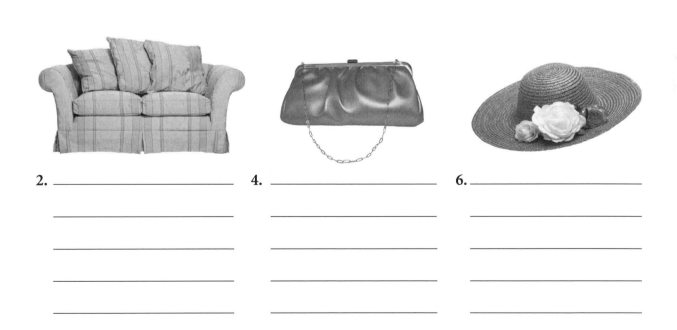

2. _____

4. _____

6. _____

D Combining Form, Meaning, and Use

D1 Thinking About Meaning and Use

A. Choose the best answer to complete each conversation. Then discuss your answers with a partner.

1. **A:** My boss is very frightening.

   B: _____

       (a.) Maybe you should look for a new job.

       b. What's he afraid of?

2. **A:** Was the actor boring?

   B: Yes. _____

       a. He fell asleep while he was on stage!

       b. I fell asleep during the play.

3. **A:** We have a great German teacher this semester.

   B: I know. His class is really ____.

       a. exciting

       b. excited

4. **A:** Did you like the magician?

   B: _____

       a. No, I thought he was pretty bored.

       b. Yes. He certainly gave an amazing performance.

5. **A:** She's really excited!

   B: _____

       a. I did, too.

       b. I am, too.

6. **A:** Would you like to hear about some of our new products?

   B: _____

       a. Thanks, but I'm not interested.

       b. Thanks, but I'm not interesting.

B. Read these pairs of sentences. Write *S* if the meaning of each pair of sentences is the same, or *D* if the meaning is different.

  S **1.** There are a lot of window seats on this flight.

         There are a lot of seats by the window on this flight.

_____ **2.** I drove a Japanese car.

         I drove a car in Japan.

_____ **3.** Sara was wearing a leather jacket.

         Sara was wearing a jacket made of leather.

_____ **4.** The rocking chair is old.

         The old chair is rocking.

_____ **5.** The musical instruments in this shop are made by hand.

         The musical instruments in this shop are handmade.

D2) Editing

Find the errors in this paragraph and correct them.

    I feel very ~~frustrating~~ *frustrated* because I never know what to buy for my father. Last year I bought him a Swiss watch expensive for his birthday. He returned it and bought several pairs of socks wool and snow new tires for his car. Last Christmas I bought him a silk long beautiful robe. It was from France, and it wasn't cheap. He returned that, too. He got a cordless new lawnmower instead. I've solved the problem for Christmas this year. I'm going to give him perfect something—money! I'm sure he'll be pleasing with that.

▶ Beyond the Classroom

Searching for Authentic Examples

Find examples of English grammar in everyday life. Look for examples of adjectives in catalogs or advertisements in English-language newspapers and magazines, or on the Internet. Bring five examples to class. What does each one describe? Discuss your findings with your classmates.

Writing

Follow these steps to write an advertisement for a product or something you want to sell.

1. Think about the topic. Make notes about what you want to say. Describe the product's size, shape, color, origin, material, or purpose. Use quality or opinion adjectives as well.

2. Write a first draft of your advertisement. Use adjectives to make people want to buy the item.

3. Read your work carefully and circle grammar, spelling, and punctuation errors. Work with a partner to help you decide how to fix your errors and improve the content.

4. Rewrite your draft.

    Are you looking for a unique Mother's Day gift? This beautiful hand-painted picture frame makes a great gift for that special woman in your life. The lovely design is perfect for any picture. . . .

Adverbs

A The Personality Compass

 Before You Read

Discuss these questions.

What kind of person are you? Are you easygoing or are you very serious? Give examples to explain the kind of person you are.

 Read

🎧 Read this magazine article to find out about personality types at work. Which personality type are you?

WORKPLACE

The Personality Compass

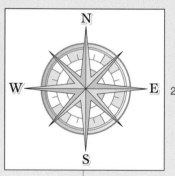

When some companies hire new workers, they look for people with certain kinds of personalities for
5 certain jobs. Fortunately, there is a test that helps these companies do this. It is called the Personality Compass. The Personality
10 Compass divides people into four basic types: Norths, Souths, Easts, and Wests.

Norths are leaders. They work very hard to reach their goals. They often
15 have strong opinions. They are so confident and independent that they can make decisions quickly. Their motto is "Get the job done fast."

20   Souths work best when they work with others. They are good team players because they understand the needs of others. They are
25 also good listeners, and they are almost always patient and helpful. Their motto is "Build the best teams."

Easts are such perfectionists that they always want to do everything right. They
30 always plan very carefully. They are very

organized and logical, and they work extremely hard. They prefer to work in a structured environment because they are good rule-followers. Their motto is "Do
35 it right the first time."

Wests are natural risk-takers; they are not afraid to take chances. Wests are often very creative. They are also flexible, so they don't mind changing a plan after
40 they have begun to work. They work very enthusiastically, especially on new projects. Their motto is "Don't be afraid to try something new today."

Everyone has some characteristics from
45 all four types, but one type is usually stronger than the others. It is also very common for some people to have both a primary personality type and a secondary one. In other words, they are not "true"
50 Norths or Souths, for example, but are instead "Northwests" or "Southeasts." However, since North-South and East-West are opposites, it is impossible for one person to have those combinations. Reread
55 the descriptions. Which personality type are you? ∎

Adapted from *The Personality Compass*

compass: a device that shows directions (i.e., N, S, E, W)
enthusiastically: with great energy
motto: a short sentence that expresses the beliefs of a person or group

primary: main or most important
secondary: less important than something else
structured: very organized, with strict rules

A3) After You Read

Look at the jobs below. Which two do you think best match each personality type? Discuss your answers with a partner. Did you both choose the same jobs?

artist	project manager	accountant	architect
pilot	construction worker	lawyer	football player

1. Norths (confident, independent leaders): _____

2. Souths (good team players): _____

3. Easts (perfectionists, rule-followers): _____

4. Wests (creative risk-takers): _____

B **Adverbs of Manner, Possibility, Time, and Opinion**

Examining Form

Look back at the magazine article on page 318 and complete the tasks below. Then discuss your answers and read the Form charts to check them.

1. Underline seven words that end in *-ly*. These are adverbs.

2. Which three underlined adverbs answer the question *How?* about the verb in the clause? These are adverbs of manner.

3. Where do the adverbs of manner occur in each clause? Do they come before or after the main verb?

Adverbs of Manner			
SUBJECT	**(AUXILIARY +) VERB**	**ADVERB**	
She	quit	**unexpectedly.**	
	has quit		

SUBJECT	**(AUXILIARY +) VERB**	**DIRECT OBJECT**	**ADVERB**
She	quit	her job	**unexpectedly.**
	has quit		

SUBJECT	**AUXILIARY**	**ADVERB**	**VERB**	
She	has	**unexpectedly**	quit	(her job).

Adverbs of Possibility			
	ADVERB	**(AUXILIARY +) VERB**	
She	**probably**	failed	the test.
		has failed	

	ADVERB	*BE*	
He	**definitely**	is	at home.

	BE	**ADVERB**	
He	is	**definitely**	at home.

	AUXILIARY	**ADVERB**	**VERB**
He	has	**definitely**	left.

MAYBE/PERHAPS	
Maybe	I'll get a raise.
Perhaps	

Adverbs of Time	
Yesterday	I found a new job.
I found a new job	**yesterday.**

Adverbs of Opinion	
Unfortunately,	I failed the test.
I failed the test,	**unfortunately.**
I	**unfortunately**	failed the test.

Overview

- Adverbs modify or change the meaning of verbs.
- Many adverbs are formed by adding *-ly* to an adjective. See Appendix 10 for the spelling of adverbs ending in *-ly*.

  quick → quick**ly**   definite → definite**ly**   unfortunate → unfortunate**ly**

- Adverbs can occur in different positions in a sentence. However, they never occur between a verb and its object.

  She quit her job **unexpectedly**.

  *She quit unexpectedly her job. (INCORRECT)

Adverbs of Manner

- Adverbs of manner usually come after the verb. In sentences with any auxiliary except *do* (that is, *be, have,* or a modal), *-ly* adverbs of manner can also be placed between the auxiliary and the verb.

  She has **unexpectedly** quit her job.   You should **carefully** consider your options.

  They are **quietly** waiting for news.   The temperature will **slowly** rise this week.

Adverbs of Possiblity

- Adverbs of possibility include words like *certainly, definitely, probably, maybe,* and *perhaps.*
- When there is no auxiliary in a sentence, *-ly* adverbs of possibility come directly before the verb. In sentences with main verb *be* or an auxiliary, *-ly* adverbs of possibility can be placed before or after *be* or the auxiliary.
- *Maybe* and *perhaps* come at the beginning of a sentence.

Adverbs of Time

- Adverbs of time can come at the beginning or end of a sentence. They include words like *yesterday, today, tomorrow, now, recently,* and *soon.*
- *Recently* can also occur before the verb or between the auxilliary and the verb.

  I **recently** found a new job.   I have **recently** found a new job.

Adverbs of Opinion

- Most adverbs of opinion can occur at the beginning or end of a sentence or before the verb. They include words like *fortunately, happily, incredibly, luckily, obviously, strangely,* and *surprisingly.*

(Continued on page 322)

Adverbs vs. Adjectives

	VERB	ADVERB		ARTICLE	ADJECTIVE	NOUN
He	runs	**fast**.	He's	a	**fast**	runner.
They don't	work	**hard**.	They aren't		**hard**	workers.
She	gets up	**early**.	She has	an	**early**	class.
I	exercise	**daily**.	I do		**daily**	exercises.
He	sang	**well**.	He was	a	**good**	singer.

Adverbs vs. Adjectives

- Some adverbs don't end in *-ly*. They look like adjectives because they have the same form. They always follow the verb.

    He runs **fast**.

- Some adjectives end in *-ly*. They look like adverbs because they have the same form.

    She has an **early** class.   (*Early* is an adjective in the sentence.)

- *Well* is the irregular adverb form of the adjective *good*. *Good* modifies nouns and stative verbs only. *Well* modifies action verbs. However, *well* can be used as an adjective when it refers to health.

    He played **well**.   (*Well* is an adverb in this sentence.)

    I don't feel **well**.   (*Well* is an adjective in the sentence.)

- Not all verbs are modified by adverbs. We modify certain stative verbs (such as *be, become, feel, seem, look,* and *appear*) with adjectives.

    It <u>tastes</u> **good**.   I <u>feel</u> **terrible**.   She <u>looks</u> **beautiful**.

⚠ Some words that end in *-ly* are never adverbs. They are adjectives that modify nouns, not verbs.

    friendly women   an **ugly** sweater   a **lonely** child   **lovely** flowers

---

B1 Listening for Form

🎧 Listen to each sentence. Choose the adjective or adverb you hear.

1. recent / (recently)

2. careful / carefully

3. careless / carelessly

4. unexpected / unexpectedly

5. slow / slowly

6. angry / angrily

7. lucky / luckily

8. certain / certainly

B2 Forming Adverbs of Manner

Change these adjectives to adverbs of manner. If there is no adverb form, leave the space blank. If necessary, see Appendix 10.

1. curious _curiously_
2. heavy _____
3. light _____
4. natural _____

5. realistic _____
6. smooth _____
7. lovely _____
8. simple _____

B3 Placing Adverbs in Sentences

Rewrite these sentences. Put the adverbs in parentheses in the correct places. More than one answer is possible in most of the sentences.

Adverbs of possibility

1. He is coming to the party. (definitely) _He is definitely coming to the party._ OR _He definitely is coming to the party._

2. We'll see you at the soccer game. (perhaps) _____

3. We have met before. (probably) _____

Adverbs of manner

4. They greeted their guest. (enthusiastically) _____

5. He explained his ideas. (carefully) _____

6. He has left the country. (unexpectedly) _____

Adverbs of time

7. I'm going to finish this project. (tomorrow) _____

8. We're going to leave. (soon) _____

9. She hasn't been around. (lately) _____

Adverbs of opinion

10. No one was hurt in the accident. (luckily) _____

11. We'll need to change our plans. (obviously) _____

12. She gave the right answer. (surprisingly) _____

A. Read each sentence. Is the underlined word an adverb or adjective? Check (✓) the correct column.

		ADVERB	ADJECTIVE
1.	This is a <u>hard</u> book; I don't really understand it.		✓
2.	The train ride seemed very <u>fast</u>.		
3.	When my sister went to college, I felt <u>lonely</u>.		
4.	I have to work really <u>hard</u> in my new job.		
5.	We left the party <u>early</u> because we were tired.		
6.	The bus to Denver leaves at 5:00 P.M. <u>daily</u>.		
7.	I'm eating <u>fast</u> because I need to get back to work.		
8.	He's catching an <u>early</u> flight to New York tomorrow.		

B. Circle the adjective or adverb that best completes each sentence.

1. Ben plays the violin (beautiful /(beautifully)).

2. The children are playing (quiet / quietly) in their room.

3. What's the matter with Lee? He looks (angry / angrily).

4. Carl sounded (terrible / terribly) when we spoke on the phone. Is he sick?

5. Rosa smiled (happy / happily) when she opened her present.

6. Your children are very friendly and (polite / politely).

7. I felt (bad / badly) after our fight.

8. You seemed (happy / happily) on the phone last night.

C. Work with a partner. Write sentences with these adverbs and adjectives.

1. ugly _That painting is ugly._____

2. recently _____

3. maybe _____

4. fast (adj.) _____

5. hard (adv.) _____

Adverbs of Manner, Possibility, Time, and Opinion

Examining Meaning and Use

Read the sentences and complete the tasks below. Then discuss your answers and read the Meaning and Use Notes to check them.

> **1a.** It rained hard while we were sleeping.
> **1b.** Unfortunately, it rained while we were sleeping.
>
> **2a.** We have made our plans. We'll definitely leave at 7 A.M.
> **2b.** We haven't made plans. Maybe we'll leave at 7 A.M.

1. Look at 1a and 1b. Underline the adverb in each sentence. Which adverb describes how the action happened? Which adverb gives an opinion?

2. Look at 2a and 2b. Underline the adverb in each sentence. In which sentence is the speaker more certain about future plans?

Meaning and Use Notes

Adverbs of Manner

1 Adverbs of manner answer the question *How?* They describe the way someone does something or the way something happens.

He works **carefully**.
It snows **heavily** in Alaska.

Adverbs of Possibility

2 Adverbs of possibility show how sure or unsure we are about something.

More Sure	• definitely, certainly	We're **definitely** going to win this game.
	• probably	If I can find a ride, I'll **probably** go.
Less Sure	• maybe, perhaps	**Perhaps** you should stay home.

(Continued on page 326)

3 Adverbs of time, such as *yesterday, today, now, recently,* and *soon,* answer the question *When?* They can refer to a specific time or a more indefinite time.

Specific Time	*Indefinite Time*
She saw him **yesterday**.	I saw him **recently**.

Adverbs of Opinion

4 Adverbs of opinion, such as *fortunately, happily, incredibly, luckily, obviously, strangely,* and *surprisingly,* give an opinion about an entire sentence or idea.

It **obviously** rained last night. The ground is still wet.

The plane had to make an emergency landing. **Surprisingly,** no one was hurt.

Adverbs with Two Forms

5 Some adverbs, such as *hard, high,* and *late,* have two forms with two meanings.

I want to pass this course. I'm studying **hard**. (*hard* = with a lot of effort)
I don't care about passing this course. I **hardly** study. (*hardly* = almost not at all)

After the storm the snow was piled **high**. (*high* = to a great height)
He is a **highly** respected writer. (*highly* = to a great degree)

He arrived at the party **late**. (*late* = not on time)
He hasn't gone to any parties **lately**. (*lately* = recently)

C1 **Listening for Meaning and Use**   ▶ Notes 2–5

🎧 Listen to each sentence. Does it have the same meaning as the sentence in the chart or a different meaning? Check (✓) the correct column.

		SAME	DIFFERENT
1.	I saw her a short time ago.	✓	
2.	It snowed a lot last night.		
3.	He's been late for our meetings recently.		
4.	It's likely we'll go to Mexico this summer.		
5.	I'm not studying very much this year.		
6.	Some buses are not arriving on time.		

C2 Using Adverbs ▶ Notes 1–4

In your notebook, rewrite each paragraph using all of the adverbs given.
Use an adverb in every sentence.

1. Adverbs of time: *recently, soon, tomorrow, yesterday*

  I joined a gym. I worked out in the weight room. My muscles are sore, but I'm going to go back to the gym. I'll be strong and healthy.

  I joined a gym recently. . . . OR Recently I joined a gym. . . .

2. Adverbs of manner and possibility: *hard, well, maybe, definitely*

  When Lee started taking my class, she didn't know English. But she really studies. She'll pass the class. She'll be ready for an advanced class next year—if she studies a lot.

3. Adverbs of opinion: *luckily, obviously, surprisingly, unfortunately*

  Children need to eat vegetables. Few children like them. My children like vegetables. They almost always ask for carrots instead of cookies.

C3 Identifying Adverbs with Different Forms ▶ Note 5

A. Choose the adverb that best completes each sentence.

 1. I think very (high /(highly) of Koji. He's a wonderful person.

 2. The door is stuck, so you have to push it (hard / hardly).

 3. I haven't seen Rita much (late / lately).

 4. The children's kites were flying (high / highly) in the sky.

 5. I'm really tired because I (hard / hardly) slept last night.

 6. The store opens early during the week, but on weekends it opens (late / lately).

B. Now write four sentences about yourself. Use these adverbs: *late, lately, hard, hardly.*

 I don't like to arrive late to class.

D Adverbs of Degree

Examining Form

Read the sentences and complete the tasks below. Then discuss your answers and read the Form charts to check them.

1a. My car runs pretty <u>smoothly</u>.
1b. They're very <u>good</u> neighbors.

2a. He was <u>so</u> smart that he got a scholarship.
2b. He was <u>such</u> a smart student that he got a scholarship.

1. Look at 1a and 1b. Is the underlined word in each sentence an adverb or an adjective? Circle the word that modifies each underlined word.

2. Look at 2a and 2b. Which of the underlined words is followed by an adjective? Which is followed by an article + adjective + noun?

Adverbs of Degree

	ADVERB	ADJECTIVE			ADVERB	ADVERB
The music is	**really**	loud.		The storm ended	**fairly**	quickly.
We were	**extremely**	tired.		He spoke	**somewhat**	formally.
The soup is	**very**	hot.		They talk	**so**	quickly.

- Adverbs of degree, such as *really, extremely, very, fairly, pretty, quite, so,* and *somewhat* come before adjectives or other adverbs.

So . . . That

	SO	ADJECTIVE	*THAT* CLAUSE			SO	ADVERB	*THAT* CLAUSE
He was	**so**	fast	(that) he won the race.		He talks	**so**	softly	(that) I can't hear him.
It was		noisy	(that) I couldn't hear.		I walked		slowly	(that) I was late for class.

- *So* modifies another adverb or an adjective that is used alone (without a noun).
- Sentences with *so* can be followed by a *that* clause. The word *that* can be omitted without a change in meaning.

			Such . . . That		
	SUCH	ARTICLE	ADJECTIVE	SINGULAR COUNT NOUN	*THAT* CLAUSE
He was	**such**	**a**	**fast**	**runner**	**(that)** he won the race.

	SUCH		ADJECTIVE	PLURAL COUNT NOUN	*THAT* CLAUSE
They were	**such**		**noisy**	**children**	**(that)** I couldn't concentrate.

	SUCH		ADJECTIVE	NONCOUNT NOUN	*THAT* CLAUSE
It was	**such**		**stormy**	**weather**	**(that)** we canceled our trip.

- *Such (a/an)* modifies an adjective that is used with a noun.
- Use *such a/an* before an adjective + a singular count noun.
- Use *such* before an adjective + a plural count noun or a noncount noun.
- Sentences with *such (a/an)* can be followed by a *that* clause. The word *that* can be omitted without a change in meaning.

D1) Listening for Form

🎧 Listen to each sentence. Write the words you hear.

1. She cooks _____*so well*_____ that everyone wants to eat at her house.

2. He's _____ right now.

3. We're _____ that I can tell her anything.

4. The kids were having _____ that they didn't want to leave.

5. They were _____ that they fell asleep during the movie.

6. The test was _____ that I don't think anyone passed.

7. She spoke _____ that I couldn't hear her.

8. We arrived _____ for the concert.

D2 Forming Sentences with Adverbs of Degree

Form sentences from these words. Punctuate your sentences correctly.

1. music/extremely/is/that/loud
   That music is extremely loud.

2. they/English/fluently/quite/speak

3. instructions/these/somewhat/are/confusing

4. he/quickly/types/really.

5. those/smell/so/flowers/nice

6. the/Jenny/well/plays/very/piano

7. the/we/news/closely/follow/fairly

8. book/it's/interesting/a/not/very

D3 Completing Conversations

Complete these conversations with *so* or *such (a/an)*. Then practice them with a partner.

1. **A:** What's wrong?

   B: Traffic moved _____so_____ slowly that it took three hours to get home.

2. **A:** Where are my jeans?

   B: They were _____ dirty that I put them in the wash.

3. **A:** Would you like to go to that Italian restaurant for dinner?

   B: I'd love to. They make _____ excellent pizzas that I could eat a

   whole pie by myself!

4. **A:** How was your test?

   B: Great! It went _____ well that I finished early. And I got _____ good

   grade that I don't have to take the final exam.

5. **A:** How did you like the movie?

   B: I thought it was _____ exciting movie that I'm going to see it again!

Adverbs of Degree

Examining Meaning and Use

Read the sentences and complete the tasks below. Then discuss your answers and read the Meaning and Use Notes to check them.

1a. Sara is an <u>extremely</u> good tennis player. She'll definitely win the match.
1b. Ana is a <u>fairly</u> good tennis player. She might win the match.

2a. It was so cold that the river froze.
2b. It was such a cold day that I couldn't start my car.

1. Look at the underlined adverbs in 1a and 1b. Who plays tennis better?

2. Look at 2a and 2b. Underline the part of each sentence that shows the result of the cold weather.

Meaning and Use Notes

> **Making Adjectives and Adverbs Weaker or Stronger**
>
> **1** Use adverbs of degree before adjectives and other adverbs to make them stronger or weaker. The adverbs *extremely, quite, really,* and *very* make adjectives and other adverbs stronger. The adverbs *fairly, pretty,* and *somewhat* usually make adjectives and other adverbs weaker.
>
> I did **very** <u>well</u> on the test. I got an A.
> I didn't get an A on the test, but I still did **fairly** <u>well</u>. I got a B.
>
> He was **extremely** <u>upset</u> about the situation. I've never heard him yell before.
> She was **somewhat** <u>upset</u> at first. Later she calmed down.

> **Reasons and Results with *So/Such* . . . + *That* Clauses**
>
> **2** *So* and *such* are used to strengthen adjectives, adverbs, and nouns that are modified by adjectives. *So* and *such* can express the reason why something happens. The *that* clause expresses the result.
>
> | *Reason* | *Result* |
> | --- | --- |
> | The necklace was **so beautiful** | **(that)** I had to buy it. |
> | It was **such a beautiful necklace** | **(that)** I had to buy it. |

Listening for Meaning and Use ► Notes 1, 2

🎧 Listen to these sentences and choose the best response.

1. **a.** I like loud music, too.
   (b.) Maybe you should talk to him.

2. **a.** Maybe she should take lessons.
   b. Can she teach me?

3. **a.** Sorry, there was a lot of traffic.
   b. Yes, there were no cars on the roads!

4. **a.** Maybe she needs extra help.
   b. That's great.

5. **a.** They're always like that on Saturdays.
   b. So long. See you later.

6. **a.** Yes, she looks beautiful.
   b. No, she's almost 16.

E2 **Using Adverbs of Degree** ► Note 1

Read each situation. Then complete the comment with the appropriate adverb in parentheses.

1. Your friend made some soup for you. It tastes delicious. What do you say when she asks you how you like it?

   It's (somewhat /(very)) good. Can you give me the recipe?

2. Your math teacher just returned your final exam. You expected an A, but you got a B instead. What do you say when your brother asks you about the exam?

   I did (fairly / quite) well, but I wanted to do better.

3. You are a football coach. You are talking to one of your players who has just played a great game. What do you tell him?

   You were (really / fairly) great tonight, Tony.

4. You were going to visit friends tonight, but you are tired. You decide to call them and cancel. What do you say?

   Hi, there. Listen, I had a long day and I'm (really / somewhat) tired. Can we get together tomorrow night instead?

5. Your co-worker is enthusiastic about a new idea. You don't think it's a good idea. What do you say to her?

   I don't know. It's (somewhat / very) interesting. Let me think about it some more.

A. You and a friend are discussing recent events in your life. Answer each question with a complaint. Use *so . . . (that)* in your answers.

1. You went to a restaurant last night.

   Friend: Was it expensive?

   You: <u>It was so expensive that we had to share a main course.</u>

   Friend: How was the food?

   You: _____

2. You just started a new job.

   Friend: What's the office like?

   You: _____

   Friend: How is the salary?

   You: _____

3. You recently moved into a new apartment.

   Friend: How expensive is it?

   You: _____

   Friend: What's your roommate like?

   You: _____

4. You just started taking classes at a local university.

   Friend: What are the professors like?

   You: _____

   Friend: What is the campus like?

   You: _____

(Continued on page 334)

B. Exchange books with a partner. Answer the questions again. Use your partner's answers from part A, but change *so . . . (that)* to *such (a/an) . . . (that)*. Make any other necessary changes.

1. You went to a restaurant last night.

   Friend: Was it expensive?

   You: <u>It was such an expensive restaurant that we had to</u>

   <u>share a main course.</u>

   Friend: How was the food?

   You: _____

2. You just started a new job.

   Friend: What's the office like?

   You: _____

   Friend: How is the salary?

   You: _____

3. You recently moved into a new apartment.

   Friend: How expensive is it?

   You: _____

   Friend: What's your roommate like?

   You: _____

4. You just started taking classes at a local university.

   Friend: What are the professors like?

   You: _____

   Friend: What is the campus like?

   You: _____

C. Think of two more situations. In your notebook, write two questions for each. Then exchange notebooks with your partner. For each situation, write one answer with *so . . . (that)* and another with *such (a/an) . . . (that)*.

F *Too* and *Enough*

Examining Form

Read the sentences and answer the questions below. Then discuss your answers and read the Form charts to check them.

   a. I type too <u>slowly</u> to work as a secretary.
   b. He's <u>good</u> enough to be on the team.
   c. We're too <u>tired</u> to go out tonight.
   d. I read <u>quickly</u> enough to finish a book in a day.

1. Look at the underlined words. Which are adverbs and which are adjectives? How do you know?

2. What is the position of *too* and *enough*? Do they come before or after the underlined words?

Too

	TOO	ADJECTIVE	INFINITIVE PHRASE
It's	**too**	hot.	
It's	**too**	hot	to eat outside.

	TOO	ADVERB	INFINITIVE PHRASE
He works	**too**	slowly.	
He works	**too**	slowly	to finish on time.

Enough

	ADJECTIVE	ENOUGH	INFINITIVE PHRASE
You aren't	strong	**enough.**	
You aren't	strong	**enough**	to pick this up.

	ADVERB	ENOUGH	INFINITIVE PHRASE
I jog	often	**enough.**	
I jog	often	**enough**	to stay fit.

- *Too* comes before an adjective or adverb.
- An infinitive phrase (a phrase that begins with *to* + base form of the verb) can follow the adverb or adjective.
- *Enough* follows an adjective or adverb.
- An infinitive phrase can follow *enough*.
- See Chapter 21 for more information on infinitives.

Listening for Form

🎧 Listen to these statements. Write the phrases you hear with *too* and *enough*.

1. You're ___*too young*___ to drive.

2. This cake is _____ for me.

3. They don't work _____ at school.

4. He drives _____, and it makes me nervous.

5. Don't buy those sweaters. They're _____.

6. He's not _____ to play basketball.

F2 **Forming Sentences with *Too* and *Enough***

Form sentences from these words and phrases. Punctuate your sentences correctly. Compare your sentences with a partner's.

1. enough/work/Pedro/carefully/doesn't

   Pedro doesn't work carefully enough. _____

2. is/too/to/that dress/wear/big

   _____

3. not/enough/slowly/you're/driving

   _____

4. be/to/young/too/he looked/her father

   _____

5. hard/Mark/worked/enough/get/to/a raise

   _____

6. too/to/Dan/to school/walk/lives/far away

   _____

G Contrasting *Too* and *Enough*

Examining Meaning and Use

Read the sentences and complete the task below. Then discuss your answers and read the Meaning and Use Notes to check them.

    a. He worked fast <u>enough</u>. He finished on time.
    b. He worked <u>too</u> fast. He made a lot of mistakes.

Look at the underlined adverbs. Which one has a positive meaning? Which one has a negative meaning?

Meaning and Use Notes

 Too

> **1A** *Too* means "to an undesirable degree." It is used before adjectives and adverbs to express a negative meaning. *Not too* expresses a positive meaning when it is used with adjectives and adverbs that are negative qualities.
>
> It's **too** crowded in here. Let's leave.
> It's **not too** humid here in the summer. In fact, it's very pleasant.

> **1B** Do not confuse *too* and *very*.
>
> | Too (*To an Undesirable Degree*) | Very (*To a Great Degree*) |
> |---|---|
> | This town is **too** small. Everyone knows each other. There's no privacy. | This town is **very** small. Everyone knows each other. It's a friendly place. |

Enough

> **2** *Enough* means "to an acceptable or sufficient degree." It expresses a positive meaning. *Not . . . enough* means "to an unacceptable or insufficient degree." It expresses a negative meaning.
>
> He explained the problem clearly **enough**. Now I understand it.
> This time I studied hard **enough** for the exam. I think I'll do well.
> This jacket doesn't fit. It's **not big enough**.
> She did**n't play well enough** to make the team. She was disappointed.

🎧 Listen to each sentence. Choose the picture that matches it.

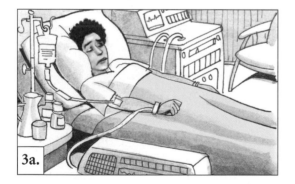

Using *Too, Very,* and *So* ▶ Note 1A–1B

Choose the word that best completes each sentence.

1. That restaurant is (too / (very)) crowded, so the food there is probably good. Let's try it.

2. He works (very / too) fast, so he never misses deadlines.

3. I finished my homework (so / very) quickly that I had time to watch a movie before bed.

4. This pudding is delicious. It's (too / very) sweet, and it has a nice chocolate flavor.

5. He drove (so / too) slowly that we missed the beginning of the play.

6. Her son is (too / very) young to see that movie.

G3 **Giving Reasons and Making Excuses** ▶ Notes 1A, 2

Read each situation. Use the words in parentheses and an infinitive phrase to give a reason or make an excuse.

1. You didn't do your homework because you were sick last night. (too)

   I was too sick to do my homework.

2. You can't go to the movies with your friend because you're very busy. (too)

   _____

3. You didn't catch the train because you were late. (not . . . enough)

   _____

4. You couldn't finish painting the kitchen because you were very tired. (too)

   _____

5. You failed the course because you didn't study very hard. (not . . . enough)

   _____

6. You didn't win the race because you couldn't swim very fast. (not . . . enough)

   _____

H Combining Form, Meaning, and Use

H1 Thinking About Meaning and Use

Choose the best answer to complete each conversation. Then discuss your answers in small groups.

1. **A:** It's too late to go to the meeting.

    B: _____

    a. Then we should hurry.

    (b.) That's OK. We'll just stay home.

2. **A:** It's such a large class that I have to go early to get a good seat.

    B: _____

    a. Is the classroom crowded?

    b. I hate crowded classes.

3. **A:** I wonder how Mark is doing. I haven't seen him lately.

    B: _____

    a. He's fine. I spoke with him last week.

    b. I know. He's always late.

4. **A:** My daughter's a fairly good student.

    B: _____

    a. Mine isn't. She's failing everything.

    b. That's too bad.

5. **A:** It was so cold that we decided not to go to the game.

    B: _____

    a. Why did you stay home?

    b. We didn't go, either.

6. A: He doesn't play piano very well.

    B: _____

        a. Well, he's only had four lessons.

        b. You should be very proud of him.

7. A: Kate dances pretty well.

    B: _____

        a. I don't think she's very pretty.

        b. Yeah. She's a good dancer.

8. A: You did fairly well on the test.

    B: _____

        a. I know, but not well enough to get an A in the class.

        b. I know. I'm so disappointed.

H2   **Editing**

Some of these sentences have errors. Find the errors and correct them.

1. He's not ~~enough handsome~~ *handsome enough* to be a movie star.

2. Andrea looks beautifully in that dress.

3. He has been recently in the hospital.

4. You are such kind woman.

5. He always works hardly.

6. She's enough shy to be a teacher.

7. You aren't tall enough to wear my clothes.

8. This ice cream tastes deliciously.

9. He's such good a player that they made him captain of the team.

10. The child smiled sweetly at the photographer.

▶ Beyond the Classroom

Searching for Authentic Examples

Find examples of English grammar in everyday life. Read an advice column in an English-language newspaper or magazine, or on the Internet. Look for examples of adverbs of manner, time, possibility, opinion, and degree. How do the adverbs change the meaning of the verbs or of the sentences? Discuss your findings with your classmates.

Writing

Follow the steps below to write a newspaper report of a sporting event such as a football game or an ice-skating competition.

1. Think about the topic. Make notes about what you want to say.

2. Write a first draft. Use a variety of adverbs and at least one sentence with *so/such (a/an) . . . (that).*

3. Read your work carefully, and circle grammar, spelling, and punctuation errors. Work with a partner to help you decide how to fix your errors and improve the content.

4. Rewrite your draft.

    The Tigers played extremely well against the Giants in the championship soccer game yesterday. The game was very close. We didn't know who would win until the last minute. . . .

Comparatives and Superlatives

Comparatives

A Early to Rise Makes Teens . . . Less Attentive?

A1 Before You Read

Discuss this question.

There is a proverb in English that says "Early to bed and early to rise, makes a man healthy, wealthy, and wise." What do you think this means? Do you agree with it?

A2 Read

Read this newspaper article about high school students. Is sleeping later a good idea?

Early to Rise Makes Teens ... Less Attentive?

PHILADELPHIA—Crystal Irwin would like to pay <u>closer</u> attention in her first-period class, but she's simply too tired. She can barely keep her eyes open. Can schools do
5 anything to help students like Crystal? One solution is to change school starting times and let teens sleep <u>longer</u>.

In the United States many high school students get less sleep than younger students.
10 This is because American high schools generally start earlier than elementary schools, and, of course, teenagers stay up later. Doctors say that teenagers need more sleep. According to a number of studies, too
15 little sleep can make students less attentive in class and more difficult to deal with. "When people don't have enough sleep, they get upset <u>more easily</u>," a researcher says.

Students are more awake when school begins later.

The first high school to change its starting
20 time was in Edina, Minnesota. In 1996 it moved its daily starting time from 7:25 A.M. to 8:30 A.M., and its finishing time from 2:05 P.M. to 3:10 P.M. The results have been positive. According to teachers, especially

first-period teachers, students are <u>more awake</u> in class. The students participate more enthusiastically, and classes seem to go more smoothly. Counselors say that students seem happier and that they are nicer to one another. There is a better climate in the school.

Despite the positive results, some parents and teachers do not want schedule changes. They think that people who sleep late are lazier than people who get up early.

Researchers believe that this way of thinking comes from the time when most people lived on farms and had to get up early to work. At that time people believed late risers weren't as hardworking or successful as early risers. This clearly isn't true of high school students today. Indeed, one student says the changes in Edina have been successful. He was in tenth grade when the school changed its starting time, and he says he immediately noticed that "everyone was more alert."

---

alert: awake and paying attention
attentive: watching or listening carefully
climate: the general attitude or feeling in a place

counselors: school employees who give students advice
smoothly: easily and without problems

A3 After You Read

Write *T* for true or *F* for false for each statement.

___T___ 1. Some students are very tired and cannot pay attention in class.

_____ 2. American high schools usually start later than elementary schools.

_____ 3. Doctors believe that teenagers need more sleep.

_____ 4. The first high school to change its schedule was in Iowa.

_____ 5. Teachers say the results have been negative.

_____ 6. Some parents and teachers do not like the schedule change.

B Comparatives

Examining Form

Look back at the article on page 346 and complete the tasks below. Then discuss your answers and read the Form charts to check them.

1. Four examples of comparative adjectives and adverbs are underlined. Which are adjectives? Which are adverbs? There are two ways to form the comparative of adjectives and adverbs. What are they?

2. Find two more examples of each underlined form.

COMPARATIVE FORMS OF ADJECTIVES, ADVERBS, AND NOUNS

Adjectives		
ONE SYLLABLE	**TWO SYLLABLES**	**THREE OR MORE SYLLABLES**
tall—tall**er**	simple—simpl**er**	beautiful—**more** beautiful
cold—cold**er**	happy—happ**ier**	expensive—**more** expensive
cute—cut**er**	famous—**more** famous	creative—**more** creative
big—big**ger**	polite—polit**er**/**more** polite	intelligent—**more** intelligent

Adverbs	
ONE SYLLABLE	**TWO OR MORE SYLLABLES**
hard—hard**er**	quickly—**more** quickly
late—later	clearly—**more** clearly

Irregular Forms		
ADJECTIVE	**ADVERB**	**COMPARATIVE**
good	well	**better**
bad	badly	**worse**

Nouns			
COUNT NOUN	**COMPARATIVE**	**NONCOUNT NOUN**	**COMPARATIVE**
a book	**more** books	homework	**more** homework

Adjectives with One Syllable

- Add *-er* to form the comparative of most one-syllable adjectives. If the adjective ends in *e*, add *-r*. If it ends with a single vowel and a consonant, double the final consonant and add *-er*.

Adjectives with Two Syllables

- If the adjective ends in *le*, add *-r*. If it ends in a consonant + *y*, change *y* to *i* and add *-er*. For most other two-syllable adjectives, use *more*.
- Some two-syllable adjectives can use either *-er* or *more*. See Appendix 11.

Adjectives with Three or More Syllables

- Use *more* with adjectives of three or more syllables.

Adverbs with One Syllable

- Add *-er* to form the comparative of most one-syllable adverbs. If the adverb ends in *e*, add *-r*.

Adverbs with Two or More Syllables

- Use *more* instead of *-er* with most adverbs of two or more syllables ending in *ly*.

Irregular Forms

- Some adjectives and adverbs have irregular comparative forms. See Appendix 12.

  She sings **better** than I do.   He is a **worse** student than I am.

Nouns

- To form the comparative, use *more* with count and noncount nouns.

THE COMPARATIVE IN SENTENCES

	COMPARATIVE	*THAN*	SUBJECT (+ VERB or AUXILIARY)
Lisa is	**taller**		**her brother (is).** **he is.**
Tony works	**harder**	**than**	**you (work).** **you (do).**
We read	**more** books		**our friends (read).** **they (do).**

	COMPARATIVE	*THAN*	OBJECT PRONOUN
Lisa is	**taller**		**him.**
Tony works	**harder**	**than**	**you.**
Lisa reads	**more** books		**them.**

(Continued on page 350)

- *Than* often follows comparative forms. If *than* is not used, it is still implied.
    I'm **older than** my sister. I'm also **taller** (than my sister).
- *Than* can be followed by a noun or by a subject pronoun + an optional verb or auxiliary.
    We read **more** books **than our friends (read).**   We read **more** books **than they (do).**
- *Than* can also be followed by an object pronoun. An object pronoun is always used alone without a verb after it.
    Lisa is **taller than him.**
- ⚠ Do not use both *-er* and *more* in a comparative.
    Lisa is **taller than he is.**   *Lisa is more taller than he is. (INCORRECT)

B1   Listening for Form

 Listen to each conversation. Which comparative form do you hear? Check (✓) the correct column.

	-ER	*MORE*
1.		✓
2.		
3.		
4.		
5.		
6.		

B2   Working on Comparative Adjectives and Adverbs

Write the correct comparative form. Use *-er* or *more.*

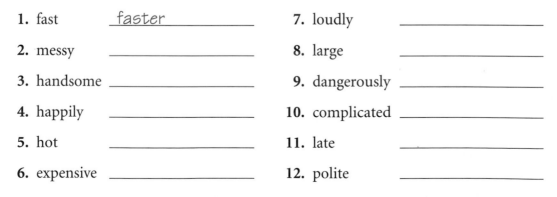

1. fast   _faster_

2. messy   _____

3. handsome   _____

4. happily   _____

5. hot   _____

6. expensive   _____

7. loudly   _____

8. large   _____

9. dangerously   _____

10. complicated _____

11. late   _____

12. polite   _____

Complete each conversation with the comparative forms of the adjectives, adverbs, or nouns in parentheses.

Conversation 1

Amy: What do you think? Should I buy the paperback or the hardcover book?

Betty: Well, the paperback is _____cheaper_____ (cheap) than the
1

hardcover, but the hardcover will last _____ (long).
2

Conversation 2

Stefan: Your newspaper is _____ (thick) than my newspaper.
1

Josh: It probably just has _____ (advertisements).
2

Conversation 3

Carlos: Is André a _____ (good) tennis player than I am?
1

Miguel: I'm not sure. He hits the ball _____ (hard) than you, but you
2

move _____ (quickly) than he does.
3

Conversation 4

Mr. Orr: So how is college compared to high school?

Yuji: It's definitely _____ (difficult) and the professors give
1

_____ (homework) than my teachers did in high school. But it's
2

getting easier. My grades were _____ (bad) last semester than
3

they are this semester.

Conversation 5

Alex: You look like your sister.

Luisa: I know. But actually, we're very different. She's _____ (tall)
1

and _____ (thin) than me. Her hair is _____ (curly)
2   3

than mine, and she has _____ (freckles).
4

Making Comparisons

Examining Meaning and Use

Read these sentences and answer the questions below. Then discuss your answers and read the Meaning and Use Notes to check them.

    a. Jake likes his new job. He's making more money.
    b. Jake's new apartment is less expensive than his old one.

Which comparison talks about a larger amount? Which comparison talks about a smaller amount?

Meaning and Use Notes

> ### Talking About Differences
>
> **1A** Use comparatives with adjectives, adverbs, and nouns to talk about differences between two things (people, objects, ideas, places, or actions).
>
> My father is **older than** my mother.
> The new computer runs **more smoothly than** the old one.
> There are **more cars than** buses on the highways.
>
> ---
>
> **1B** You can use the comparative without *than* when the meaning is clear from context.
>
> She's a good student, but I think he's **smarter**. (= smarter than she is)
> We sang well, but they sang **better**. (= better than we did)

> ### Expressing Greater and Lesser Degrees
>
> **2A** Use *more* or *-er* with adjectives and adverbs to show that something is a larger quantity, degree, or size than something else. Use *less* with adjectives and adverbs to show that something is a smaller quantity, degree, or size than something else.
>
> | More/-er . . . Than | Less . . . Than |
> |---|---|
> | Diamonds are **more expensive** than rubies. | Rubies are **less expensive than** diamonds. |
> | He works **more quickly than** she does. | She works **less quickly than** he does. |

⚠️ *Less* can sound awkward with adjectives and adverbs that have one syllable. To avoid this, use the comparative form of an adjective or adverb with the opposite meaning.

I'm **shorter than** my brother.

* I'm less tall than my brother. (NOT USUAL)

2B Use *more* with count or noncount nouns to talk about larger quantities. Use *fewer* with count nouns and *less* with noncount nouns to talk about smaller quantities.

Count Nouns

Mexico City has **more people than** Seattle.

Seattle has **fewer people than** Mexico City.

Noncount Nouns

The Smiths have **more money than** the Johnsons.

The Johnsons have **less money than** the Smiths.

Pronouns and Formality

3 When *than* is followed by a subject pronoun alone, the sentence has a more formal tone. When it is followed by a subject pronoun + verb or auxiliary, it is neutral in tone (neither formal nor informal). When it is followed by an object pronoun, it has a more informal tone.

More Formal

He is **older than** I.

Neutral

He is **older than** I am.

More Informal

He is **older than** me.

Changing Situations

4 A comparative form can be repeated and joined with *and* to show that a situation is changing. This use of the comparative is common with verbs of change such as *get, become,* and *grow,* especially in the present continuous.

He looks **older and older** every day.

I have **less and less time** to study.

Taxes are getting **higher and higher**.

Car engines are becoming **more and more efficient**.

C1 Listening for Meaning and Use

🎧 Listen to each situation and the question that follows. Choose the correct answer.

1. **a.** Dan is.
   b. Mike is. (circled)

2. **a.** Ana's coat was.
   b. Rick's coat was.

3. **a.** Our team did.
   b. Their team did.

4. **a.** Betty did.
   b. Her classmates did.

5. **a.** Maria does.
   b. Frank does.

6. **a.** The B4 bus is.
   b. The D2 bus is.

C2 Expressing Differences

Read the two sentences. Then write a comparative sentence with the adjective, adverb, or noun in parentheses.

1. Texas has an area of 267,277 square miles.
   California has an area of 158,869 square miles.

   (larger) _Texas has a larger area than California (has/does)._

2. Cheetahs can run up to 70 miles per hour.
   Greyhounds can run up to 40 miles per hour.

   (quickly) _____

3. There are exactly 36 inches in a yard.
   There are a little more than 39 inches in meter.

   (long) _____

4. Earth travels around the Sun in 365 days.
   Mercury travels around the Sun in 88 days.

   (slowly) _____

5. A kilogram has 1,000 grams.
   A pound has 454 grams.

   (heavy) _____

6. China's population is more than 1.3 billion.
   India's population is more than 845 billion.

   (people) _____

C3 Rephrasing Comparatives ▶ Note 3

Make each sentence more formal, more informal, or more neutral in tone.

1. My son is taller than me.

   (more neutral) <u>My son is taller than I am.</u>

2. I take more classes than he does.

   (more informal) _____

3. I've been waiting longer than them.

   (more neutral) _____

4. Jack has more experience than I.

   (more informal) _____

5. He worked harder than she did.

   (more formal) _____

6. He got more presents than me.

   (more neutral) _____

7. They've lived here for more years than we have.

   (more informal) _____

8. She's more friendly than he is.

   (more formal) _____

C4 Talking About Changing Situations ▶ Note 4

Think about the place where you live. Choose six of the topics below to make sentences about how things are changing. Use the present continuous with *get, become,* or *grow* and the comparative form of an adjective with *and.*

the air	the economy	my neighborhood	the prices	the stores
the buses	the houses	the people	the schools	the traffic

The air is getting more and more polluted.

D *As . . . As* with Adjectives, Adverbs, and Nouns

Examining Form

Look at the sentences and complete the tasks below. Then discuss your answers and read the Form charts to check them.

    a. My car isn't as new as your car.
    b. Sara looks as young as he looks.
    c. We walked as fast as them.
    d. Dan doesn't talk as loudly as Mark does.

1. Underline the adjectives and circle the adverbs.

2. Which sentences end with an auxiliary or a verb? Which ends with a noun? Which ends with an object pronoun?

Adjectives

	AS + ADJECTIVE + AS	SUBJECT (+ VERB or AUXILIARY)
She is	as tall as	Dan (is).

	AS + ADJECTIVE + AS	OBJECT PRONOUN
She is	as tall as	him.

Adverbs

	AS + ADVERB + AS	SUBJECT (+ VERB or AUXILIARY)
He works	as hard as	Eve (works). she (does).

	AS + ADVERB + AS	OBJECT PRONOUN
He works	as hard as	her.

Plural Count Nouns

	AS MANY + NOUN + AS	SUBJECT (+ VERB or AUXILIARY)
I have	as many CDs as	they (have). they (do).

	AS MANY + NOUN + AS	OBJECT PRONOUN
I have	as many CDs as	him.

Noncount Nouns

	AS MUCH + NOUN + AS	SUBJECT (+ VERB or AUXILIARY)
He has	as much money as	Carla (has). she (does).

	AS MUCH + NOUN + AS	OBJECT PRONOUN
He has	as much money as	her.

- Use *as . . . as* with adjectives and adverbs.

- Use *as many . . . as* with plural count nouns. Use *as much . . . as* with noncount nouns.

- The second *as* can be followed by a noun or a subject pronoun + an optional verb or auxiliary.

- The second *as* can also be followed by an object pronoun. An object pronoun is always used alone.

- To form a negative statement with *as . . . as,* use the negative form of the verb + *as (much/many) . . . as.*

    She <u>is not</u> **as tall as he is.**   He <u>doesn't have</u> **as much money as I do.**

D1 **Listening for Form**

Listen to each conversation. What form of *as . . . as* does the second speaker use? Write the *as . . . as* phrase you hear.

1. My college isn't small. It's _____<u>as big as</u>_____ your college.

2. Yes, but it's going to take me a while to finish it. I don't read _____ you do.

3. I'm _____ you are.

4. Not great. It seems to have _____ my old car.

5. It's hard. The other kids already did this stuff. I can't work _____ they can.

D2 **Rephrasing Sentences with *As . . . As***

In your notebook, rewrite each sentence in three different ways.

1. Lee works as hard as <u>his sister</u>.

    Lee works as hard as she.   *Lee works as hard as she does.*   *Lee works as hard as her.*

2. We've spent as much money as <u>the Swansons</u>.

3. Rita's son isn't as old as <u>Sara's son</u>.

4. Rick didn't take as many classes as <u>his brother</u>.

5. He doesn't have as many stamps as <u>I do</u>.

6. They played better than <u>Mike and I</u>.

E *As . . . As* with Adjectives, Adverbs, and Nouns

Examining Meaning and Use

Read the sentences and answer the questions below. Then discuss your answers and read the Meaning and Use Notes to check them.

    a. Ben is as tall as Matt.
    b. Dan isn't as tall as Ben.

1. In which sentence are the boys the same height?

2. In which sentence are the boys different heights?

Meaning and Use Notes

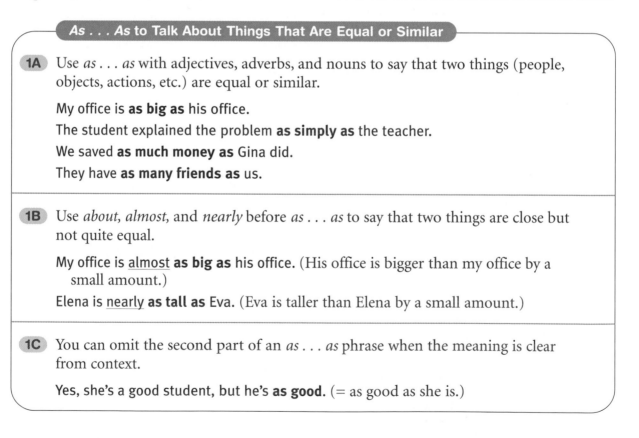

> ### *As . . . As* to Talk About Things That Are Equal or Similar
>
> **1A** Use *as . . . as* with adjectives, adverbs, and nouns to say that two things (people, objects, actions, etc.) are equal or similar.
>
> My office is **as big as** his office.
> The student explained the problem **as simply as** the teacher.
> We saved **as much money as** Gina did.
> They have **as many friends as** us.
>
> ---
>
> **1B** Use *about, almost,* and *nearly* before *as . . . as* to say that two things are close but not quite equal.
>
> My office is <u>almost</u> **as big as** his office. (His office is bigger than my office by a small amount.)
> Elena is <u>nearly</u> **as tall as** Eva. (Eva is taller than Elena by a small amount.)
>
> ---
>
> **1C** You can omit the second part of an *as . . . as* phrase when the meaning is clear from context.
>
> Yes, she's a good student, but he's **as good.** (= as good as she is.)

2 Use negative statements with *as . . . as* to talk about differences between two things. A negative statement with *as . . . as* has the same meaning as a comparative sentence with *less* or *fewer*.

Ken <u>is not</u> **as athletic as** Tom. (= Ken is less athletic than Tom.)

He <u>didn't finish</u> **as quickly as** us. (= He finished less quickly than us.)

I <u>don't have</u> **as much energy as** they do. (= I have less energy than they do.)

He <u>doesn't know</u> **as many students as** I do. (= He knows fewer students than I do.)

⚠️ *Less* can sound awkward with adjectives and adverbs that have one syllable. Use a negative statement with *as . . . as* instead.

I'm <u>not</u> **as tall as** my brother.

* I'm less tall than my brother. (NOT USUAL)

E1 **Listening for Meaning and Use** ▶ Notes 1A, 2

🎧 Listen to each statement and the question that follows. Choose the correct answer to the questions. Choose *c* if neither *a* nor *b* is correct.

1. **a.** Atlanta Braves
   b. New York Yankees *(circled)*
   c. neither

2. **a.** Russian
   b. Chinese
   c. neither

3. **a.** Carlene
   b. Janet
   c. neither

4. **a.** Techno computers
   b. Quantum computers
   c. neither

5. **a.** teenage girls
   b. teenage boys
   c. neither

6. **a.** teachers
   b. nurses
   c. neither

7. **a.** Paul's children
   b. Bob's children
   c. neither

8. **a.** rattlesnakes
   b. king cobras
   c. neither

A. Look at the pictures of Derek's and Koji's apartments. In your notebook, write sentences about the two men. Use the words below and *as . . . as, nearly/almost as . . .* , and *not as . . . as.*

Derek's apartment

Koji's apartment

1. Derek's apartment/messy

   Derek's apartment isn't as messy as Koji's.

2. Koji/clean/frequently

3. Koji/eat/junk food

4. Koji/books/bookcase

5. Derek/dress/casually

6. Derek/interested/sports

B. Work with a partner. Look at the pictures again. Make at least four more comparisons with *as . . . as* phrases.

Koji's furniture isn't as nice as Derek's.

Vocabulary Notes

Using Descriptive Phrases with *As ... As*

There are many common descriptive phrases with *as ... as* in English. These phrases are used to compare a subject to something (such as an animal or object) that people associate with a certain quality or feeling.

An example of one of these phrases is *as free as a bird*. We use this phrase to express the idea that someone or something is or feels very free: for example, *I have finished my exams, and now I'm as free as a bird.*

We sometimes use these phrases in speech and writing to make a description more lively and colorful. Here is a list of some of these phrases:

as free as a bird	as cold as ice	as tough as nails
as strong as an ox	as gentle as a lamb	as hungry as a bear
as old as the hills	as quiet as a mouse	as light as a feather

E3 Using Descriptive Phrases with *As ... As*

Complete the sentences with one of the descriptive phrases from the Vocabulary Notes above.

1. Can we turn up the heat? It's freezing in here. My hands are <u>as cold as ice</u> .

2. Don't be afraid of the dog. He's big and he looks mean, but he wouldn't hurt anyone. He's _____ .

3. Wow! I can lift this bicycle with one hand. It's _____ .

4. No one heard me come in. I didn't make any noise. I was _____ .

5. Don't try to move that big TV by yourself. It's really heavy. Ask Mike to help you. He's _____ .

6. My kids are all in college now. I don't have to cook meals or spend hours cleaning. These days I feel _____ .

7. I haven't had anything to eat all day. I'm _____ .

8. Our dog is 16 or 17 years old. He's _____ .

9. That old, retired army officer still insists on ordering everyone around. He's _____ .

F Combining Form, Meaning, and Use

F1 Thinking About Meaning and Use

Read each sentence and choose the best response. Then discuss your answers in small groups.

1. **A:** Your son doesn't seem as interested in sports as your daughter.

   B: _____

   (a.) You're right. He's definitely less interested in sports.

   b. Yes. They're both very interested in sports.

2. **A:** I don't run as fast as Greg.

   B: _____

   a. Good, then you should win the race easily.

   b. That's OK. You could still get second place.

3. **A:** The red dress is more expensive than the blue one.

   B: _____

   a. Well, if you want to save money, get the blue one.

   b. I like the red one better and it's cheaper, too.

4. **A:** You're as smart as I am.

   B: _____

   a. Then why are my grades worse?

   b. You're always criticizing me.

5. **A:** My grades are getting better and better.

   B: _____

   a. Maybe you're trying too hard.

   b. That's because you've been studying.

6. A: He's not arriving as early as we thought.

    B: _____

        a. That's good. I haven't finished cleaning the house yet.

        b. Oh, dear! Will we be ready in time?

7. A: I don't have as much money as you do.

    B: _____

        a. OK. Then I'll pay for dinner.

        b. OK. Then you pay for dinner

8. A: Ana doesn't work as quickly as Sara.

    B: _____

        a. That's why Sara stays later.

        b. That's why Ana stays later.

F2) Editing

Find the errors in this paragraph and correct them.

    My new job is ~~more good~~ *better* than my old one. I am more happyer here. There are several reasons why. For one thing, we have flextime. That means that we can arrive at work anytime between seven and ten and leave eight hours later. In general, this company doesn't have as much rules as my old company does. Also, the building is nicer of the old building, and my office is biger than my old office. There are more windows in this building than in my old building. The work is more hard than the work at my old job, but I like the challenge of hard work. I like my new boss more than my old boss. She's less bad tempered than he was, and she's helpfuler. Finally, I really like my co-workers. They are so much more nice that the people I used to work with. We have a lot of fun together. The day goes by more quicker. I'm glad I came here.

▶ Beyond the Classroom

Searching for Authentic Examples

Find examples of English grammar in everyday life. Look at advertisements in English-language magazines and newspapers or on the Internet. Find at least three examples of comparative adjectives or adverbs. Bring them to class. What two things are compared in each advertisement? Do you believe the advertisement? Discuss your findings with your classmates.

Writing

Follow these steps to write a letter to a friend comparing teenagers in your country to teenagers in another country that you are familiar with.

1. Think about the topic. Make notes about what you want to say. Use these questions to help you.

   • How are teenagers in your country similar to teenagers in the other country?

   • How are they different?

2. Write a first draft. Use comparative adjectives, adverbs, and nouns. Try to use at least one sentence with *less* and one sentence with *as . . . as*.

3. Read your work carefully and circle grammar, spelling, and punctuation errors. Work with a partner to decide how to fix your errors.

4. Rewrite your draft.

   There are many differences between the teenagers in the United States and the teenagers in Japan. In general, the teenagers in Japan are more serious about life. . . .

Superlatives

A Strange but True

 A1 Before You Read

Discuss these questions.

What is the tallest building in the world? What is the longest river? Which country has the most people? If you need information like this, where can you look?

A2 Read

Read this magazine article to find out the story behind the first *Guinness* record book.

Strange but True

H ow big was the world's biggest lollipop? (4,016 pounds) What is the driest place in the world? (The Atacama Desert in Chile) Who has climbed a 100-
5 foot tree the fastest? (Guy German; 24.82 seconds, up and down) If you would like to know the answers to thousands of questions like these, you can find them in *Guinness World Records*™. For over 40 years
10 *Guinness* has recorded the world's superlatives: the strongest person, the most valuable stamp, the fastest talker, the most

The driest place in the world

expensive meal, the ugliest dog, the most dangerous ant, the worst pollution, and
15 the world's tallest building.

The History of a Best-Seller

A little over 50 years ago Sir Hugh Beaver, the managing director of Guinness Brewery, had a problem. He wanted to know whether a certain bird, the
20 golden plover, was the fastest of all the birds that people hunt in Europe. He looked everywhere, but he couldn't find the answer to his question. He thought that other people must have similar
25 questions, so he got the idea for a book that would answer them. On August 27, 1955, the first *Guinness* record book was printed. By Christmas of that year it was selling the most copies of any book.
30   Two years later the first U.S. version of *Guinness* appeared. By 1974 the book had sold more copies than any other book except the Bible. By 1989 sales around the world had risen to over 60 million. That equals 163

35 piles of books, each as high as Mount Everest. So far the book has sold more than 90 million copies in 37 languages.

Getting into *Guinness*

I t's not easy to be a world record holder, in any category. For example, do you
40 think you can collect the most bus tickets? You'll have to collect more than 14,000 of them. Or what about dribbling a basketball the farthest without stopping? As Mark Young, the publisher of the American
45 version of *Guinness*, points out, that record is 97 miles in 24 hours. "I get tired driving a car that far," Young says.

You can try to set a record, though, and be successful. In 1979 Ashrita Furman
50 decided to set a *Guinness* record, and he now has set 58 of them—the most *Guinness* records that one person has set.

---

dribbling: bouncing a basketball up and down with short repeated bounces

lollipop: a piece of hard candy on a stick

set a record: do something better than anyone has done before

---

A3 After You Read

Match each number with what it represents.

__c__ **1.** 4,016 pounds

_____ **2.** 1955

_____ **3.** 58

_____ **4.** over 90 million

_____ **5.** 97

_____ **6.** over 14,000

a. the number of miles someone dribbled a basketball

b. the number of bus tickets someone has collected

c. the weight of the biggest lollipop

d. the number of *Guinness* books sold so far

e. the most *Guinness* records one person has set

f. the year the first *Guinness* record book was published

B Superlatives

Examining Form

Look back at the article on page 366 and complete the tasks below. Then discuss your answers and read the Form charts to check them.

1. Find the superlative form of these adjectives: *big, strong, valuable,* and *expensive.*

2. There are two ways to form the superlative of adjectives. What are they?

3. Find one more example of each form.

SUPERLATIVE FORMS OF ADJECTIVES, ADVERBS, AND NOUNS

Adjectives					
ADJECTIVE	COMPARATIVE	SUPERLATIVE	ADJECTIVE	COMPARATIVE	SUPERLATIVE
tall	taller	**the** tall**est**	famous	more famous	**the most** famous
cute	cuter	**the** cut**est**	polite	politer more polite	**the** polite**st** **the most** polite
big	bigger	**the** big**gest**	beautiful	more beautiful	**the most** beautiful
simple	simpler	**the** simpl**est**	expensive	more expensive	**the most** expensive
happy	happier	**the** happ**iest**	intelligent	more intelligent	**the most** intelligent

Adverbs		
ADVERB	COMPARATIVE	SUPERLATIVE
hard	harder	**the** hard**est**
late	later	**the** lat**est**
quickly	more quickly	**the most** quickly
clearly	more clearly	**the most** clearly

Irregular Forms		
ADJECTIVE	COMPARATIVE	SUPERLATIVE
good	better	**the best**
bad	worse	**the worst**

ADVERB	COMPARATIVE	SUPERLATIVE
well	better	**the best**
badly	worse	**the worst**

Nouns					
COUNT NOUN	COMPARATIVE	SUPERLATIVE	NONCOUNT NOUN	COMPARATIVE	SUPERLATIVE
a book	more books	**the most** books	money	more money	**the most** money

Adjectives with One Syllable

- Use *the* + adjective + *-est* to form the superlative of most one-syllable adjectives. If the adjective ends in *e*, add *-st*. If it ends with a single vowel and a consonant, double the consonant and add *-est*.

Adjectives with Two Syllables

- If the adjective ends in *le*, add *-st*. If it ends in a consonant + *y*, change *y* to *i* and add *-est*. For most other two-syllable adjectives, use *the most* + adjective.
- Some two-syllable adjectives can use either *-est* or *the most*. See Appendix 11.

Adjectives with Three or More Syllables

- Use *the most* + adjective with adjectives of three or more syllables.

Adverbs with One Syllable

- Use *the* + adverb + *-est* to form the superlative of most one-syllable adverbs. If the adverb ends in *e*, add *-st*.

Adverbs with Two or More Syllables

- For most adverbs with two or more syllables ending in *ly*, use *the most* + adverb.
- Use *the most* + adverb with adverbs of three or more syllables.

Irregular Adjectives and Adverbs

- Some adjectives and adverbs have irregular superlative forms. See Appendix 12.

Nouns

- To form the superlative, use *the most* with count and noncount nouns.

PREPOSITIONAL PHRASES AFTER SUPERLATIVES

	SUPERLATIVE	PREPOSITIONAL PHRASE
My sister is	**the tallest**	**in the family.**
He works	**the hardest**	**of all the employees.**
They have	**the most children**	**on the block.**

⚠ Do not use *than* after a superlative.

He works **the hardest** <u>of</u> all the employees.
*He works the hardest than all the employees. (INCORRECT)

Listening for Form

 Listen to each sentence. Which form of the adjective or adverb do you hear? Check (✓) the correct column.

	COMPARATIVE	SUPERLATIVE
1.		✓
2.		
3.		
4.		
5.		
6.		

B2 Forming Adjectives and Adverbs

Complete this chart with the missing forms of each adjective or adverb.

	BASE FORM	COMPARATIVE FORM	SUPERLATIVE FORM
1.	beautifully	more beautifully	the most beautifully
2.		higher	
3.	badly		
4.		more rapidly	
5.			the sleepiest
6.		more famous	
7.	early		
8.	good		
9.			the happiest
10.		more softly	
11.	wet		
12.	lovely		

Complete this paragraph with the superlative form of the words in parentheses.

Today's planetarium show begins with a guided tour of the planets in our solar

system. Mercury is ___the closest___ (close) planet to the Sun and also the one
                         1

with _____ (short) orbiting time. Mercury takes just 88 Earth days to
            2

complete a trip around the Sun. Venus is _____ (bright) planet in the
                                                   3

solar system and the one with _____ (hot) surface temperature.
                                       4

Earth is _____ (dense) and has _____ (intense)
                5   6

magnetic field. Leaving Earth, we come to Mars, _____ (red) of
                                                          7

all the planets, and then to Saturn and Jupiter. Many people say that Saturn is

_____ (beautiful) planet in the solar system because of its amazing
        8

ring system. Jupiter is _____ (massive), with a diameter 11.2 times
                                9

greater than Earth's. Uranus and Neptune are _____ (blue) of all
                                                        10

the planets. Neptune is also _____ (windy), with storms that are
                                     11

five times more powerful than _____ (strong) tornadoes on Earth.
                                       12

Finally, there is Pluto, _____ (cold) and _____ (tiny)
                                13   14

of all the planets.

Superlatives

Examining Meaning and Use

Read these sentences and answer the questions below. Then discuss your answers
and read the Meaning and Use Notes to check them.

a. August was warmer than July.   **b.** August was the warmest month of the year.

Which sentence compares things in a group of three or more things? Which compares only
two things?

Meaning and Use Notes

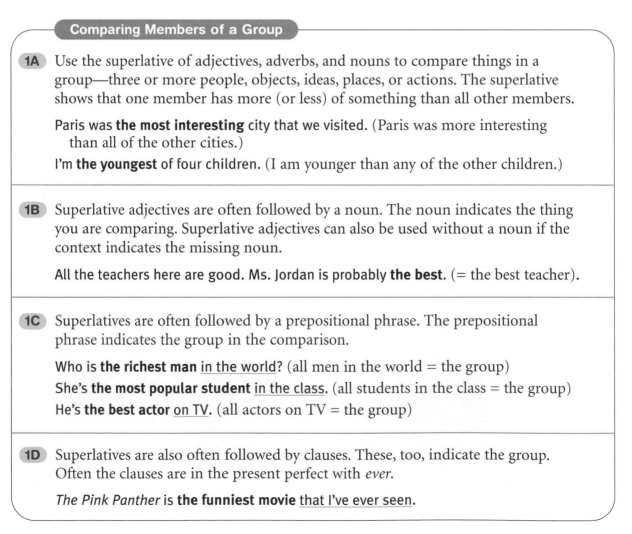

Comparing Members of a Group

1A Use the superlative of adjectives, adverbs, and nouns to compare things in a
group—three or more people, objects, ideas, places, or actions. The superlative
shows that one member has more (or less) of something than all other members.

Paris was **the most interesting** city that we visited. (Paris was more interesting
than all of the other cities.)

I'm **the youngest** of four children. (I am younger than any of the other children.)

1B Superlative adjectives are often followed by a noun. The noun indicates the thing
you are comparing. Superlative adjectives can also be used without a noun if the
context indicates the missing noun.

All the teachers here are good. Ms. Jordan is probably **the best**. (= the best teacher).

1C Superlatives are often followed by a prepositional phrase. The prepositional
phrase indicates the group in the comparison.

Who is **the richest man** in the world? (all men in the world = the group)

She's **the most popular student** in the class. (all students in the class = the group)

He's **the best actor** on TV. (all actors on TV = the group)

1D Superlatives are also often followed by clauses. These, too, indicate the group.
Often the clauses are in the present perfect with *ever*.

The Pink Panther is **the funniest movie** that I've ever seen.

2A The prepositional phrase *of all* gives the superlative more emphasis. It means "of all the people, places, or other things in the group." It doesn't change the meaning of the superlative.

I think mountain climbing is **the most dangerous sport** <u>of all</u>.

Everyone made an effort, but John tried **the hardest** <u>of all</u>.

2B You can use *one of* before the superlative of an adjective. *One of* weakens the superlative because it means that the thing you are talking about is not unique by itself, but is part of a group of things that are unique.

New York is <u>one of</u> **the most famous cities** in the world. (New York and some other cities are more famous than the rest of the cities in the world.)

3A Use *the most* or *-est* with adjectives and adverbs to show that something is a higher degree, quantity, or size than all the other members of a group. Use *the least* to show that something is a lower degree, quantity, or size than all the other members of a group.

Diamonds are **the most expensive gems** in this shop.

He's **the richest man** in the world.

He's **the least talkative** of any of our friends.

⚠ *The least* sometimes sounds awkward with one-syllable adjectives and adverbs. To avoid this, use the superlative form of an adjective or adverb with the opposite meaning.

I'm **the shortest** in my family.

* I'm the least tall in my family. (INCORRECT)

3B Use *the most* with count or noncount nouns to talk about the largest quantities. Use *the fewest* with count nouns and *the least* with noncount nouns to talk about the smallest quantities.

Count Nouns	*Noncount Nouns*
He made **the most mistakes**.	I had **the most trouble** with the test.
You made **the fewest mistakes**.	She had **the least trouble** with the test.

🎧 Read the situations and questions below. Then listen to the conversations and answer the questions.

Situation 1

A woman has three daughters: Alison, Caitlin and Megan. One of them is five years old, one is seven, and one is eleven.

1. Who is five years old? _Caitlin_

2. Who is eleven years old? _____

Situation 2

There are three restaurants: Isabelle's, Sun Palace, and Seaview. One of them is a block away, one is two miles away, and one is five miles away.

1. Which restaurant is a block away? _____

2. Which restaurant is five miles away? _____

Situation 3

Three boys played in a practice basketball game: Ed, Pete, and Tom. One of them made two baskets, one made ten, and one made fifteen.

1. Who made two baskets? _____

2. Who made fifteen baskets? _____

A. Use each set of words and phrases to write a question with *what* or *who*. Use a superlative and a clause with *ever* and the present perfect.

1. easy subject/study _What is the easiest subject that you've ever studied?_

2. interesting book/read _____

3. unusual person/know _____

4. pretty place/visit _____

5. bad movie/see _____

B. Work with a partner. Take turns asking and answering the questions in part A.

A: What is the easiest subject that you have ever studied?
B: The easiest subject that I've ever studied is geography.

Read the situations. Write sentences with *one of . . .* + superlative.

1. You have just moved to New York. When you call your family, your sister asks if the New York subway system is larger than any other subway system in the United States. You know that Boston and Chicago have large subway systems, too. You say:

   <u>New York has one of the largest subway systems in the U.S.</u>

2. You're talking about sports with your friend. You say that basketball is more popular than any other sport in the world. Your friend knows that basketball is very popular, but he thinks that soccer may be more popular. He says:

   <u>Basketball is</u>

3. You wonder whether diamonds are more valuable than other gems. You research the subject and find out that diamonds are valuable, but other gems are sometimes more valuable. What have you learned?

   <u>Diamonds are</u>

4. You and your friend are driving through Death Valley in California. It is very hot! Your friend asks if Death Valley is hotter than any other place on earth. You're not really sure. You say:

   <u>Death Valley is</u>

Work with a partner. Imagine that you have a new neighbor. Use the words in parentheses to make recommendations with superlatives.

1. (beautiful/place) <u>The most beautiful place in town is Memorial Park.</u>

2. (good/restaurant) _____

3. (near/supermarket) _____

4. (nice/hotel) _____

5. (popular/club) _____

6. (big/mall) _____

7. (cheap/movie theater) _____

8. (interesting/store) _____

A. Complete this note with the superlative of the words in parentheses.

Dear Carol,

Thank you so much for the birthday gift! I received many fabulous presents this year, but yours was ___the most wonderful___ (wonderful) of all! You
1

can imagine my smile when I tore off the wrapping and saw

_____ (late) edition of *Guinness World Records*! Only you
2

could have chosen something so appropriate for the one who was voted "girl

with _____ (weird) sense of humor" in high school!
3

It may not be _____ (serious) reference in the world,
4

but it's certainly one of _____ (enjoyable). I loved reading
5

about _____ (long) surviving headless chicken,
6

_____ (smelly) flower in the world, and the man with
7

_____ (wide) waist! But you know us library science majors!
8

The book appeals to my serious side as well. Did you know that Switzerland has

_____ (high) use of solar energy in the world and that
9

World War II was _____ (bloody) war in history?
10

Again, many thanks for the wonderful surprise. You really are

_____ (great)! This was one of _____ (nice)
11 12

birthdays I've ever had.

Regards to you and the family,

Rita

B. Use the example in part A to help you write a thank-you note to someone who has given you a gift recently. Use superlatives where possible.

Dear Kim,

Thank you very much for the beautiful gift. It's the nicest sweater that I've ever seen. . . .

D Combining Form, Meaning, and Use

D1 Thinking About Meaning and Use

Read each sentence and choose the best answer. Then discuss your answers in small groups.

1. **A:** Bill works more quickly than Bob. Elena works more quickly than Bill.

   B: _____

   a. So Elena is the quickest worker of all.

   b. Can Elena work more quickly than Bob?

2. **A:** Jan is one of the fastest runners on the team.

   B: _____

   a. Who else is fast?

   b. Is anyone else fast?

3. **A:** Their youngest son is 12 years old.

   B: _____

   a. How old are their other sons?

   b. How old is their other son?

4. **A:** John got an A, and the rest of us got B's and C's.

   B: _____

   a. So John did the best of all.

   b. So John got one of the highest grades.

5. **A:** She's the best dancer I know.

   B: _____

   a. Who is better?

   b. She must be great!

6. **A:** Are any of your other TVs less expensive than this one?

   B: _____

   a. Yes, this is one of our least expensive TVs.

   b. No, this is our least expensive TV.

Find the errors in this paragraph and correct them.

I think that Paris is _the_ most wonderful~~est~~ city in the world. It certainly is the more romantic. It has some of the most good art museums in the world. It also has some of the interestingest architecture, such as the Eiffel Tower. Then there is French food. I've been to many cities, and Paris has the best restaurants than all. Of course, Paris is not the most cheap place to visit. In fact, it is one of the most expensive place in the world, especially for hotels. But there are a few cheap hotels. Youth hostels cost the less of all, so I stay in youth hostels.

The Eiffel Tower

▶ Beyond the Classroom

Searching for Authentic Examples

Find examples of English grammar in everyday life. Look in a book or on the Internet for information on world records, or for information that compares members of a group (rivers, cities, etc.). Find five facts that use superlatives. Bring them to class and discuss them with your classmates.

Speaking

Work with a group of classmates to create a list of group or class records. Then write questions. For example: Who is the fastest swimmer in the group? Who can eat the most ice cream? Who has visited the most countries? Who speaks the loudest? After you have completed your questions, take turns reading them to the whole class. Then ask the class to try to guess who holds the record.

Gerunds, Infinitives, and Phrasal Verbs

Gerunds

A 10 Easy Ways to Start Saving Money

A1 Before You Read

Discuss these questions.

Do you try to save money? How do you do it? Is it easy or difficult?

A2 Read

Read this magazine article to learn ten things that you can do to save money.

Saving money is very difficult for many people. Here are some ways to make it easier.

1

5 Before starting, write down your expenses. For one week, every time you spend money write down how much money you 10 spent and what you spent it on. This will help you save by showing you where your money goes.

2

Divide your expenses 15 into two groups—the things that you need and the things that you want. Think about cutting some of your "wants." 20 These cuts will help you save money.

3

Make a monthly budget. A budget is a plan for spending the money you 25 have. Include in your budget all your needs and some of your wants. Each month stay within your budget. This is very 30 important. Many people love making budgets but hate staying within them.

Saving is a need, so include it in your budget. 35 Save some money each month, and put this money in the bank; even small amounts of money add up.

4

40 Start taking your lunch to work or to school. How much do you save by not buying lunch? Each day put this money 45 in a large jar.

5

Save all of your change. Instead of spending your coins, put them in the jar, too. You won't notice 50 the difference, and by the end of the year you could have several hundred dollars. Each time your jar is full, put 55 the money in the bank.

6

Make it difficult to spend money. Before going out, check your wallet. Don't take much money 60 with you and leave your credit cards at home.

7

Don't go shopping when you don't need to buy anything. Do you find it 65 hard to be in stores without buying things? If so, stay away from stores.

8

Wait a while before making a large purchase. 70 Give yourself time to change your mind. If you wait 24 hours, you may decide not to make the purchase.

9

75 If you get unexpected money, don't spend it.

Put any gifts of money in the bank. You didn't expect this money, so 80 you won't miss it.

10

When you do have to buy something, use the Internet. Shopping on the Internet not only 85 saves money, it saves time.

If you are tired of not having any money in the bank, try these ten easy 90 ways to start saving money. You will be surprised at how quickly your situation will change.

Adapted from "Ten Easy Ways to Start Saving Money"

---

expenses: money spent for specific purposes   **purchase:** something bought

A3 **After You Read**

Write *T* for true and *F* for false for each statement.

__T__ **1.** Writing down your expenses will help you save money.

_____ **2.** Your wants are more important than your needs.

_____ **3.** A budget is a plan for earning money.

_____ **4.** You don't have to stay within your budget every month.

_____ **5.** Saving works only with large amounts of money.

_____ **6.** Taking your lunch to work is cheaper than buying lunch.

_____ **7.** Always carry a lot of money so that you will be ready for an emergency.

_____ **8.** Waiting to make large purchases is a good idea.

B Gerunds as Subjects and Objects

Examining Form

Read the sentences and complete the tasks below. Then discuss your answers and read the Form charts to check them.

1a. <u>Saving</u> is difficult for many people.   **2a.** I started <u>taking my lunch to work</u>.
1b. She <u>is saving</u> a lot of money.   **2b.** <u>Taking my lunch to work</u> saves money.

1. Look at the underlined forms in 1a and 1b. Which one is in the present continuous? Which one is a gerund? How do you know?

2. Look at the underlined gerund phrases in 2a and 2b. In which sentence is the underlined phrase the subject? In which sentence is the underlined phrase the object of the main verb?

3. Are gerunds singular or plural? How do you know?

OVERVIEW

Affirmative Gerunds	
GERUND	
Exercising	is important.
Budgeting carefully	is difficult.
Budgeting your money	

Negative Gerunds	
NOT + GERUND	
Not exercising	is bad for you.
Not budgeting carefully	is a mistake.
Not budgeting your money	

GERUNDS AS SUBJECTS AND OBJECTS

Gerunds as Subjects		
GERUND (SUBJECT)	THIRD-PERSON SINGULAR VERB	
Learning math	is	difficult.
Exercising	isn't	fun.

Gerunds as Objects		
SUBJECT	VERB	GERUND (OBJECT)
I	enjoy	shopping.
We	discussed	moving to Ohio.

Overview

- A gerund is the base form of a verb + *-ing*. It can be one word (*exercising*), or it can be part of a longer phrase with an adverb (*budgeting carefully*), a noun (*budgeting your money*), or a prepositional phrase (*moving to Ohio*).
- A gerund functions as a singular noun.
- All verbs except modal auxiliaries have gerund forms.
- See Appendix 3 for the spelling of verbs ending in *-ing*.

Gerunds as Subjects

- A gerund can function as the subject of a sentence. A subject gerund takes a third-person singular verb.

  Listening <u>is</u> an important skill.   **Learning math** <u>takes</u> time.

Gerunds as Objects

- A gerund can be the object of certain verbs. These verbs include:

avoid	discuss	finish	like	prefer
begin	dislike	go	love	quit
continue	enjoy	hate	miss	start

- See Appendix 13 for a list of verbs that can be followed by gerunds.

B1 **Listening for Form**

 Listen to each statement. Listen carefully for the *-ing* form in the chart. Do you hear a gerund or the present continuous? Check (✓) the correct column.

		GERUND	PRESENT CONTINUOUS
1.	shopping	✓	
2.	saving		
3.	working		
4.	eating		
5.	buying		
6.	taking		
7.	having		
8.	spending		

Complete these sentences with gerunds. Use the words in parentheses.

1. <u>Finding a job</u> (find/a job) isn't easy.

2. _____ (take/classes) can help improve job skills.

3. _____ (not/have/money) isn't much fun.

4. _____ (stay/within a budget) can be difficult.

5. _____ (not/carry/credit cards) is a way to spend less.

6. _____ (shop/on the Internet) saves time and money.

7. _____ (travel) costs less with student discounts.

8. _____ (save/a lot of money) takes time.

B3 **Working on Gerunds as Objects**

Complete each conversation with a verb + gerund. Use the words in parentheses.

1. **A:** You lost a lot of weight. How did you do it?

   B: It was easy. I <u>quit eating</u> (quit/eat) sweets.

2. **A:** I thought you and Jim were moving to California.

   B: We often _____ (discuss/move), but I don't think

   we'll ever leave Philadelphia.

3. **A:** That dinner was expensive. What happened to our new budget?

   B: It's OK. We can _____ (start/budget) tomorrow.

4. **A:** We don't have much money in the bank right now.

   B: Maybe we should _____ (consider/not/go) on vacation.

5. **A:** Do you like college?

   B: I'm not sure yet. I _____ (miss/be) with my family.

6. **A:** I couldn't get tickets for the basketball game.

   B: That's OK. It will be on TV. I _____ (like/watch)

   basketball on TV.

C Gerunds After Prepositions

Examining Form

Look at the sentences and complete the tasks below. Then discuss your answers and read the Form charts to check them.

    a. He won a prize for swimming the fastest.
    b. She wasn't accustomed to getting bad grades.
    c. I don't approve of lying.
    d. Do you worry about making enough money?

Underline the gerund in each sentence. Circle the word that comes directly before each gerund. What kind of word is it?

Preposition + Gerund		
	PREPOSITION	**GERUND**
I'll call	**before**	**leaving town.**
We walked	**instead of**	**driving.**

Verb + Preposition + Gerund		
	VERB + PREPOSITION	**GERUND**
We	worried **about**	**losing.**
I	believe **in**	**telling the truth.**

Be + Adjective + Preposition + Gerund		
	***BE* + ADJECTIVE + PREPOSITION**	**GERUND**
We	were tired **of**	**studying hard.**
He	was afraid **of**	**losing his job.**

Preposition + Gerund

• Gerunds can follow prepositions such as *about, for, in, instead of, of,* and *to.*

Verb + Preposition + Gerund

• Many verb + preposition combinations can be followed by gerunds. These include *approve of, believe in, disapprove of, plan on, think about,* and *worry about.*

• See Appendix 13 for a list of verb + preposition combinations that can be followed by gerunds.

(Continued on page 388)

> **Be + Adjective + Preposition + Gerund**
>
> • Many *be* + adjective + preposition combinations can be followed by a gerund. These include *be accustomed to/be used to, be afraid of, be fond of, be good at, be interested in, be surprised at,* and *be tired of.* See Appendix 13 for a list of more *be* + adjective + preposition phrases that are followed by gerunds.

C1 Listening for Form

🎧 Listen and complete these sentences with the words you hear.

1. Are you __interested in going__ to a movie tonight?

2. You should drink tea _____ coffee.

3. John is talking _____ his job.

4. I'm looking _____ Mr. Johnson's class.

5. I'm _____ TV.

C2 Working on Gerunds After Verb + Preposition

Match each sentence beginning on the left to its correct sentence ending on the right.

__d__ 1. Jorge is talking   **a.** of being in school.

_____ 2. I believe   **b.** at explaining things.

_____ 3. We're looking forward   **c.** in treating people fairly.

_____ 4. We're planning   **d.** about buying an apartment.

_____ 5. He's tired   **e.** on leaving early today.

_____ 6. She's good   **f.** to traveling to Europe next summer.

C3 Working on Gerunds After Adjective + Preposition

Work in pairs. Take turns asking and answering these questions. Answer with adjective + preposition combinations and gerunds.

1. What are you afraid of doing?

   A: *What are you afraid of doing?*
   B: *I'm afraid of flying.*

2. What are you good at doing?

3. What are you interested in doing?

4. What are you tired of doing?

5. What are you fond of doing?

Gerunds

Examining Meaning and Use

Read the sentences and answer the questions below. Then discuss your answers and read the Meaning and Use Notes to check them.

  a. I don't like playing tennis, but I love watching it.
  b. Would you mind opening the door, please? My hands are full.
  c. You can stop the elevator by pressing this button.

1. In which sentence is the speaker expressing a like or dislike?

2. In which sentence is the speaker making a polite request?

3. In which sentence is the speaker explaining how to do something?

Meaning and Use Notes

Referring to Activities and States

1A Use a gerund to refer to an activity or state.

Activity
Learning a foreign language is hard work.

State
I don't like **being hungry**.

1B Use *go* + gerund to refer to common activities. *Go* can be used in any tense.

I <u>went</u> **sightseeing** when I was in Paris.
When you visit a national park, you can <u>go</u> **hiking**, **camping**, and **fishing**.

1C Use verbs such as *like, dislike, hate,* and *enjoy* + gerund to talk about liking or disliking activities and states.

I <u>hate</u> **eating alone**.
In his spare time, John <u>enjoys</u> **fixing old cars**.

(Continued on page 390)

2A The verb *mind* means "dislike, feel bothered." *Mind* + gerund is usually used in questions and negative statements to express likes and dislikes.

Expressing Likes and Dislikes

A: <u>Do you mind</u> **getting up early for work?** (= Does getting up early bother you?)
B: No, <u>I don't mind</u>. I'm used to it. (= No, it doesn't bother me.)
<u>I don't mind</u> **driving at night**. (= Driving at night doesn't bother me.)

2B Use the phrase *would you mind* + gerund to make polite requests. An answer of *no* means that the listener agrees to the request.

Making Polite Requests

A: Sorry to bother you, but <u>would you mind</u> **closing that window**?
B: No, not at all. (= OK. I'll close it.)

Other Common Uses

3A Use *by* + gerund to explain how to do something.

Explaining How to Do Something
You can make better cookies <u>by</u> **adding extra butter.**

3B Gerunds are often used in signs that permit or forbid an activity.

Signs
Taking photos is not allowed.   **Smoking** is strictly forbidden.

D1 ▶ Listening for Meaning and Use

▶ Notes 1A, 1C, 2A, 2B, 3A

 Listen to each sentence. Is the speaker expressing a like or dislike, making a polite request, or explaining how to do something? Check (✓) the correct column.

	LIKE OR DISLIKE	POLITE REQUEST	HOW TO DO SOMETHING
1.	✓		
2.			
3.			
4.			
5.			
6.			

Look at the pictures. Take turns making and responding to a polite request for each situation. Use *would you mind* and a gerund in your requests.

1.

4.

A: *Would you mind passing the salt?*
B: *No, not at all.*

2.

5.

3.

6.

Work with a partner. Take turns asking and answering these questions.
Use *by* + gerund. Compare answers with two other students.

1. How do you find a job?

   By going to an employment service.

2. How do you keep your money safe?

3. How do you lose weight?

4. How do you get a raise?

5. How do you find out the meaning of unknown words?

6. How do you choose a roommate?

D4 Making Lists of Activities ▶ Notes 1A, 1B

Complete these lists with gerunds.

Relaxing Activities

1. Reading a novel
2. _____
3. _____
4. _____

Stressful Activities

1. Taking an exam
2. _____
3. _____
4. _____

Healthy Activities

1. Swimming
2. _____
3. _____
4. _____

Not Allowed in Class

1. Cheating on tests
2. _____
3. _____
4. _____

E Combining Form, Meaning, and Use

E1 Thinking About Meaning and Use

Choose the best answer to complete each conversation. Then discuss your answers in small groups.

1. **A:** Would you mind opening the window?

   B: _____
   a. No, not at all.
   b. Sure, go ahead and open it.

2. **A:** What kind of housework do you dislike the most?

   B: _____
   a. Doing the laundry.
   b. Do the laundry.

3. **A:** Instead of serving steak, why don't we serve pizza?

   B: _____
   a. I hate steak.
   b. That's a good idea.

4. **A:** What do you like doing at night?

   B: _____
   a. Watching television.
   b. By watching television.

5. **A:** These days I have to get up early for work.

   B: _____
   a. Do you mind getting up early?
   b. Would you mind getting up early?

6. **A:** I need to save money, but keeping to a budget won't be easy.

   B: _____
   a. Yes, they will. Don't worry.
   b. Yes, it will. Don't worry.

E2 Editing

Some of these sentences have errors. Find the errors and correct them.

1. We avoid ~~to drive~~ *driving* at night.

2. Save money can be difficult.

3. Walking are good exercise.

4. He got sick by stand out in the rain.

5. Shopping and eating are my two favorite activities.

6. No buying everything you want is a good way to save money.

▶ Beyond the Classroom

Searching for Authentic Examples

Find examples of English grammar in everyday life. Look in English-language magazines or on the Internet for examples of gerunds (including subject and object gerunds) in advice columns, instructions, and signs. Bring at least five examples to class. What verbs do your object gerunds follow? Do any of the gerunds follow prepositions? Discuss your findings with your classmates.

Writing

Follow the steps below to write a paragraph about your plans for the near future.

1. Think about the topic, and make notes about what you want to say. Use these questions to help you.

   • What are you looking forward to doing?

   • What do you plan on doing?

   • What are you worried about doing?

2. Write a first draft. Use gerunds with verbs and gerunds with verb + preposition combinations.

3. Read your work carefully and circle grammar, spelling, and punctuation errors. Work with a partner to decide how to fix your errors and improve the content.

4. Rewrite your draft.

   I'm planning on getting my own apartment next year. Living with my parents is fine, but I'm looking forward to living on my own. I'm worried about having enough money for the rent. Maybe I can manage better by getting a roommate. . . .

Infinitives

He agreed **to speak slowly.**
He taught me **to cook.**
(In order) to win, he cheated.
It took two years **to learn the truth.**

Referring to Activities and States

Giving Reasons with *In Order* + Infinitive

Sentences with *It* Subject . . . + Infinitive

Verbs Taking Only Gerunds

Verbs Taking Only Infinitives

Verbs Taking Gerunds or Infinitives with No Difference in Meaning

Verbs Taking Gerunds or Infinitives with a Difference in Meaning

A The *Twenty-One* Quiz Show Scandal

A1 Before You Read

Discuss these questions.

What are television quiz shows? Do you ever watch them? Do you enjoy them?
Why or why not?

A2 Read

Read this magazine article to find out about a famous scandal involving a quiz show.

The *Twenty-One* Quiz Show Scandal

In the 1950s, television quiz shows were
very popular. Each week families turned on
their TVs to watch their favorite quiz shows.
If a show was very popular, up to one-third
5 of all Americans watched it. One of the most
popular shows was *Twenty-One*. *Twenty-One*
worked like this: two contestants tried to
answer questions for points. In order to win,
a contestant needed to get 21 points. The
10 winning contestant got money and could
choose to play again the next week.

In the beginning *Twenty-One* was not
very popular. Dan Enright, the producer,
was in trouble because the show's
15 commercial sponsor expected a hit. Enright
had an idea: if a contestant kept winning,
TV viewers might become interested in that
contestant and would keep watching in
order to see him. He found a student
20 named Herb Stempel who wanted to appear
on the show. Enright thought Stempel was
perfect because he was a very ordinary

Charles Van Doren (right) on *Twenty-One*

person. Viewers often want an ordinary
person to win. Before each show Enright
25 gave Stempel the questions. Stempel was on
Twenty-One for eight weeks. He pretended
not to know the questions, and the viewers
believed this. Stempel won more than
$69,000 and became famous. *Twenty-One*
30 became a hit.

Soon, however, people started to get tired of Stempel. Enright decided not to keep Stempel on the show anymore. This time he looked for someone who was not ordinary.
35 He found Charles Van Doren—a handsome English professor from a famous family. Enright convinced Van Doren to cheat. He then told Stempel to give the wrong answer on the next show. Stempel was unhappy, but
40 he agreed to lose by not answering correctly.

Van Doren became the new champion of *Twenty-One*. He stayed on the show for 15 weeks and won almost $130,000. Each week millions of people watched Van Doren win
45 more money.

The show's ratings were high, and everyone was happy—except Herb Stempel. He told newspaper reporters his story, but no one believed him. Finally, the government
50 began to investigate. It took two years to learn the whole story. In the end, Charles Van Doren admitted cheating and apologized.

The TV station canceled *Twenty-One*. Enright lost his job and left the United States.
55 Van Doren lost his job, too, and he refused to say anything more about the show. The TV viewers were surprised and angry. The show seemed so real. Van Doren seemed so wonderful. It was hard to accept the truth.
60 For many years Stempel and Enright were forgotten. Then, in 1994 the famous actor Robert Redford turned this strange story into a movie titled *Quiz Show*. To find out more about the scandal, as well as
65 Stempel and Enright, watch Redford's award-winning movie.

---

contestant: a person who participates in a quiz show

hit: a very popular TV show

ratings: a measure of how popular a TV show is

scandal: a situation that shocks people

sponsor: a company that pays for a TV show in return for being able to advertise on the show

---

A3 **After You Read**

Write *T* for true or *F* for false for each statement.

__F__ **1.** In the 1950s few Americans watched game shows on TV.

_____ **2.** *Twenty-One* was not popular before Herb Stempel appeared on it.

_____ **3.** Herb Stempel was happy when Charles Van Doren won on the show.

_____ **4.** When Herb Stempel told everyone how he won on *Twenty-One*, they immediately believed him.

_____ **5.** Charles Van Doren was sorry that he cheated.

_____ **6.** *Twenty-One* was canceled.

B Infinitives

Examining Form

Read the sentences and complete the tasks below. Then discuss your answers and read the Form charts to check them.

1a. They <u>speak</u> to the producer before the show.   **2a.** He wanted <u>to be</u> on the show.
1b. The producer told them <u>to speak</u> clearly.   **2b.** The producer wanted him <u>to cheat</u>.

1. Look at the underlined forms in 1a and 1b. Which is in the simple present? Which is an infinitive?

2. Look at 2a and 2b. In which does the infinitive directly follow the verb? In which does the infinitive follow the object of the verb? Look back at lines 31–40 of the article on page 397. Find a verb + infinitive and a verb + object + infinitive.

OVERVIEW

Affirmative Infinitives		
SUBJECT	**VERB**	**INFINITIVE**
He	agreed	**to leave.** **to speak slowly.** **to help me.**

Negative Infinitives		
SUBJECT	**VERB**	***NOT* + INFINITIVE**
He	agreed	**not to leave.** **not to speak quickly.** **not to bother me.**

INFINITIVES

Infinitives After Verbs			
SUBJECT	**VERB**	**INFINITIVE**	
I	learned	**to cook.**	

SUBJECT	**VERB**	**OBJECT**	**INFINITIVE**
He	taught	me	**to cook.**

SUBJECT	**VERB**	**(OBJECT)**	**INFINITIVE**
I	wanted	him	**to cook.**

(*In Order* +) Infinitive		
SUBJECT	VERB	(*IN ORDER* +) INFINITIVE
He	cheated	**(in order) to win.**

(*IN ORDER* +) INFINITIVE	SUBJECT	VERB
(In order) to win,	he	cheated.

It Subject . . . + Infinitive			
SUBJECT	VERB	ADJECTIVE	INFINITIVE
It	was	difficult	**to lie.**

SUBJECT	VERB	NOUN	INFINITIVE
It	took	two years	**to learn the truth.**

Overview

- An infinitive is *to* + the base form of the verb. It can be two words (*to leave*), or it can be part of a longer phrase with an adverb (*to speak slowly*) or an object (*to help me*).
- All verbs except modal auxiliaries have infinitive forms.

Infinitives After Verbs

- Infinitives follow verbs in three main patterns:

  VERB + INFINITIVE

agree	continue	hate	learn	wait
begin	decide	hope	plan	

  VERB + OBJECT + INFINITIVE

advise	cause	order	teach
allow	invite	remind	tell

  VERB + (OBJECT) + INFINITIVE

ask	expect	need	promise	prefer
choose	help	pay	want	

- See Appendix 14 for a list of verbs that can be followed by infinitives.

In Order + Infinitive

- Infinitives can follow the expression *in order*.
- With affirmative infinitives, we often leave out *in order* and use the infinitive alone.

It Subject . . . + Infinitive

- An infinitive can function as the subject of a sentence: *To lie is wrong*. However, this form is not common. It is more usual to start the sentence with *It* and use the infinitive at the end of the sentence. *It* refers to the infinitive.

  It is wrong **to lie.** (*It* = to lie)

- *It* is followed by a limited group of verbs, including *be*, *cost*, *seem*, and *take*.

🎧 Listen to each sentence. Does it have an infinitive? Check (✓) the correct column.

	INFINITIVE	NO INFINITIVE
1.	✓	
2.		
3.		
4.		
5.		
6.		
7.		
8.		

Complete these sentences by choosing the correct answers. In some of the sentences, both answers are correct.

1. I agreed _____.
   a. not to tell
   b. him not to tell

2. I asked _____.
   a. to leave
   b. him to leave

3. I allowed _____.
   a. to go
   b. him to go

4. They decided _____.
   a. to study
   b. him to study

5. We want _____.
   a. to look at it
   b. him to look at it

6. We told _____.
   a. not to ask
   b. him not to ask

7. I expect _____.
   a. to finish soon
   b. him to finish soon

8. We plan _____.
   a. to help
   b. him to help

9. They invited _____.
   a. to come
   b. him to come

10. I need _____.
    a. to stay
    b. him to stay

B3 Working on *In Order* + Infinitive

In your notebook, write each sentence in two different ways.

1. I need to sit in front of the class in order to see.

   In order to see, I need to sit in front of the class.   I need to sit in front of the class to see.

2. In order to get good seats, we left early.

3. I drink coffee to stay awake.

4. To get a scholarship, you need to do well in school.

5. In order to get a better job, she's going to study English.

6. I didn't tell her about losing the money in order to avoid an argument.

B4 Working on *It* Subject . . . + Infinitive

Use these words to write sentences with *It* subject . . . + infinitive.

1. be/useful/know/foreign languages

   It is useful to know foreign languages.

2. take/time/learn/a language well

3. be/expensive/eat/in restaurants

4. cost/a lot/fly/first class

5. be/important/not/tell/lies

6. seem/better/talk/about your problems

7. be/dangerous/drive/on icy roads

8. be/wise/not/smoke

Infinitives

Examining Meaning and Use

Look at the sentences and complete the tasks below. Then discuss your answers
and read the Meaning and Use Notes to check them.

> **a.** I left the house early in order to arrive on time.
> **b.** She hated to eat alone.
> **c.** It isn't easy to leave your family.

1. Underline the infinitive in each sentence.

2. Which sentences express a feeling about an activity? In which sentence does the infinitive express a reason for doing something?

Meaning and Use Notes

Referring to Activities and States

1 An infinitive usually follows a verb and refers to an activity or state. Use verbs such as *like, love, hate, prefer,* and *want* + infinitive to express likes, dislikes, and other feelings toward these activities and states.

I hate **to go to parties alone**.
He wants **to own his own home**.

Giving Reasons with *In Order* + Infinitive

2A Use *in order* + infinitive to express a reason for doing something. This is called the purpose infinitive. It can answer the question *Why?*

A: Why did you go to your son's school?
B: I went **in order to meet his teacher**.
In order to finish my Christmas shopping early, I started in November.

2B *In order* is often left out, especially in conversations or in instructions.

A: Why did you leave work early?
B: **To go to the doctor.** I had a 3:00 appointment.
Call the number below **to get more information**.

Sentences with *It* Subject . . . + Infinitive

3A In sentences with *It* subject . . . + infinitive, *it* refers to the infinitive at the end of the sentence.

It takes a long time **to learn another language**. (*It* = to learn another language)
It wasn't easy **to find an apartment**. (*It* = to find an apartment)
It is better **not to say anything**. (*It* = not to say anything)

3B *It* subject . . . + infinitive sentences can have the same meaning as sentences with subject gerunds.

It was difficult **to lie**. = <u>Lying</u> was difficult.
It took two years **to learn the truth**. = <u>Learning the truth</u> took two years.

C1 ▸ Listening for Meaning and Use

► Notes 1, 2A, 2B

 Listen to each sentence. How is the infinitive used? Check (✓) the correct column.

	TO EXPRESS A LIKE, DISLIKE, OR WANT	TO GIVE A REASON FOR DOING SOMETHING
1.	✓	
2.		
3.		
4.		
5.		
6.		
7.		
8.		

Expressing Likes and Dislikes

Complete these sentences with infinitives. Share your answers with another student. Do you agree with each other?

1. Most children hate _to go to bed on time._

2. Teenagers often prefer _____

3. Some adults don't like _____

4. Many Americans like _____

5. Most of my friends like _____

6. Few people hate _____

C3 **Giving Reasons** ► Notes 2A, 2B

Answer these questions with at least one reason. Use (*in order* +) infinitive.

1. Why do stores raise their prices?

   In order to make more money. OR
   To pay for their expenses.

2. Why do people climb mountains?

3. Why do people take vacations?

4. Why are you taking this class?

5. Why do people go to libraries?

6. Why do people work?

C4 **Rephrasing Gerunds and Infinitives** ► Notes 3A, 3B

A. Rewrite these sentences. Change sentences with *It* subject . . . + infinitive to sentences beginning with gerunds. Change sentences beginning with gerunds to sentences with *It* subject . . . + infinitive.

1. It's fun to learn a language.

   Learning a language is fun.

2. Learning to type is not easy.

3. It will take several days to drive across the country.

4. Going camping will be fun.

5. Ignoring people isn't nice.

6. It doesn't have to cost a lot to take a vacation.

B. Work with a partner. Write two more sentences beginning with a gerund or *It* subject . . . + infinitive. Ask your partner to rephrase them as in part A.

D **Contrasting Gerunds and Infinitives**

Examining Meaning and Use

Read the sentences and answer the questions below. Then discuss your answers and read the Meaning and Use Notes to check them.

1a. When I <u>stopped eating</u> ice cream every day, I lost five pounds.
1b. When I <u>stopped to eat</u> ice cream every day, I gained five pounds.

2a. It <u>started raining</u> a few minutes ago. Take an umbrella.
2b. It <u>started to rain</u> a few minutes ago. Take an umbrella.

Compare the underlined phrases in each pair of sentences. Which pair has the same meaning? Which pair has different meanings?

Meaning and Use Notes

Verbs Taking Only Gerunds

1 Some verbs take only gerunds. These verbs include *avoid, dislike, enjoy, finish, miss, prohibit,* and *resist.* See Appendix 13 for a list of more verbs.

Paul <u>enjoys</u> **swimming.**   I <u>finished</u> **reading the book.**

Verbs Taking Only Infinitives

2 Some verbs take only infinitives. These verbs include *agree, expect, need, offer, plan, promise* and *want.* See Appendix 14 for a list of more verbs.

Joe <u>wants</u> **to leave.**   I <u>expect</u> **to receive her letter** today.

Verbs Taking Gerunds or Infinitives with No Difference in Meaning

3 Some verbs can take either gerunds or infinitives with no difference in meaning. These verbs include *begin, continue, hate, like, love, prefer,* and *start.* See Appendix 15 for a list of more verbs.

Gerund		*Infinitive*
I <u>began</u> **feeling sick** after dinner.	=	I <u>began</u> **to feel sick** after dinner.
It <u>starts</u> **snowing** in December.	=	It <u>starts</u> **to snow** in December.

(Continued on page 406)

⚠️ After continuous forms of *begin* or *start*, use an infinitive, not a gerund.

Infinitive	*Gerund*
I <u>was beginning</u> **to feel** sick.	*I was beginning feeling sick. (INCORRECT)
He <u>was starting</u> **to get** better.	*He was starting feeling better.

Verbs Taking Gerunds or Infinitives with a Difference in Meaning

4A Some verbs can take either gerunds or infinitives, but with a difference in meaning. After *stop, forget,* and *remember,* the gerund refers to something that happened <u>before</u> the action of the main verb. The infinitive refers to something that happened <u>after</u> the action of the main verb.

Gerund	*Infinitive*
I <u>stopped</u> **smoking.** (I was a smoker. Then I stopped.)	I <u>stopped</u> **to smoke.** (I stopped what I was doing. Then I smoked.)
He <u>remembered</u> **mailing the letter.** (He mailed the letter. Then he remembered doing it.)	He <u>remembered</u> **to mail the letter.** (He remembered the letter. Then he mailed it.)

4B The verb *forget* is usually used with an infinitive. With a gerund, *forget* is most common in sentences with *will never.*

Infinitive	*Gerund*
I <u>forgot</u> **to go to her party.** She was mad at me. (First = I forgot. Second = I didn't go.)	I'll <u>never forget</u> **going to her party.** It was so much fun! (First = I went to the party. Second = I won't forget it.)

D1 **Listening for Meaning and Use**   ▶ Notes 3, 4A, 4B

🎧 Listen to these pairs of sentences. Do they have the same meaning or different meanings? Choose the correct answer.

1. same   (different)   4. same   different

2. same   different   5. same   different

3. same   different   6. same   different

Complete each sentence with a gerund or infinitive.

1. I finished ____reading____ (read) the book you lent me. It was really good.

2. She expects us _____ (finish) our essays by Friday.

3. Do you miss _____ (see) your family and friends?

4. They dislike _____ (get) phone calls late at night.

5. He promised _____ (make) less noise after I complained.

6. Jim says he wants _____ (quit) his job.

A. Replace the underlined words with a verb + gerund without changing the meaning of the sentence. If this is not possible, write *no change possible*.

Conversation 1

A: I'll <u>start to load</u> the car.   ____start loading____
      1

   Did you <u>remember to turn off</u> the light?   ____no change possible____
                              2

B: Yes, but I <u>forgot to lock</u> the front door.   _____
              3

Conversation 2

A: Do you <u>like to cook</u>?   _____
          1

B: Yes, but I <u>prefer to eat out</u>.   _____
              2

B. Replace the underlined words with an infinitive without changing the meaning of the sentence. If this is not possible, write *no change possible*.

Conversation 1

A: Do you <u>like working</u> at home?   _____
          1

B: Yes. I've been much happier since I

   <u>stopped working</u> in an office.   _____
        2

Conversation 2

A: I <u>finished writing</u> my paper this morning. _____
       1

B: That's great! I just <u>began writing</u> mine.   _____
                        2

A. Work in small groups. Choose one of the topics below. Make suggestions by completing each sentence with either a gerund or an infinitive.

Starting an Exercise Program

Organizing Your Time

Choosing a Marriage Partner

Learning a Language

Studying for Final Exams

Choosing a University

Suggestions for <u>Starting an Exercise Program</u>

1. Start <u>thinking about different exercises.</u>

2. Plan <u>to join a gym.</u>

3. Remember _____

4. Avoid _____

5. Try _____

6. Consider _____

7. Don't stop _____

8. Finally, don't forget _____

B. Work with a partner from a different group. Share your suggestions. Can you add any ideas to your partner's list?

E Combining Form, Meaning, and Use

E1 Thinking About Meaning and Use

Choose the best answer to complete each conversation. Then discuss your answers in small groups.

1. **A:** She stopped _____ when she saw the accident.

   B: How brave!
   a. to help
   b. helping

2. **A:** I went out to buy some paint.

   B: _____
   a. Why did you go out?
   b. How much did you buy?

3. **A:** We stopped _____ you, but there was no answer.

   B: I went out for a while.
   a. to call
   b. calling

4. **A:** I'll never forget _____ my baby daughter for the first time.

   B: I feel the same way.
   a. to see
   b. seeing

5. **A:** _____ cheap tickets, come back an hour before the show.

   B: Thanks for the advice!
   a. To get
   b. Getting

6. **A:** Do you remember _____ to me about your boss?

   B: Yes, last week in the lunch room. Why?
   a. to talk
   b. talking

Some of these sentences have errors. Find the errors and correct them.

driving
1. We avoid to ~~drive~~ at night.

2. It is useful have an extra key for your house.

3. I was starting saying something when he interrupted.

4. He continued to ask questions.

5. In order get your driver's license, you have to take a test.

6. She stopped to smoke a few years ago. She feels much better now.

7. I'm looking forward to finish this report.

8. She needs to pass this course for to graduate.

▶ Beyond the Classroom

Searching for Authentic Examples

Find examples of English grammar in everyday life. Look in English-language
newspaper articles, advice columns, instructions, or on the Internet. Find five
examples of infinitives and bring them to class. Do any of your examples contain
in order to? Are any of them sentences with *It* subject . . . + infinitive? Discuss your
findings with your classmates.

Speaking

Work with a partner. Write a six-question survey about likes and dislikes. Use
some of the verbs below with gerunds or infinitives. (You can use the verbs more
than once.) Your survey can be on one topic (for example, TV or food) or on
various topics. Ask at least ten people to respond to your survey. Report your
results to the class.

    dislike   enjoy   hate   like   prefer   want

What TV programs do you enjoy watching?
Do you prefer to play sports or to watch sports?

Phrasal Verbs

A ## "Eggstraordinary" Breakfasts Are Easy!

 Before You Read

Discuss these questions.

What's your favorite breakfast? Do you like to eat eggs? If you do, how do you cook them?

A2 **Read**

Read the website article on the following page to find out the best way to fry an egg.

A3 **After You Read**

Look at the information again and number these steps for cooking a fried egg.

_____ Take the egg out of the pan.

_____ Turn the heat down to low.

_____ Wait until the white is slightly hard.

_____ Wait about 15 seconds.

_____ Put oil or butter in the pan.

__1__ Turn on the stove to medium heat.

_____ Turn the egg over.

_____ Break the egg into the pan.

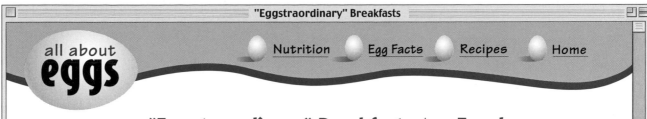

all about **eggs**

Nutrition   Egg Facts   Recipes   Home

"Eggstraordinary" Breakfasts Are Easy!

Do you start each day with a boring bowl of cereal? Do you try to get by without breakfast? Why put up with an ordinary breakfast—or no breakfast at all—when you can eat eggs? Eggs are one of the most popular breakfast foods in the United States. There are many different ways to prepare them. Most of these ways are easy. Consider, for example, fried (over easy) eggs. Follow these simple steps
5 (remember to start out with fresh eggs) and you can count on delicious fried eggs every time.

Heat up the pan

Put a frying pan on the stove, and turn the stove on to medium. Figure out the amount of butter or oil you will need. (Use about two teaspoons of butter or one teaspoon of oil per egg.
10 To cut down on fat, use less butter or oil and a nonstick pan.) Put the butter or oil in the pan, and heat up the pan for a couple of minutes.

Cook the eggs

To crack an egg, gently hit it against the side of the pan. Then break
15 it open and let the white and yolk fall out. Turn the heat down to low, so the eggs will cook slowly. This is very important. If the heat is too high, your eggs won't turn out well. When the whites are slightly hard, use a spatula to turn the eggs over. Wait about 15 seconds and your eggs will be ready. If you prefer a harder yolk, wait up to one minute.

20 ## Take the eggs out and season them

Once the eggs are ready, take them out with a spatula and put them on a warm plate. Season them with salt and pepper. Now sit down, pick up a fork, and enjoy your "eggstraordinary" breakfast!

Adapted from Learn2.com

"eggstraordinary": a made-up word that sounds like *extraordinary* (special, not ordinary)

nonstick pan: a pan with a special surface that food does not stick to

season: to add flavor to something

spatula: a cooking tool for lifting and turning food

yolk: the yellow part of the egg

B Phrasal Verbs

Examining Form

Read the sentences and complete the tasks below. Then discuss your answers and read the Form charts to check them.

1a. He <u>turned off</u> the stove.   **2a.** Turn on the stove.
1b. The eggs <u>turned out</u> well.   **2b.** Turn the stove on.

1. Look at the underlined phrasal verbs in 1a and 1b. In which sentence does the phrasal verb have an object? Circle it. In which sentence does the phrasal verb not have an object?

2. Look at 2a and 2b. Circle the objects in these sentences. In which sentence does the object come after the phrasal verb? In which sentence does the object separate the phrasal verb?

TRANSITIVE PHRASAL VERBS

Separable Transitive Phrasal Verbs		
SUBJECT	VERB + PARTICLE	OBJECT NOUN
I	**left out**	the sugar.

SUBJECT	VERB	OBJECT NOUN	PARTICLE
I	**left**	the sugar	**out.**

SUBJECT	VERB	OBJECT PRONOUN	PARTICLE
I	**left**	it	**out.**

Inseparable Transitive Phrasal Verbs		
SUBJECT	VERB + PARTICLE	OBJECT NOUN or PRONOUN
She	**looked after**	the children.
He	**counts on**	you.
We	**cut down on**	fat.
They	**dropped out of**	school.

INTRANSITIVE PHRASAL VERBS

SUBJECT	VERB + PARTICLE	
We	**grew up**	overseas.
He	**dropped by**	yesterday.

Overview

- A phrasal verb consists of a verb and a particle. *Up, down, on, off, after, by, in,* and *out* are examples of particles.
- Particles look like prepositions, but they often have different meanings. Unlike prepositions, particles often change the meaning of the verb they combine with.

  VERB + PREPOSTION   PHRASAL VERB

  I ran out the door.   Can I borrow some paper? **I ran out.**
  (I left quickly.)   (I used all of my paper. I have no more.)
- See Appendix 17 for a list of phasal verbs and their meanings.

Transitive Phrasal Verbs

- Transitive phrasal verbs take objects.
- Most transitive phrasal verbs are separable; that is, we can put an object noun after the phrasal verb or between the verb and the particle.

  VERB + PARTICLE + <u>NOUN</u>   VERB + <u>NOUN</u> + PARTICLE

  She **turned on** <u>the stove</u>.   She **turned** <u>the stove</u> **on.**
- If the object of a separable transitive phrasal verb is a pronoun, it must separate the verb and the particle. It cannot follow the phrasal verb.

  She **turned** <u>it</u> **on.**
  *She turned on it. (INCORRECT)
- Separable transitive phrasal verbs include *call up, figure out, fill out, leave out, pick up, put down, try on,* and *turn down.*
- Some transitive phrasal verbs are inseparable; that is, you cannot place the object between the verb and the particle. Inseparable phrasal verbs include *call for, come across, count on, go over,* and *look after.*

  She **looked after** <u>the children</u>.   She **looked after** <u>them</u>.
  *She looked the children after. (INCORRECT) *She looked them after. (INCORRECT)
- Some inseparable transitive phrasal verbs consist of three words. The verb + particle is followed by a preposition. The object always follows the preposition. These verbs include *cut down on, drop out of, go along with, look up to, put up with, run out of,* and *stick up for.*

  We **cut down on** fat.   They **dropped out of** school.

Intransitive Phrasal Verbs

- Phrasal verbs that do not take objects are called intransitive phrasal verbs. These verbs include *break down, come out, drop by, grow up, run out, show up,* and *watch out.*

  We **grew up** overseas.   He **dropped by** yesterday.

🎧 Listen to these sentences with phrasal verbs. Write the particle you hear.

1. take ____out____   5. give _____

2. grows _____   6. made _____

3. ran _____ of   7. turn _____

4. look _____   8. get _____ with

In your notebook, rewrite these sentences in two different ways. First, place the object between the verb and the particle. Then, replace the object with a pronoun.

1. We picked up the children from school.

    We picked the children up from school.
    We picked them up from school.

2. Fill out the application.

3. He tried on his new suit.

4. You should call up Bill after lunch.

5. She dropped off her daughter.

6. I put on my warm coat.

7. Please take out the garbage.

8. I can't figure out this problem.

Complete each conversation with the correct form of the phrasal verb in parentheses and an appropriate object pronoun.

1. **A:** Did I leave my gloves here?

    B: Yes. I ____came across them____ (come across) when I cleaned.

2. **A:** I'm going away for the weekend, and I can't take my dog.

    B: Why don't you leave him with me? I _____ (look after).

3. **A:** How are you getting to the airport?

    B: A car from my company _____ (come by for) in

    about an hour.

4. **A:** Your children seem to get along well.

   B: They do. Rachel is five years older than Alex, and he really

   _____ (look up to).

5. **A:** Did you finish your report?

   B: Yes, but I want _____ (go over) once more.

6. **A:** Do you drink coffee in the morning?

   B: Yes. I can't _____ (do without).

7. **A:** Do you have any of those new stamps?

   B: I'm sorry, but we _____ (run out of) earlier today.

8. **A:** The food here is terrible!

   B: I know! We shouldn't _____ (put up with)!

B4 Working on Transitive and Intransitive Phrasal Verbs

A. Underline the phrasal verb in each sentence and identify it as transitive or intransitive.

1. <u>Look up</u> the number in the phone book.   _____transitive_____

2. I came across your watch while I was cleaning.   _____

3. My friend Chris is going to drop by this afternoon.   _____

4. We have to be there at 11, so I'll pick up the boys at 10.   _____

5. The weather was terrible, so they called off the race.   _____

6. Next week we'll go over phrasal verbs again.   _____

7. You might have left out a word here.   _____

8. His plane took off on time.   _____

B. Look at the sentences with transitive phrasal verbs again. Where possible, change each sentence so that the object is between the verb and particle. Why is it not possible to change some of the sentences?

Look the number up in the phone book.

C Phrasal Verbs

Examining Meaning and Use

Read the sentences and complete the task below. Then discuss your answers and read the Meaning and Use Notes to check them.

   a. Please pick up the chair and move it over there.
   b. I pick up the children at 3:00 every day.
   c. He'll pick up French easily because he's a good language learner.

1. The phrasal verb *pick up* has more than one meaning. In which sentence does it mean "learn"?

2. In which sentence does it mean "lift"?

3. In which sentence does it mean "go somewhere and get somebody"?

Meaning and Use Notes

> ### Idiomatic Meanings

1A Many phrasal verbs are like idiomatic expressions. Their meaning is different from the meaning of the individual words combined. See Appendix 17 for a list of phrasal verbs and their meanings.

Keep up the good work. (*keep up* = continue)
The plane **took off** late. (*took off* = left)

1B Some phrasal verbs have more than one meaning. Some meanings may be transitive, and others may be intransitive.

Transitive	*Intransitive*
It was warm, so I **took off** my coat. (*took off* = removed)	The plane **took off** at 10:00. (*took off* = left)
He's not telling the truth. He **made up** that story. (*made up* = created, invented)	Last night they had a big fight. This morning they **made up.** (*made up* = became friends again)

1C Many phrasal verbs have the same meaning as an equivalent one-word verb. Phrasal verbs are more common in conversation. Their one-word equivalents sometimes sound more formal.

Phrasal Verbs		*One-Word Verbs*
I **took off** my coat because I was hot.	=	I <u>removed</u> my coat because I was hot.
The dress didn't fit so she **took it back**.	=	The dress didn't fit so she <u>returned</u> it.

Predictable Meanings

2 With certain particles, you can use the meaning of the particle to guess the meaning of the phrasal verb. Some examples are *through* (from beginning to end), *over* (again), and *up/down* (completely). *Up* and *down* can also mean a change in amount (increase or decrease).

Don't make a quick decision. You need to **think** the problem **through** first.
My speech is finished, but I wish I could **do** it **over**. It was a disaster.
He **tore up** the letter. Then he threw all the little pieces in the garbage.
Their house **burned down**. They lost everything.
Turn down the music. It's too loud.

C1 Listening for Meaning and Use

► Notes 1A, 1B

🎧 Listen to each sentence. Choose the meaning of the phrasal verb you hear.

1. take off
   a. leave
   b. remove *(circled)*

2. take off
   a. leave
   b. remove

3. let out
   a. finish
   b. make bigger

4. let out
   a. finish
   b. make bigger

5. turn down
   a. refuse
   b. make lower

6. turn down
   a. refuse
   b. make lower

7. work out
   a. be OK
   b. exercise

8. work out
   a. be OK
   b. exercise

9. make up
   a. invent
   b. end a fight

10. make up
    a. invent
    b. end a fight

11. pick up
    a. lift
    b. learn

12. pick up
    a. lift
    b. learn

► Note 1C

C2 Rephrasing Phrasal Verbs

Replace the phrasal verb in each sentence with one of the verbs below.

choose   delay   postpone   remove   return   review

1. If you need to go, I don't want to hold you up.

   <u>If you need to go, I don't want to delay you.</u>

2. Before you give me your test, you should go over your work very carefully.

   _____

3. If you've finished your dinner, I'll take away your plates.

   _____

4. If some people can't come today, maybe we should put off the meeting.

   _____

5. I need the dictionary for a minute; I'll give it back to you right away.

   _____

6. Can you help me pick out a dress for tonight?

   _____

C3 Understanding Phrasal Verbs

► Notes 1A, 2

Complete this paragraph by choosing the correct phrasal verbs.

I (ran into / ran over) an old friend by
1
accident the other day. I was going to
(pick up / pick out) my son from school, when
2
suddenly my car (broke up / broke down).
3
I (called up / called in) my husband on my
4
cell phone. While I was waiting for him to

(turn down / turn up), a truck crashed into my car. The driver (got into / got out) of
5   6
the truck to (check in / check out) the damage. It was my friend Patrick. I hadn't seen
7
him since college. Fortunately, nobody was hurt. It was nice to (catch up / catch on)
8
while we were waiting for my husband and the tow truck.

D Combining Form, Meaning, and Use

D1 Thinking About Meaning and Use

Choose the best answer to complete each conversation. Then discuss your answers in small groups.

1. **A:** Did anyone else see that note?

   B: No, I _____ after I read it.
   - **a.** tore it
   - **b.** tore it up

2. **A:** Hey, Bob! It's great to see you.

   B: It's great to see you, too! Come on in! _____ your jacket.
   - **a.** Take off
   - **b.** Remove

3. **A:** What happened? Why were you so late?

   B: Our flight didn't take _____ until 11:30.
   - **a.** up
   - **b.** off

4. **A:** What is the homework for tomorrow?

   B: Read the story _____, but this time read only the important parts.
   - **a.** over
   - **b.** up

5. **A:** Do you want to go clothes shopping this week?

   B: I'd rather wait until they mark _____ the prices.
   - **a.** down
   - **b.** up

6. **A:** Doctor, how is the patient progressing?

   B: His condition remains serious. However, I plan to _____ again soon.
   - **a.** look him up
   - **b.** examine him

Some of these sentences have errors. Find the errors and correct them.

1. I can look ^*after* your children ~~after~~ tomorrow if you want.

2. Tom is always on time; you can count out him.

3. I haven't seen your book, but I'll tell you if I come across.

4. The doctor told me to cut salt down on.

5. I'm not going to put up with that noise any longer.

6. It's not a very good paper; I might do over it.

▶ Beyond the Classroom

Searching for Authentic Examples

Look up these phrasal verbs in an English-language dictionary. Write down two meanings for each, and indicate whether the meanings are transitive or intransitive. Then write a sentence for each meaning.

blow up   call up   check out   get down   turn out   work out

Speaking

Follow these steps to prepare a demonstration of how to do something. You can use one of the ideas below or an idea of your own.

bathe a dog   make a paper airplane   polish shoes   wrap a package

1. First make notes on cards for the different steps. You can use some of the phrasal verbs below or any other phrasal verbs. Try to use at least six phrasal verbs.

brush off	dry off	fold down	make up	sit down
check out	end up with	fold over	pick up	start out
clean up	figure out	hold down	put down	throw away
do over	fill up	look over	put together	tie up

2. Bring objects to class to demonstrate the activity as you are explaining it. If this is not possible, draw pictures or diagrams to illustrate the steps. Show a small group of your classmates how to do the task you have chosen.

I'm going to explain how to polish shoes. First, pick up one of the shoes. Then, take a stiff brush and brush off any dried mud or dirt. . . .

Appendices

① Spelling of Verbs and Nouns Ending in *-s* and *-es*

1. For most third-person singular verbs and plural nouns, add *-s* to the base form.

Verbs	Nouns
swim — swims	lake — lakes

2. If the base form ends with the letter *s, z, sh, ch,* or *x,* add *-es.*

Verbs	Nouns
miss — misses	box — boxes

3. If the base form ends with a consonant + *y,* change *y* to *i* and add *-es.* (Compare vowel + *y*: obey — obeys; toy — toys.)

Verbs	Nouns
try — tries	baby — babies

4. If the base form ends with a consonant + *o,* add *-s* or *-es.* Some words take *-s,* some words take *-es,* some take both *-s* and *-es.* (Compare vowel + *o*: radio — radios; zoo — zoos.)

   -s
   auto — autos
   photo — photos
   piano — pianos
   solo — solos

   Both -s and -es
   tornado — tornados/tornadoes
   volcano — volcanos/volcanoes
   zero — zeros/zeroes

   -es
   do — does
   echo — echoes
   go — goes
   hero — heroes
   potato — potatoes
   tomato — tomatoes

5. If the base form of certain nouns ends with a single *f* or *fe,* change the *f* or *fe* to *v* and add *-es.*

   calf — calves
   shelf — shelves
   knife — knives

   Exceptions
   belief — beliefs
   chief — chiefs
   roof — roofs
   scarf — scarfs/scarves

2 Pronunciation of Verbs and Nouns Ending in *-s* and *-es*

1. If the base form of the verb or noun ends with the sound /s/, /z/, /ʃ/, /ʒ/, /tʃ/, /dʒ/, or /ks/, then pronounce *-es* as an extra syllable /ɪz/.

   Verbs

   slice — slices   watch — watches

   lose — loses   judge — judges

   wash — washes   relax — relaxes

   Nouns

   price — prices   inch — inches

   size — sizes   language — languages

   dish — dishes   tax — taxes

   garage — garages

2. If the base form ends with the voiceless sound /p/, /t/, /k/, /f/, or /θ/, then pronounce *-s* and *-es* as /s/.

   Verbs

   sleep — sleeps   work — works

   hit — hits   laugh — laughs

   Nouns

   grape — grapes   cuff — cuffs

   cat — cats   fifth — fifths

   book — books

3. If the base form ends with any other consonant or with a vowel sound, then pronounce *-s* and *-es* as /z/.

   Verbs

   learn — learns

   go — goes

   Nouns

   name — names

   boy — boys

3 Spelling of Verbs Ending in *-ing*

1. For most verbs, add *-ing* to the base form of the verb.

   sleep — sleeping   talk — talking

2. If the base form ends in a single *e*, drop the *e* and add *-ing* (exception: be – being).

   live — living   write — writing

3. If the base form ends in *ie*, change *ie* to *y* and add *-ing*.

   die — dying   lie — lying

4. If the base form of a one-syllable verb ends with a single vowel + consonant, double the final consonant and add *-ing*. (Compare two vowels + consonant: eat — eating.)

   hit — hitting   stop — stopping

5. If the base form of a verb with two or more syllables ends in a single vowel + consonant, double the final consonant only if the stress is on the final syllable. Do not double the final consonant if the stress is not on the final syllable.

   admít — admitting   begín — beginning   devélop — developing   lísten — listening

6. Do not double the final consonants *x, w,* and *y*.

   fix — fixing   plow — plowing   obey — obeying

Spelling of Verbs Ending in *-ed*

1. To form the simple past and past participle of most regular verbs, add *-ed* to the base form.

   brush — brushed   play — played

2. If the base form ends with *e*, just add *-d*.

   close — closed   live — lived

3. If the base form ends with a consonant + *y*, change the *y* to *i* and add *-ed*. (Compare vowel +*y*: play — played; enjoy — enjoyed.)

   study — studied   dry — dried

4. If the base form of a one-syllable verb ends with a single vowel + consonant, double the final consonant and add *-ed*.

   plan — planned   shop — shopped

5. If the base form of a verb with two or more syllables ends with a single vowel + consonant, double the final consonant and add *-ed* only when the stress is on the final syllable. Do not double the final consonant if the stress is not on the final syllable.

   prefér — preferred   énter — entered

6. Do not double the final consonants *x, w,* and *y*.

   coax — coaxed   snow — snowed   stay — stayed

Pronunciation of Verbs Ending in *-ed*

1. If the base form of the verb ends with the sounds /t/ or /d/, then pronounce *-ed* as an extra syllable /ɪd/.

/t/	/d/
start — started	need — needed
wait — waited	decide — decided

2. If the base form ends with the voiceless sounds /f/, /k/, /p/, /s/, /ʃ/, /tʃ/, or /ks/, then pronounce *-ed* as /t/.

laugh — laughed	jump — jumped	wish — wished	fax — faxed
look — looked	slice — sliced	watch — watched	

3. If the base form ends with the voiced sounds /b/, /g/, /dʒ/, /m/, /n/, /ŋ/, /l/, /r/, /ð/, /v/, /z/, or with a vowel, then pronounce *-ed* as /d/.

rob — robbed	hum — hummed	call — called	wave — waved
brag — bragged	rain — rained	order — ordered	close — closed
judge — judged	bang — banged	bathe — bathed	play — played

6 Irregular Verbs

Base Form	Simple Past	Past Participle	Base Form	Simple Past	Past Participle
arise	arose	arisen	grow	grew	grown
be	was/were	been	hang	hung	hung
beat	beat	beaten	have	had	had
become	became	become	hear	heard	heard
begin	began	begun	hide	hid	hidden
bend	bent	bent	hit	hit	hit
bet	bet	bet	hold	held	held
bind	bound	bound	hurt	hurt	hurt
bite	bit	bitten	keep	kept	kept
bleed	bled	bled	know	knew	known
blow	blew	blown	lay (= put)	laid	laid
break	broke	broken	lead	led	led
bring	brought	brought	leave	left	left
build	built	built	lend	lent	lent
buy	bought	bought	let	let	let
catch	caught	caught	lie (= recline)	lay	lain
choose	chose	chosen	light	lit	lit
come	came	come	lose	lost	lost
cost	cost	cost	make	made	made
creep	crept	crept	mean	meant	meant
cut	cut	cut	meet	met	met
deal	dealt	dealt	pay	paid	paid
dig	dug	dug	prove	proved	proven/proved
dive	dove/dived	dived	put	put	put
do	did	done	quit	quit	quit
draw	drew	drawn	read	read	read
drink	drank	drunk	ride	rode	ridden
drive	drove	driven	ring	rang	rung
eat	ate	eaten	rise	rose	risen
fall	fell	fallen	run	ran	run
feed	fed	fed	say	said	said
feel	felt	felt	see	saw	seen
fight	fought	fought	sell	sold	sold
find	found	found	send	sent	sent
fit	fit	fit	set	set	set
flee	fled	fled	sew	sewed	sewn
fly	flew	flown	shake	shook	shaken
forget	forgot	forgotten	shine	shone	shone
forgive	forgave	forgiven	shoot	shot	shot
freeze	froze	frozen	show	showed	shown
get	got	gotten	shrink	shrank	shrunk
give	gave	given	shut	shut	shut
go	went	gone	sing	sang	sung

Base Form	Simple Past	Past Participle	Base Form	Simple Past	Past Participle
sink	sank	sunk	sweep	swept	swept
sit	sat	sat	swim	swam	swum
sleep	slept	slept	swing	swung	swung
slide	slid	slid	take	took	taken
speak	spoke	spoken	teach	taught	taught
speed	sped	sped	tear	tore	torn
spend	spent	spent	tell	told	told
spin	spun	spun	think	thought	thought
split	split	split	throw	threw	thrown
spread	spread	spread	understand	understood	understood
spring	sprang	sprung	undertake	undertook	undertaken
stand	stood	stood	upset	upset	upset
steal	stole	stolen	wake	woke	woken
stick	stuck	stuck	wear	wore	worn
stink	stank	stunk	weep	wept	wept
strike	struck	struck	wet	wet	wet
string	strung	strung	win	won	won
swear	swore	sworn	write	wrote	written

7 Common Stative Verbs

Emotions and Attitudes	Senses and Sensations	Knowledge and Beliefs	Descriptions and Measurements
admire	ache	agree	appear
appreciate	burn	believe	be
care	feel	consider	cost
desire	hear	disagree	equal
despise	hurt	expect	look (like)
dislike	itch	feel (=think)	measure
doubt	notice	find	resemble
envy	see	forget	seem
fear	smell	guess	sound (like)
hate	sound	hope	taste
like	sting	imagine	weigh
love	taste	know	
mind		mean	**Possession and Relationships**
need		notice	belong
prefer		realize	consist of
regret		recognize	contain
respect		remember	depend on
want		suppose	have
		think	include
		understand	own
			possess

8 Common Irregular Plural Nouns

Singular	Plural
child	children
fish	fish
foot	feet
man	men
mouse	mice
person	people
tooth	teeth
woman	women

9 Common Adjectives Ending in *-ed* and *-ing*

-ed	*-ing*	*-ed*	*-ing*
amazed	amazing	relaxed	relaxing
amused	amusing	satisfied	satisfying
annoyed	annoying	shocked	shocking
bored	boring	surprised	surprising
confused	confusing	terrified	terrifying
depressed	depressing	tired	tiring
disappointed	disappointing		
embarrassed	embarrassing		
excited	exciting		
fascinated	fascinating		
frightened	frightening		
interested	interesting		

10 Spelling Rules for Adverbs Ending in *-ly*

1. Many adverbs of manner are formed by adding *-ly* to an adjective.

   careful — carefully
   quick — quickly

2. If the adjective ends with a consonant + *y*, change the *y* to *i* and add *-ly*.

   easy — easily
   happy — happily

3. If the adjective ends in *le*, drop the *e* and add *-y*.

   gentle — gently
   suitable — suitably

4. If the adjective ends in *ic*, add *-ally*.

   fantastic — fantastically
   terrific — terrifically

11 Adjectives with Two Comparative and Superlative Forms

Adjective	Comparative	Superlative
common	commoner	the commonest
	more common	the most common
friendly	friendlier	the friendliest
	more friendly	the most friendly
handsome	handsomer	the handsomest
	more handsome	the most handsome
happy	happier	the happiest
	more happy	the most happy
lively	livelier	the liveliest
	more lively	the most lively
lovely	lovelier	the loveliest
	more lovely	the most lovely
narrow	narrower	the narrowest
	more narrow	the most narrow
polite	politer	the politest
	more polite	the most polite
quiet	quieter	the quietest
	more quiet	the most quiet

12 Irregular Comparative and Superlative Forms

Adjective	Adverb	Comparative	Superlative
bad	badly	worse	the worst
far	far	farther/further	the farthest/furthest
good	well	better	the best
(a) little	(a) little	less	the least
much/many	much/many	more	the most

 **Gerunds**

Verb + Gerund

These verbs may be followed by gerunds, but not by infinitives:

acknowledge	detest	keep (= continue)	recall
admit	discuss	loathe	recollect
anticipate	dislike	mean (= involve)	recommend
appreciate	endure	mention	regret
avoid	enjoy	mind (= object to)	report
can't help	escape	miss	resent
celebrate	excuse	omit	resist
consider	feel like	postpone	resume
defend	finish	practice	risk
defer	go	prevent	suggest
delay	imagine	prohibit	tolerate
deny	involve	quit	understand

Verb with Preposition + Gerund

These verbs or verb phrases with prepositions may be followed by gerunds, but not by infinitives:

adapt to	believe in	depend on
adjust to	blame for	disapprove of
agree (with someone) on	care about	discourage (someone) from
apologize (to someone) for	complain (to someone) about	engage in
approve of	concentrate on	forgive (someone) for
argue (with someone) about	consist of	help (someone) with
ask about	decide on	

Be + Adjective + Preposition + Gerund

Adjectives with prepositions typically occur in *be* + adjective phrases. These phrases may be followed by gerunds, but not by infinitives:

be accustomed to	be familiar with	be nervous about
be afraid of	be famous for	be perfect for
be angry (at someone) about	be fond of	be proud of
be ashamed of	be glad about	be responsible for
be capable of	be good at	be sad about
be certain of/about	be happy about	be successful in
be concerned with	be incapable of	be suitable for
be critical of	be interested in	be tired of
be discouraged from	be jealous of	be tolerant of
be enthusiastic about	be known for	be upset about

Infinitives

These verbs may be followed by infinitives, but not by gerunds:

Verb + Infinitive

agree	decide	offer	struggle
aim	decline	plan	swear
appear	demand	pledge	tend
arrange	fail	pretend	volunteer
care	hope	refuse	wait
claim	intend	resolve	
consent	manage	seem	

Verb + Object + Infinitive

advise	get	persuade	tell
command	hire	remind	trust
convince	invite	require	urge
force	order	teach	warn

Verb + (Object) + Infinitive

ask	desire	need	want
beg	expect	pay	wish
choose	help	prepare	would like
dare	know	promise	

Verb + Infinitive or Gerund

These verbs may be followed by infinitives or gerunds:

attempt	continue	neglect	start
begin	forget	prefer	stop
can't bear	hate	propose	try
can't stand	like	regret	
cease	love	remember	

16 Contractions with Verb and Modal Forms

Contractions with *Be*

I am	= I'm
you are	= you're
he is	= he's
she is	= she's
it is	= it's
we are	= we're
you are	= you're
they are	= they're

I am not	= I'm not
you are not	= you're not / you aren't
he is not	= he's not / he isn't
she is not	= she's not / she isn't
it is not	= it's not / it isn't
we are not	= we're not / we aren't
you are not	= you're not / you aren't
they are not	= they're not / they aren't

Contractions with *Be Going To*

I am going to	= I'm going to
you are going to	= you're going to
he is going to	= he's going to
she is going to	= she's going to
it is going to	= it's going to
we are going to	= we're going to
you are going to	= you're going to
they are going to	= they're going to

you are not going to	= you're not going to / you aren't going to

Contractions with *Will*

I will	= I'll
you will	= you'll
he will	= he'll
she will	= she'll
it will	= it'll
we will	= we'll
you will	= you'll
they will	= they'll

will not	= won't

Contractions with *Would*

I would	= I'd
you would	= you'd
he would	= he'd
she would	= she'd
we would	= we'd
you would	= you'd
they would	= they'd

would not	= wouldn't

Contractions with *Was* and *Were*

was not	= wasn't
were not	= weren't

Contractions with *Have*

I have	= I've
you have	= you've
he has	= he's
she has	= she's
it has	= it's
we have	= we've
you have	= you've
they have	= they've

have not	= haven't
has not	= hasn't

Contractions with *Had*

I had	= I'd
you had	= you'd
he had	= he'd
she had	= she'd
we had	= we'd
you had	= you'd
they had	= they'd

had not	= hadn't

Contractions with *Do* and *Did*

do not	= don't
does not	= doesn't
did not	= didn't

Contractions with Modals and Phrasal Modals

cannot	= can't
could not	= couldn't
should not	= shouldn't

have got to	= 've got to
has got to	= 's got to

Separable Transitive Phrasal Verbs

Many two-word transitive phrasal verbs are separable. This means that a noun object can separate the two words of the phrasal verb or follow the phrasal verb. If the object is a pronoun *(me, you, him, her, us, it,* or *them),* the pronoun must separate the two words of the phrasal verb. Pronoun objects cannot follow the phrasal verb.

Noun Object	**Pronoun Object**
She **turned** the offer **down**.	She **turned** it **down**.
She **turned down** the offer.	*She **turned down** it. (INCORRECT)

These are some common separable transitive phrasal verbs and their meanings:

Phrasal Verb	**Meaning**
bring (someone) up	raise someone (a child)
bring (something) up	introduce a topic
brush (something) off	remove something by brushing
call (something) off	cancel something
call (someone) up	telephone someone
clean (something) up	clean something completely
do (something) over	do something again
dry (something) off	dry something with a towel
fill (something) out	complete a form with information
get (someone) up	awaken someone
give (something) back	return something
hand (something) in	give something to a person in authority
hold (something) up	delay something
leave (something) out	omit something
let (something) out	alter clothes to make them larger
look (something) over	examine something carefully or review it
look (something) up	look for information in a book or on the Internet
make (something) up	invent something
mark (something) down/up	decrease/increase the price of something
pick (something) out	choose something
pick (something/someone) up	lift something or someone; stop to get something or someone
put (something) away	put something in its usual place
put (something) off	postpone something
put (something) together	assemble something
take (something) away	remove something
take (something) back	return something
take (something) off	remove an article of clothing
talk (something) over	discuss something
tear (something) up	destroy something by ripping
think (something) through	consider something thoroughly
throw (something) away	get rid of something

Phrasal Verb	Meaning
try (something) on	put on clothing to see how it looks
turn (something) down	refuse a request; lower the heat or volume
turn (something) in	give something to a person in authority
turn (something) off	stop a machine or a light
turn (something) on	start a machine or a light
turn (something) over	turn something so that its top is facing down
use (something) up	use something until no more is left

Nonseparable Transitive Phrasal Verbs

Some two-word and most three-word transitive phrasal verbs cannot be separated. This means that a noun object or pronoun object cannot separate the parts of the phrasal verb.

Noun Object	Pronoun Object
The teacher **called on** Sally.	The teacher **called on** her.
*The teacher **called** Sally **on**. (INCORRECT)	*The teacher **called** her **on**. (INCORRECT)

These are some common nonseparable transitive phrasal verbs and their meanings:

Phrasal Verb	Meaning
break into (something)	enter something illegally, such as a car or house
call on (someone)	ask someone to speak, especially in a class or meeting
come across (something)	find something unexpectedly
come by for (someone)	pick someone up, especially in a car
count on (someone)	depend on someone
cut down on (something)	use less of something
do without (something)	manage without having something
drop out of (something)	quit something, especially school
end up with (something)	have or get something in the end
find out (something)	discover something
get around (something)	avoid something
get on with (something)	continue something
go along with (someone/something)	agree with someone/something
get over (something)	recover from something, such as an illness
go over (something)	review something, such as a report
look after (someone)	take care of someone
look into (something)	research a subject
look up to (someone)	admire someone
put up with (something/someone)	tolerate something or someone
run into (someone)	meet someone unexpectedly
take after (someone)	resemble someone; act like someone

Intransitive Phrasal Verbs

Intransitive phrasal verbs do not take objects.

My car **broke down** yesterday.   What time do you usually **get up**?

These are some common intransitive phrasal verbs and their meanings:

Phrasal Verb	Meaning
blow up	explode
break down	stop working properly
burn down	burn completely
catch up	find out the latest news
come back	return
come over	visit
drop by	visit, especially unexpectedly
eat out	eat in a restaurant
fall down	suddenly stop standing
get up	get out of bed
give up	stop trying, lose hope
go down	(of computers) stop functioning; (of prices or temperature) become lower; (of ships) sink; (of the sun or moon) set
go off	(of lights or machines) stop functioning; (of alarms) start functioning; explode or make a loud noise
grow up	become an adult
hold on	wait on the telephone
look out	be careful
make out	manage or progress
move out	stop living somewhere, especially by removing all of your possessions
pass out	lose consciousness
show up	appear
start out	begin
take off	leave (usually by plane)
talk back	answer in a rude way
turn up	appear or arrive
wake up	stop sleeping
work out	exercise

18 Phonetic Symbols

Vowels

i	see /si/	u	too /tu/	oʊ	go /goʊ/
ɪ	sit /sɪt/	ʌ	cup /kʌp/	ər	bird /bərd/
ɛ	ten /tɛn/	ə	about /əˈbaʊt/	ɪr	near /nɪr/
æ	cat /kæt/	eɪ	say /seɪ/	ɛr	hair /hɛr/
ɑ	hot /hɑt/	aɪ	five /faɪv/	ɑr	car /kɑr/
ɔ	saw /sɔ/	ɔɪ	boy /bɔɪ/	ɔr	north /nɔrθ/
ʊ	put /pʊt/	aʊ	now /naʊ/	ʊr	tour /tʊr/

Consonants

p	pen /pɛn/	f	fall /fɔl/	m	man /mæn/
b	bad /bæd/	v	voice /vɔɪs/	n	no /noʊ/
t	tea /ti/	θ	thin /θɪn/	ŋ	sing /sɪŋ/
t̬	butter /ˈbʌt̬ər/	ð	then /ðɛn/	l	leg /lɛg/
d	did /dɪd/	s	so /soʊ/	r	red /rɛd/
k	cat /kæt/	z	zoo /zu/	y	yes /yɛs/
g	got /gɑt/	ʃ	she /ʃi/	w	wet /wɛt/
tʃ	chin /tʃɪn/	ʒ	vision /ˈvɪʒn/	x	Chanukah /ˈxɑnəkə/
dʒ	June /dʒun/	h	how /haʊ/		

Glossary of Grammar Terms

ability modal *See* **modal of ability.**

action verb A verb that describes a thing that someone or something does. An action verb does not describe a state or condition.

> Sam **rang** the bell.
> I **eat** soup for lunch.
> It **rains** a lot here.

active sentence In active sentences, the agent (the noun that is performing the action) is in subject position and the receiver (the noun that receives or is a result of the action) is in object position. In the following sentence, the subject **Alex** performed the action, and the object **letter** received the action.

> Alex mailed the letter.

adjective A word that describes or modifies the meaning of a noun.

> the **orange** car
> a **strange** noise

adverb A word that describes or modifies the meaning of a verb, another adverb, an adjective, or a sentence. Many adverbs answer such questions as *How? When? Where?* or *How often?* They often end in **-ly.**

> She ran **quickly**.   She ran **very** quickly.
> a **really** hot day   **Maybe** she'll leave.

adverb of degree An adverb that makes adjectives or other adverbs stronger or weaker.

> She is **extremely** busy this week.
> He performed **very** well during the exam.
> He was **somewhat** surprised by her response.

adverb of frequency An adverb that tells how often a situation occurs. Adverbs of frequency range in meaning from *all of the time* to *none of the time.*

> She **always** eats breakfast.
> He **never** eats meat.

adverb of manner An adverb that answers the question *How?* and describes the way someone does something or the way something happens. Adverbs of manner usually end in **-ly.**

> He walked **slowly**.
> It rained **heavily** all night.

adverb of opinion An adverb that expresses an opinion about an entire sentence or idea.

> **Luckily,** we missed the traffic.
> We couldn't find a seat on the train, **unfortunately.**

adverb of possibility An adverb that shows different degrees of how possible we think something is. Adverbs of possibility range in meaning from expressing a high degree of possibility to expressing a low degree of possibility.

> He'll **certainly** pass the test.
> **Maybe** he'll pass the test.
> He **definitely** won't pass the test.

adverb of time An adverb that answers the question *When?* and refers to either a specific time or a more indefinite time.

> Let's leave **tonight** instead of **tomorrow**.
> They've **recently** opened a new store.

adverbial phrase A phrase that functions as an adverb.

> Amy spoke **very softly**.

affirmative statement A sentence that does not have a negative verb.

> Linda went to the movies.

agreement The subject and verb of a clause must agree in number. If the subject is singular, the verb form is also singular. If the subject is plural, the verb form is also plural.

> **He comes** home early.   **They come** home early.

article The words **a, an,** and **the** in English. Articles are used to introduce and identify nouns.

> **a** potato   **an** onion   **the** supermarket

auxiliary verb A verb that is used before main verbs (or other auxiliary verbs) in a sentence. Auxiliary verbs are usually used in questions and negative sentences. **Do, have,** and **be** can act as auxiliary verbs. Modals (**may, can, will,** and so on) are also auxiliary verbs.

> **Do** you have the time?
> I **have** never been to Italy.
> The car **was** speeding.
> I **may** be late.

base form The form of a verb without any verb endings; the infinitive form without *to*. Also called *simple form.*

> sleep   be   stop

clause A group of words that has a subject and a verb. *See also* **dependent clause** and **main clause.**

> If I leave, . . .
> The rain stopped.
> . . . when he speaks.
> . . . that I saw.

common noun A noun that refers to any of a class of people, animals, places, things, or ideas. Common nouns are not capitalized.

> man   cat   city   pencil   grammar

comparative A form of an adjective, adverb, or noun that is used to express differences between two items or situations.

> This book is **heavier than** that one.
> He runs **more quickly than** his brother.
> A CD costs **more money than** a cassette.

complex sentence A sentence that has a main clause and one or more dependent clauses.

> When the bell rang, we were finishing dinner.

conditional sentence A sentence that expresses a real or unreal situation in the *if* clause, and the (real or unreal) expected result in the main clause.

> If I have time, I will travel to Africa.
> If I had time, I would travel to Africa.

consonant A speech sound that is made by partly or completely stopping the air as it comes out of the mouth. For example, with the sounds /p/, /d/, and /g/, the air is completely stopped. With the sounds /s/, /f/, and /l/, the air is partly stopped.

contraction The combination of two words into one by omitting certain letters and replacing them with an apostrophe.

> I will = **I'll**   we are = **we're**   are not = **aren't**

count noun A common noun that can be counted. It usually has both a singular and a plural form.

> orange — oranges
> woman — women

definite article The word **the** in English. It is used to identify nouns based on assumptions about what information the speaker and listener share about the noun. The definite article is also used for making general statements about a whole class or group of nouns.

> Please give me **the** key.
> **The** scorpion is dangerous.

dependent clause A clause that cannot stand alone as a sentence because it depends on the main clause to complete the meaning of the sentence. Also called *subordinate clause.*

> I'm going home **after he calls**.

determiner A word such as **a, an, the, this, that, these, those, my, some, a few,** and **three** that is used before a noun to limit its meaning in some way.

> **those** videos

direct object A noun or pronoun that refers to a person or thing that is directly affected by the action of a verb.

> John wrote **a letter**.
> Please buy **some milk**.

first person One of the three classes of personal pronouns. First person refers to the person *(I)* or people *(we)* who are actually speaking or writing.

future A time that is to come. The future is expressed in English with **will, be going to,** the simple present, or the present continuous. These different forms of the future often have different meanings and uses.

> I **will** help you later.
> David **is going to** call later.
> The train **leaves** at 6:05 this evening.
> **I'm driving** to Toronto tomorrow.

general quantity expression A quantity expression that indicates whether a quantity or an amount is large or small. It does not give an exact amount.

> **a lot of** cookies   **a little** flour
> **a few** people   **some** milk

general statement A generalization about a whole class or group of nouns.

> Whales are mammals.
> A daffodil is a flower that grows from a bulb.

generic noun A noun that refers to a whole class or group of nouns.

> I like **rice**.
> **A bird** can fly.
> **The laser** is an important tool.

gerund An -**ing** form of a verb that is used in place of a noun or pronoun to name an activity or a state.

> **Skiing** is fun.   He doesn't like **being sick**.

if **clause** A dependent clause that begins with **if** and expresses a real or unreal situation.

> **If I have the time,** I'll paint the kitchen.
> **If I had the time,** I'd paint the kitchen.

imperative A type of sentence, usually without a subject, that tells someone to do something. The verb is in the base form.

> **Open** your books to page 36.
> **Be** ready at eight.

impersonal *you* The use of the pronoun **you** to refer to people in general rather than a particular person or group of people.

> Nowadays **you** can buy anything on the Internet.

indefinite article The words **a** and **an** in English. Indefinite articles introduce a noun as a member of a class of nouns or make generalizations about a whole class or group of nouns.

> Please hand me **a** pencil.
> **An** ocean is **a** large body of water.

independent clause *See* **main clause.**

indirect object A noun or pronoun used after some verbs that refers to the person who receives the direct object of a sentence.

> John wrote a letter to **Mary**.
> Please buy some milk for **us**.

infinitive A verb form that includes **to** + the base form of a verb. An infinitive is used in place of a noun or pronoun to name an activity or situation expressed by a verb.

> Do you like **to swim**?

information question A question that begins with a **wh-** word.

> Where does she live?   Who lives here?

intonation The change in pitch, loudness, syllable length, and rhythm in spoken language.

intransitive verb A verb that cannot be followed by an object.

> We finally **arrived**.

irregular verb A verb that does not form the simple past by adding a -*d* or -*ed* ending.

> put — put — put   buy — bought — bought

main clause A clause that can be used by itself as a sentence. Also called *independent clause*.

> I'm going home.

main verb A verb that can be used alone in a sentence. A main verb can also occur with an auxiliary verb.

> I **ate** lunch at 11:30.
> Kate can't **eat** lunch today.

mental activity verb A verb such as **decide, know,** and **understand** that expresses an opinion, thought, or feeling.

> I don't **know** why she left.

modal The auxiliary verbs **can, could, may, might, must, should, will,** and **would.** They modify the meaning of a main verb by expressing ability, authority, formality, politeness, or various degrees of certainty. Also called *modal auxiliary*.

> You **should** take something for your headache.
> Applicants **must** have a high school diploma.

modal of ability **Can** and **could** are called modals of ability when they express knowledge, skill, opportunity, and capability.

> He **can** speak Arabic and English.
> **Can** you play the piano?
> Yesterday we **couldn't** leave during the storm.
> Seat belts **can** save lives.

modal of necessity **Should** and **must** are called modals of necessity along with the phrasal modals **ought to, have to**, and **have got to**. They express various degrees of necessity in opinions, obligations, rules, laws, and other requirements.

> Students **must** take two upper-level courses in order to graduate.
> Employees **should** wear identification tags at all times.
> We**'ve got to** arrive before the ceremony starts.

modal of possibility **Could, might, may, should, must,** and **will** are called modals of possibility when they express various degrees of certainty ranging from slight possibility to strong certainty.

> It **could / might / may / will** rain later.

modal of prohibition **Must not** is called a modal of prohibition when it means that something is not allowed (prohibited).

> Drivers **must not** change lanes without signaling.

modal of request **Can, could, will,** and **would** are called modals of request when they are used for asking someone to do something. They express various degrees of politeness and formality.

> **Can** you **pass** the sugar, please?
> **Would** you **tell** me the time?

modify To add to or change the meaning of a word. Adjectives modify nouns (**expensive** cars). Adverbs modify verbs (**very** fast).

negative statement A sentence with a negative verb.

> I **didn't see** that movie.
> He **isn't** happy.

noncount noun A common noun that cannot be counted. A noncount noun has no plural form and cannot occur with **a, an,** or a number.

> information   mathematics   weather

nonseparable Refers to two- or three-word verbs that don't allow a noun or pronoun object to separate the two or three words in the verb phrase. Certain two-word verbs and almost all three-word verbs are nonseparable.

> Amy **got off** the bus.
> We **cut down on** fat in our diet.

noun A word that typically refers to a person, animal, place, thing, or idea.

> Tom   rabbit   store   computer   mathematics

noun clause A dependent clause that can occur in the same place as a noun, pronoun, or noun phrase in a sentence. Noun clauses begin with **wh-** words, **if, whether,** or **that.**

> I don't know **where he is.**
> I wonder **if he's coming.**
> I don't know **whether it's true.**
> I think **that it's a lie.**

noun phrase A phrase formed by a noun and its modifiers. A noun phrase can substitute for a noun in a sentence.

> She drank **milk.**
> She drank **chocolate milk.**
> She drank **the milk.**

object A noun, pronoun, or noun phrase that follows a transitive verb or a preposition.

> He likes **pizza.**
> She likes **him.**
> Go with **her.**
> Steve threw **the ball.**

particle Words such as **up, out,** and **down** that are linked to certain verbs to form phrasal verbs. Particles look like prepositions but don't express the same meanings.

> He got **up** late.
> Tom works **out** three times a week.
> They turned **down** the offer.

passive sentence Passive sentences emphasize the receiver of an action by changing the usual order of the subject and object in a sentence. In the sentence below, the subject (**The letter**) does not perform the action; it receives the action or is the result of an action. The passive is formed with a form of **be** + the past participle of a transitive verb.

> The letter was mailed yesterday.

past continuous A verb form that expresses an action or situation in progress at a specific time in the past. The past continuous is formed with **was** or **were** + verb + **-ing.** Also called *past progressive.*

> A: What **were** you **doing** last night at eight o'clock?
> B: I **was studying.**

past participle A past verb form that may differ from the simple past form of some irregular verbs. It is used to form the present perfect, for example.

> I have never **seen** that movie.

past progressive *See* **past continuous.**

phrasal modal A verb that is not a true modal, but has the same meaning as a modal verb. Examples of phrasal modals are **ought to, have to,** and **have got to.**

phrasal verb A two- or three-word verb such as **turn down** or **run out of.** The meaning of a phrasal verb is usually different from the meanings of its individual words.

> She **turned down** the job offer.
> Don't **run out of** gas on the freeway.

phrase A group of words that can form a grammatical unit. A phrase can take the form of a noun phrase, verb phrase, adjective phrase, adverbial phrase, or prepositional phrase. This means it can act as a noun, verb, adjective, adverb, or preposition.

> The **tall man** left.
> Lee **hit the ball.**
> The child was **very quiet.**
> She spoke **too fast.**
> They ran **down the stairs.**

plural The form of a word that refers to more than one person or thing. For example, **cats** and **children** are the plural forms of **cat** and **child.**

possibility modal *See* **modal of possibility.**

preposition A word such as **at, in, on,** or **to,** that links nouns, pronouns, and gerunds to other words.

prepositional phrase A phrase that consists of a preposition followed by a noun or noun phrase.

> on Sunday
> under the table

present continuous A verb form that indicates that an activity is in progress, temporary, or changing. It is formed with **be** + verb + **-ing.** Also called *present progressive.*

> **I'm watering** the garden.
> Ruth **is working** for her uncle.
> He**'s getting** better.

present perfect A verb form that expresses a connection between the past and the present. It indicates indefinite past time, recent past time, or continuing past time. The present perfect is formed with **have** + the past participle of the main verb.

> **I've seen** that movie.
> The manager **has** just **resigned.**
> We**'ve been** here for three hours.

present progressive *See* **present continuous.**

pronoun A word that can replace a noun or noun phrase. **I, you, he, she, it, mine,** and **yours** are some examples of pronouns.

proper noun A noun that is the name of a particular person, animal, place, thing, or idea. Proper nouns begin with capital letters and are usually not preceded by **the.**

> Peter   Rover   India   Apollo 13   Buddhism

purpose infinitive An infinitive that expresses the reason or purpose for doing something.

> **In order to operate this machine,** press the green button.

quantity expression A word or words that occur before a noun to express a quantity or amount of that noun.

> **a lot of** rain   **few** books   **four** trucks

real conditional sentence A sentence that expresses a real or possible situation in the **if** clause and the expected result in the main clause. It has an **if** clause in the simple present, and the **will** future in the main clause.

> If I get a raise, I won't look for a new job.

regular verb A verb that forms the simple past by adding **-ed, -d,** or changing **y** to **i** and then adding **-ed** to the simple form.

> hunt — hunted
> love — loved
> cry — cried

rejoinder A short response used in conversation.

> A: I like sushi.
> B: **So do I.**
> C: **Me too.**

response An answer to a question, or a reply to other types of spoken or written language. *See also* **rejoinder**.

    A: Are you hungry?
    B: Yes, **I am**. Let's eat.

    A: I'm tired of this long winter.
    B: **So am I.**

second person One of the three classes of personal pronouns. Second person refers to the person (**you,** singular) or people (**you,** plural) who are the listeners or readers.

separable Refers to certain two-word verbs that allow a noun or pronoun object to separate the two words in the verb phrase.

    She **gave** her job **up.**

short answer An answer to a **Yes/No** question that has **yes** or **no** plus the subject and an auxiliary verb.

    A: Do you speak Chinese?
    B: **Yes, I do. / No, I don't.**

simple past A verb form that expresses actions and situations that were completed at a definite time in the past.

    Carol **ate** lunch.
    She **was** hungry.

simple present A verb form that expresses general statements, especially about habitual or repeated activities and permanent situations.

    Every morning I **catch** the 8:00 bus.
    The earth **is** round.

singular The form of a word that refers to only one person or thing. For example, **cat** and **child** are the singular forms of **cats** and **children.**

stative verb A type of verb that is not usually used in the continuous form because it expresses a condition or state that is not changing. **Know, love, resemble, see,** and **smell** are some examples.

subject A noun, pronoun, or noun phrase that precedes the verb phrase in a sentence. The subject is closely related to the verb as the doer or experiencer of the action or state, or closely related

to the noun that is being described in a sentence with *be*.

    Erica kicked the ball.
    He feels dizzy.
    The park is huge.

subordinate clause *See* **dependent clause.**

superlative A form of an adjective, adverb, or noun that is used to rank an item or situation first or last in a group of three or more.

    This perfume has **the strongest** scent.
    He speaks **the fastest** of all.
    That machine makes **the most noise** of the three.

tag question A type of question that is added to the end of a statement in order to express doubt, surprise, and certainty. Certain rising or falling intonation patterns accompany these different meanings.

    You're feeling sick, **aren't you**?
    He didn't leave, **did he**?

tense The form of a verb that shows past, present, and future time.

    He **lives** in New York now.
    He **lived** in Washington two years ago.
    He**'ll live** in Toronto next year.

third person One of the three classes of personal pronouns. Third person refers to some person (**he, she**), thing (**it**), or people or things (**they**) other than the speaker/writer or listener/reader.

three-word verb A phrasal verb such as **break up with, cut down on,** and **look out for.** The meaning of a three-word verb is usually different from the individual meanings of the three words.

time clause A dependent clause that begins with a word such as **while, when, before,** or **after.** It expresses the relationship in time between two different events in the same sentence.

    Before Sandy left, she fixed the copy machine.

time expression A phrase that functions as an adverb of time.

    She graduated **three years ago.**
    I'll see them **the day after tomorrow.**

transitive verb A verb that is followed by an object.

> I **read** the book.

two-word verb A phrasal verb such as **blow up, cross out,** and **hand in.** The meaning of a two-word verb is usually different from the individual meanings of the two words.

used to A special past tense verb. It expresses habitual past situations that no longer exist.

> We **used to** go skiing a lot. Now we go snowboarding.

verb A word that refers to an action or a state.

> Gina **closed** the window.
> Tim **loves** classical music.

verb phrase A phrase that has a main verb and any objects, adverbs, or dependent clauses that complete the meaning of the verb in the sentence.

> Who **called you**?
> He **walked slowly.**
> I **know what his name is.**

voiced Refers to speech sounds that are made by vibrating the vocal cords. Examples of voiced sounds are /b/, /d/, and /g/.

> **b**at   **d**ot   **g**et

voiceless Refers to speech sounds that are made without vibrating the vocal cords. Examples of voiceless sounds are /p/, /t/, and /f/.

> u**p**   i**t**   i**f**

vowel A speech sound that is made with the lips and teeth open. The air from the lungs is not blocked at all. For example, the sounds /a/, /o/, and /i/ are vowels.

***wh-* word** Who, whom, what, where, when, why, how, and which are **wh-** words. They are used to ask questions and to connect clauses.

***Yes/No* question** A question that can be answered with the words **yes** or **no.**

> Can you drive a car?   Does he live here?

Index

meaning and use of, 208, 210, 214

have to
forms of, 203–204, 207
meaning and use of, 208, 210, 214, 215

hear, in statements about ability, 163

high, 326

highly, 326

how many, 265, 266

how much, 265, 266

hurt, in present continuous, 37

I

I, vs. *me,* in short responses, 252

-ic, adjectives formed with, 305

Identifying nouns, with articles, 288–289

Idioms, phrasal verbs as, 418

I don't mind . . ., 390

if clauses, for future
forms of, 141–142
meaning and use of, 146–147

Imperatives, 17–28
forms of, 20
meaning and use of, 22–23

Impossibility, *see*
Possibility/impossibility

I'm sorry, in refusing requests, 187

in, in future time expressions, 122

incredibly, 321, 326

Indefinite articles, *see also* No article
and adjectives, 305
forms of, 284–285
with nouns, 264–265
meaning and use of, 287
in general statements, 293–294

Indefinite nouns, 287
in general statements, 294

Indefinite past time, and present perfect, 100–101

Infinitives, 395–410
forms of, 398–399
with *too* and *enough,* 335, 337

with *would like* and *would prefer,* 183
meaning and use of, 402–403, 405–406

Informality, *see* Formality/informality

Information, *see also* Background information; Certainty/uncertainty; Classification; Definitions; Facts; General truths; Introducing topics; Plans; Predictions; Reasons

Information questions
in future
with *be going to,* 115
with *will,* 126
with *how many* and *how much,* 265, 266
with modals of ability
with *can* for present and future ability, 159
with *could* for past ability, 160
with modals of advice, necessity, and prohibition, 202, 203
with modals of future possibility, 168
with modals of permission, 181
in past continuous, 73
with phrasal modals of advice and necessity, 205
in present continuous, 33, 40
in present perfect, 93
with adverbs, 104
in simple past, 51
in simple present, 7
with *used to,* 63
with *would like, would prefer,* and *would rather,* 182–183

-ing, see also Gerunds; Past continuous; Present continuous
adjectives formed with, 305, 310

in order, with infinitives, 399, 402

Inseparable phrasal verbs, 414, 415

Instructions, and imperatives, 22

Intentions, and *be going to* and present continuous, 119

Interrupted events, 83

Intonation, with tag questions,

231–232

Intransitive verbs, phrasal verbs as, 414–415, 418

Introducing topics, with indefinite articles, 287

Irregular comparatives, 348, 349

Irregular superlatives, 368

Irregular verbs
past participles of, 92–93
in simple past, 40–51

-ish, adjectives formed with, 305

is/isn't, 81, see also *be*
vs. present perfect, 93

it
as subject, with infinitives, 399, 403
and tag questions, 228

I think, with advice and opinions, 209

K

know, 37, 77

know how to, vs. *can,* 166

L

Lack of necessity, with modals and phrasal modals, 202–204, 214–215

late, 326

lately, 326

Laws, 214

least, 373

leave out, 415

less, with comparatives, 352–353, 359

-less, adjectives formed with, 305

like, see also *would like*
with gerunds or infinitives, 389, 402, 405
vs. *would like,* 193

little, in quantity expressions, 265, 266, 270–272

look
and adjectives, 305